スチュワードシップコードの目的とその多様性
（令和元年9月10日開催）

報告者 後 藤 　 元

（東京大学大学院法学政治学研究科教授）

目　　次

スチュワードシップコードの目的とその多様性

神作会長　まだお見えでない方もおられますけれども、定刻になりましたので、第11回金融商品取引法研究会を始めさせていただきます。

　本日は、既にご案内させていただいておりますとおり、後藤元先生から「スチュワードシップコードの目的とその多様性」というテーマでご報告いただくこととなっております。

　それでは、早速でございますけれども、後藤先生、ご報告よろしくお願いいたします。

［後藤委員の報告］

後藤報告者　東京大学の後藤でございます。本日は報告の機会をいただき、ありがとうございます。

　きょうは「スチュワードシップコードの目的とその多様性」ということでお話をさせていただければと思います。

　まずお手元にレジュメと、あと大部になってしまって恐縮ですが、資料をお配りさせていただきました。資料は、私が前に書きました英語の論文が1つと、あと日本、イギリス、シンガポール、韓国、台湾、アメリカのスチュワードシップコードの原文をつけてございますので、適宜ご参照いただければと思います。報告自体はレジュメに沿ってお話をさせていただきます。

Ⅰ．問題意識

1．スチュワードシップコードの国際的な流行

　まず、どういう問題意識で始めた研究かということですが、皆様ご承知のとおり、スチュワードシップコードはイギリスで2010年に初めて策定されまして、それ以来、日本を含め、世界各国でそれを採択するという動きが広まっております。

日本は割と早目にその流れに乗ったほうで、2014年に策定し、2017年に改訂して、さらに次の改定のためのフォローアップ会議が始まっております。3年に一度見直すということですので、順調にいけば、2020年に改訂されることになります。

　イギリスは、2010年の後、2012年に改訂されまして、さらに再改訂の作業がもうすぐ大詰めというところまで来ておりまして、2019年中にまた新しくなるということでございます。

　アメリカでは、連邦政府や州政府ではなくて、Investor Stewardship Groupという投資家の団体がスチュワードシップコードに当たるようなものを2017年にまとめて、2018年の1月から発効しております。また、レジュメの記載にはひょっとしたら漏れがあるかもしれないのですけれども、これらの他にも世界各国で採択が進んでおります。

　特に、マレーシアが2014年、台湾が2016年、シンガポールも2016年、韓国も2016年、香港も2016年にスチュワードシップコードを採択しており、さらに中国も昨年、コーポレートガバナンスコードの中に機関投資家の役割というような章を設けておりまして、日本風に言えばスチュワードシップコードに当たるようなものをまとめているところでございます。またインド、フィリピン、ベトナムなどでも検討が進んでいると報じられておりまして、特にアジアでいろいろと進んでいるという状況にあります。

　これらの動きの背景について、注をつけましたように、シンガポール国立大学のDan W. Puchniak准教授とNanyang工科大学のAlan K. Koh助教授と共同研究を進めておりまして、本日はその共同研究の成果に、私自身で行った検討も含めてご報告をさせていただければと思っております。

2．日英のスチュワードシップコードの違い

　このようにスチュワードシップコードは広まってきているのですけれども、それが全く同じものなのだろうかというところが私の問題意識の出発点でございまして、手始めにやったのが、日本とイギリスのスチュワードシッ

プコードが果たして同じものと言えるかという研究で、それをまとめたのが資料1の論文です。

　特に私が着目をしましたのは、スチュワードシップコードが何のために策定されたのかという「コードの目的」というところです。まず日本版のコードにおきましては、スチュワードシップ責任の定義という形で目的が述べられております。そこでは、引用しておりますとおり、「『スチュワードシップ責任』とは、機関投資家が、投資先企業やその事業環境等に関する深い理解に基づく建設的な『目的を持った対話』（エンゲージメント）などを通じて、当該企業の企業価値の向上や持続的成長を促すことにより、『顧客・受益者』（最終受益者を含む）の中長期的な投資リターンの拡大を図る責任を意味する」とされています。

　ここで二重下線を引いたところですけれども、投資先企業の企業価値の持続的な成長という要素と、「顧客・受益者（最終受益者）」の利益という2つの要素があるわけですが、「ことにより」というフレーズからわかるように、最終的な目的というのは、「顧客・受益者（最終受益者）」の中長期的な投資リターンの拡大というところに置かれておりまして、投資先企業の企業価値の持続的成長はその手段という構造の文になっています。

　これに対して、日本のスチュワードシップコードの策定において大いに参照されたイギリスの2012年版コードを参照しますと、そこでは、下線部を引いたところですけれども、Stewardship aims to promote the long term success of companies in such a way that the ultimate providers of capital also prosper. となっております。日本版よりも文章の構造ははっきりしていませんが、1つ目に目的として掲げられているのは、投資先企業の長期的な成功という要素であり、それに追加して、also という形で、資本の最終的な拠出者の利益も、付随的に掲げられているというような形の文章になっております。

　このように、日本とイギリスは、投資先の持続的成長という要素と、最終受益者の利益という2つの要素を挙げているところでは共通しているわけで

3

すけれども、どちらに重点を置いた文章になっているかというところが違うように思えるというのが私の出発点でございました。

　他方で、コードの中身を見ますと、田中亘さんが、日本の 2014 年版のコードができた後に、イギリスとの比較をされた論文があります[1]。資料 2 が日本版コードで、資料 3 － 2 か 3 － 3 のイギリスの 2010 年版か 2012 年版のコードと比較していただければと思うのですが、幾つかの違いがあるというふうに田中さんが指摘されておられます。

　まず、どちらのコードも 7 つの原則を掲げているわけですけれども、7 原則の柱書きに当たるような部分で、投資先企業の持続的成長が大事なのだということを日本版コードでは強調しているのに対して、イギリス版のコードではそのような言及がなく、むしろ最終受益者の利益のためにということが強調されている。

　また、イギリス版では、必要があれば、エンゲージメントを段階的に強化していくとか、集団的なエンゲージメントをすることも考えるべきであるというようなことが言われているわけですけれども、日本の最初の 2014 年版のコードでは、この 2 つは言及されていないという状況にありました。この 2 つは、投資家・株主目線での圧力を強化していくという観点から非常に重要であるにもかかわらず、それへの言及がないということは、株主目線のガバナンスという観点からすると、日本版のスチュワードシップコードには不十分な点があると田中さんは指摘されています。

　さらに、イギリス版のコードでは、機関投資家は投資先企業の経営をモニタリングしなければいけないということが言われております。配付はしていませんが、日本版コードの英語版では、同じくモニタリング、monitor という言葉が使われているのですけれども、日本語版では「監視」という訳語は避けて、「適切に把握」と言いかえられていることが指摘されています。「適切に把握」と「監視」では、語感が大分違うわけで、日本語版であえて語感

---

[1]　田中亘「日本版スチュワードシップコードの検討」月刊監査役 629 号 66 頁（2014 年）。

4

を弱めたところに、問題があるというわけではありませんけれども、日本版コードの踏み込みの弱さがあるということを田中さんが言っておられます。

　この他、日本版コードでは、イギリスにはない原則として、原則7で、機関投資家は投資先企業に対する理解をしていなければいけないし、それに基づいて行動する実力が必要であるということが要求されています。これは投資先企業に対して理解が不十分であると弁解する余地を認めるもので、余り望ましくないのではないかということも田中さんは言っておられるわけです。

　以上のように、イギリスと日本のコードを比較しますと、目的のレベルでは、日本版のコードは、投資先企業の持続的成長よりも顧客・受益者の利益のほうに重点を置きながら、内容面ではイギリスのほうが投資先企業への配慮が少ないというところで、何かずれがあるような気がする。それは何で起きているのだろうかというのが第1の問題意識でございます。

3．各国における株式所有構造の違い

　また、先ほどの国際的な広がりに話を戻しますと、各国において株式所有構造はいろいろ違っていて、それに伴ってコーポレートガバナンス上生じる問題点にも違いがあるということが認識されるようになって久しいわけですが、イギリス、アメリカでは分散保有が進んでおりまして、特に機関投資家による保有が増大している状況であるのに対して、日本では、解消の動きはあるわけですけれども、持ち合いによる安定株主が多い。それに対して、アジア諸国や大陸・ヨーロッパ諸国では、支配株主が多いことが問題となっているわけです。特にアジアでは、支配株主はオーナー一族であることもあれば、政府が支配株主として存在することもある。そうすると、それぞれで問題は違ってくるはずなのに、イギリスという所有構造が違うところで始まったスチュワードシップコードというソリューションを他の国が一様に採用しているのはなぜなのか、そんなにうまくいくのだろうかという問題が出てきます。

そういうわけで、スチュワードシップコードは各国で採択されているわけですけれども、その目的は実はばらばらなのではないかということを思いついて始めたのが以下でお話しする研究ということになります。

II．スチュワードシップコードの目的の多様性

1．イギリス

まず、出発点としてイギリスの状況からご紹介をしたいと思います。イギリスの最初の 2010 年版コードは、2009 年に発行されたいわゆる Walker Review の提言を受けて採択されたものになります。Walker Review はどういう文書だったかと申しますと、2008 年に金融危機があって、イギリスの金融機関も大きな影響を受けたわけですけれども、その中で幾つかの金融機関は政府によって救済されるということがございました。その中で、金融機関のガバナンスを改革しなければいけないのではないかという声が出てきてまとめられたのが Walker Review ですが、そこでは、有限責任を享受している株主が、短期的業績を追求してリスクを取ることを要求してくるプレッシャーに耐えかねて金融機関の経営陣が過大なリスクをとってしまったのが金融危機の一因であるという認識が基礎となっています。その結果として、結局、負担は債権者と納税者のところに降ってきたということを強く批判しまして、こういうことを再び起こさないためにはどうするかというと、金融機関を含む上場企業の経営者の過度のリスクテイクを抑制する必要がある。それは株主の利益ではなくて、社会とか経済全般の公益的な観点から要請されるのだということを言いながら、Walker Review は、それを実現するための方策の一つとして機関投資家の役割を取り上げているわけです。

ここでのポイントは、Walker Review の問題意識は、株主の利益という目線よりも、むしろ公益的な観点のほうに重点があるというところです。その中で、機関投資家は、株主として影響力があるのに、金融機関の過度のリスクテイクを抑えられなかったので、今度は抑えられるようにしようというのがスチュワードシップ責任であるということが言われているわけです。

ところで、イギリスには、投資家の自主的な団体である Institutional Shareholders' Committee という団体がまとめていた、ISC Code on the Responsibilities of Institutional Investors という文書が既に存在していました。資料 3 - 1 です。Walker Review は、この文書に着目し、金融危機の直後で迅速な行動が求められるところ、ここに機関投資家の責任という文書があるが、民間団体が自分たちでつくったものにすぎないので、イギリスの財務報告評議会（FRC：Financial Reporting Council）が、ISC がつくった文書をオーソライズすれば、手早く対策がとれるので、そうしてはどうかということを提言しました。これを受けて、FRC が、ISC のコードを政府がスチュワードシップコードとしてまとめることでどうかというパブコメをして、その結果、まとめられたのが 2010 年版コードになります。

　それではイギリスのスチュワードシップコードの前身である ISC コードはどういうものだったかということですが、実は ISC コードは、機関投資家の責任を中身としては書いているのですけれども、その序文の中で、我々がここで書いている機関投資家の義務というのは、あくまで機関投資家の顧客と最終受益者に対するものであって、一般社会に対するものではないのだということを明言していました。何でこの文書ができたかというと、ISC コードは 2009 年にできているのですが、そのさらに前身となる文書が 2002 年から存在しています。2002 年に何があったかといいますと、年金基金に顧客の利益の観点からの議決権行使を義務づけることを提案した Myners Report という文書がありまして、それに対応して、政府による規制を避けるために、自分たちでちゃんとやりますという形での自主規制として作成されたのが ISC コードの前身であったわけです。

　これは、Myners Report 自身もそうですけれども、年金基金などの機関投資家に顧客の利益の観点から行動することを要請するもので、まさに ISC コードの序文に書かれているように、あくまで顧客と最終受益者に対する責任であったわけです。それがイギリスの 2010 年版コードによってどうなったかといいますと、最終的には序文のところをざっくりと全部削って、新し

い序文をつけて、中身はそのままという形で採択されています。

　特に、機関投資家の義務は顧客と最終受益者に対するもので、一般社会に対するものではないという部分も削られています。Walker Review のもともとの目的からすると、むしろ機関投資家に社会的な責任を負わせようという話ですので、そこは削らざるを得なかったわけですが、そういうものとして、ただ、中身はそのまま出てきたというのがイギリス版コードであったわけです。

　この傾向はその後も維持されておりまして、2012 年にいわゆる Kay Review が出されましたが、Kay Review では、さらに株式市場の短期主義的傾向が批判されており、これを改めるためには、拡大されたスチュワードシップが必要であるということが提言されています。拡大されたスチュワードシップコードというのはよくわからない概念ですけれども、その中で 1 つ挙げられているのは、機関投資家は経営者を単に批判するのではなくて、信頼しなければならず、もちろん経営者の側もその負託に応えなければいけないということがうたわれています。具体的な提言ではないのですけれども、機関投資家の経営者に対する圧力を弱めるような方向での提言と言えるように思います。

　Kay Review の提言を受けてまとめられたのがイギリスの 2012 年版のコードです。先ほど冒頭でご紹介したイギリスのスチュワードシップコードの目的は、この 2012 年版コードから取ったものですけれども、そこでは、投資先企業の長期的な成功を最初に持ってくるような形で、まさに Kay Review の全体的なメッセージを受け入れたような形での規定がなされているわけでございます。

　現在進行中のイギリスの 2019 年版の改訂案はどうなっているかというと、スチュワードシップコードの目的がさらに修正されています。何で修正するのかという理由の説明は、今のところ見つけられずにいるのですけれども、今度は少し揺り戻しがあったようにも見えなくもありません。抜粋した部分の最後のところですが、primary purpose of stewardship as looking after

the assets of beneficiaries ということが書いてあって、最終受益者のことば
かりを言っているように読めなくもありません。

　ただ、他方で、最近ヨーロッパで特に話題になっておりますけれども、気
候変動への対策などのＥＳＧ関連の課題を、スチュワードシップの実施にお
いて考慮しなければいけないということも明示しておりまして、社会的・公
益的な要請という側面は、イギリスのコードからは依然として消えていない
という状況にあるということでございます。

　次に、このようなイギリス版コードが、特に 2010 年に最初に導入された
後に、イギリスの学界でどのような議論がなされていたかということですが、
まずケンブリッジ大学の Cheffins 教授は、イギリス版コードがやろうとして
いることはいいのだけれども、外国の機関投資家に公益的な責任を果たさせ
ることは無理なので、結局無意味だということで批判していました。また
UCL の Chiu 教授と KCL の Katelouzou 教授は、同じように機関投資家に社
会的責任を果たさせる必要があるのだけれども、ソフトローではだめなので、
もっと公的規制を強める必要がある。どういう規制なのかは余りはっきりと
は言われていないのですが、ソフトローではなくてハードローとして、まず
は開示をもっと強化することが必要であると提言しています。スチュワード
シップコード自体に対しては批判もしているのですけれども、目指す方向性
としては、機関投資家に社会経済のことを考えさせるという点で、Walker
Review の方向性が共有されていたわけです。

　エンフォースメントはどうなっているかということも、ごく簡単にですが
見ておきたいと思います。2010 年版コードでは、賛同するかどうかは全く
の任意であり、賛同した署名者のリストを FRC が開示することになってお
り、コードの中身自体については comply or explain であるということで、
日本と同じような形だったわけです。ただ、これでは実効性がないとの批判
もあった中で、2012 年版コードでは、まずイギリスにベースがある asset
manager には、任意ではなくて強制的に適用するということが導入された。
また、2016 年には、comply or explain の開示の質によって３つの Tier に分

けるということを始めまして、一番開示の質が悪い Tier は、もはや賛同者とは言えないということで、一定の猶予期間を置いた後に、署名者リストから削除するということで、圧力を強めるということもやっております。さらに、2019 年版コードでは、基本原則のような発想は全員が適用しなければいけないのだということで、apply and explain という考え方に変えるということが言われたりもしていますので、規制色をだんだんと強める方向に向かいつつあるというのがイギリスのお話でございます。

２．日本

　他方、我が日本はどうかということです。まずイギリスと同様に、策定の経緯を見ていきたいと思うのですが、日本版のスチュワードシップコードの策定経緯として、各種の文献で出発点としてよく挙げられているのが、レジュメの４ページの一番下にある、2013 年６月に公表されました日本再興戦略という政策文書です。そこに引用しておりますように、「企業の持続的な成長を促す観点から、幅広い範囲の機関投資家が企業との建設的な対話を行い、適切に受託者責任を果たすための原則」について取りまとめるということで作られたのがスチュワードシップコードとされるわけです。

　ただ、日本再興戦略では、なぜここで急にスチュワードシップコードが必要だと言われたのか、その背景が全く説明されていませんし、何でこういうフレームが出てきたのかもわからない。そういうことで、もう少しさかのぼってみますと、私が調べた限りでは、その３カ月前の 2013 年３月に産業競争力会議という会議が官邸でありまして、その競争力会議のサブグループというか、テーマ別会合の中で、ローソンの新浪剛史さんがスチュワードシップコードに言及されたのが最初ではないかと思っております。

　その中で新浪さんがどういうことを言われていたかということですが、全体としてはコーポレートガバナンスを、ポイズンピルのようなものをつくって守るだけではなくて、むしろ攻めていくことができる仕組みにすることが必要である。攻めていくというのは何を意味しているのか、これだけだとよ

くわからないところもあるのですが、買収とか合併がしやすい法制度に見直すことが必要であるということを言いながら、ガバナンスについては、イギリスのスチュワードシップコードのように、「むしろ厳しく制度を設けて、企業そのものが生産性の高い経営ができるという制度設計も必要なのではないか」ということです。厳しくというのがどういう趣旨なのかということですけれども、これはすぐ後でご説明したいと思います。

　こういう議論に対して、政府側では、当時の甘利明経済再生担当大臣が、投資家側の圧力を強めることに対しては、アクティビストの要求で内部留保を吐き出してしまうと、長期的な成長のための研究開発資金がなくなってしまう。それはよくないのであって、むしろ短期主義ではなくて、長期的な経営ができるようにすべきであるという趣旨のことを反論されました。

　それに対して、新浪さんが再反論として、「アクティビストもある意味では悪くはない」のであり、むしろ長期経営と言いながらROEも上がっていないこと、企業がお金をちゃんと使ってないことが問題であって、それを意識させるという点では、アクティビストも必要だということを言われている。そうすると、先ほどのスチュワードシップコードの話も、アクティビストのような株式市場からの経営に対する圧力を強めるようなものとして新浪さんが認識していたということが示唆されるわけであります。

　テーマ別会合の1週間後ぐらいに親会議のほうに行きまして、また新浪さんがスチュワードシップコードに言及されているのですが、その中でも、物言う株主が重要ですということで、アクティビストとは区別をされていて、少し修正をされていますけれども、「中長期に株主として将来を見据えた機関投資家が、企業経営にしっかりと介入し、新陳代謝をすべき」であり、そのためにスチュワードシップコードが要るのだということを言っておられて、ここでもスチュワードシップコードは株主からの圧力を強めるためのものとして認識されています。

　一方で、先ほど新浪さんに反論していた甘利大臣は、ここでも反論されていたのですが、その裏で、2013年4月に開催された経済財政諮問会議で、

別の流れを作ろうとされています。この会議は甘利経済再生担当大臣が副議長ですが、当日は安倍首相がいなかったので、司会をされていたのですが、そこで、アメリカでベンチャーキャピタルをやっている原丈人さんという方が、公益資本主義、簡単に言うと、シェアホルダープライマシーではない経営モデルを標榜されているのですが、この原さんに「持続的成長を実現するための市場経済システムの構築に向けて」という講演をしてもらい、それを受けて、それは非常に大事なので、これをもっと考えるための専門調査会をつくるべきだということを甘利大臣自身が提案して、認められています。

その2カ月後に出たのが、先ほどお話ししました日本再興戦略ですけれども、そこでは「企業の持続的な成長」という言葉が入ってきまして、持続的な成長を促す観点から対話を行い、そのための原則について、「我が国の市場経済システムに関する経済財政諮問会議の議論も踏まえながら」検討を進めるということで、最終的に安倍総理の指示までいっているということになっております。

裏でどういう調整があったかは想像するしかないわけですけれども、もともとのスチュワードシップコードというアイデアを出してきた新浪さんのように、株主や資本市場からの経営に対する圧力を強めていくという路線に対して、それに対抗する形で、甘利大臣が投資先企業の持続的成長という発想を入れてくる。それのせめぎ合いの中ででき上がったのが日本再興戦略という文書なのではないかということが考えられるわけでございます。

こういう形の総理指示が出ましたので、スチュワードシップコードの有識者会議の中では専門調査会の話を聞かざるを得ないわけですけれども、専門調査会の報告書が紹介された際に、有識者会議のメンバーであった田中亘さんが、この報告書に対しても非常に批判的な意見を述べられて、これは結局、経営者に言いわけを許すだけであるということを言っておられました。それに対して、専門調査会を担当した内閣府の佐久間参事官が、それはわかるのだけれども、もともと専門調査会が立ち上がった問題意識は、原さんの公益資本主義から出発しているので、それで取りまとめるしかなかったというこ

ともご理解くださいということを言ってしまっているところがありまして、ここでも2つの流れのせめぎ合いが見えてくるわけです。

　この結果が最初に日本版スチュワードシップコードの「目的」としてご紹介した、スチュワードシップ責任の定義になるのですけれども、その中では、最終受益者の投資リターンの拡大ということが目的とされており、投資先企業の企業価値の持続的成長というのはあくまで手段として位置づけられているわけですが、この2つの要素は最初からセットであったわけではなくて、対立するようなものとして位置づけられていたわけです。

　では、どちらが究極的な目的なのだろうかということが問題となるのですが、まずコードの目的の書き方自体は、最終受益者の投資リターンのほうを上位に置いているわけですし、例えば田中さんの2014年版コードの一種の緩さへの批判などのように、どちらかというと株主からの経営への介入というものをもっと強化すべきであるというような路線で議論がされていた。少なくとも私自身はその方向性に余り疑問を持っていなかったのですけれども、そういう流れで議論がされていたように感じております。

　また、2017年版コードが改訂されたときも、株主からの介入を強めるような形で、運用機関による利益相反管理や、議決権行使結果の個別開示が導入されました。これらは、結局、より中立的な判断を機関投資家がすることを促すものということですので、全体的に最終受益者の投資リターンを強調する形で動いてきていると言えます。そうしますと、やはりイギリス版のコードとは目的が違ってくる。資料1の論文では、英語で書いたこともあって、「正反対」というような強い言い方をしているのですけれども、少なくとも大分違った方向を向いていると言うことができるのかなと思っています。

　その中で、日本版スチュワードシップコードの主たるターゲットとされていたのは、国内の機関投資家で、どちらかというと経営者寄りの行動をとりがちであったものを、個別開示などをさせることによって、もっと中立的に、最終受益者の目線で行動させるようにしたというのが、日本版スチュワードシップコードだったと言うことができるわけです。もっとも、それでは足り

13

なくて、株式持ち合いというものもあるのだから、本当はそれも含めないと目的が達成できないのではないかということが、大崎先生などからも指摘されていたところでありました。イギリスでは、国外機関投資家が入ってないことについて Cheffins が批判していたのに対して、日本では、そこは全く問題にされずに、むしろ銀行や取引先の株式持ち合いが入ってないことが批判されていたのが非常に対照的であって、着眼点の違いを示していると感じております。

　ただ、最終受益者の投資リターンを何のために強調しているのかということですが、例えば 2017 年版コードでは、パッシブファンドがもっとしっかりやらなければいけないということが言われるようになったわけです。しかし、パッシブファンド自体は、投資戦略として、そこまでお金をスチュワードシップにかけられないという可能性が指摘されています。本来、最終受益者の投資リターンだけを考えるのであれば、そこに口を出す必要はないはずです。にもかかわらず、もっとやれと言っているということは、結局、日本版スチュワードシップコードの最終的な目的は、最終受益者の投資リターンだけではなくて、それを言うことによって株主利益をベースとしたガバナンスシステムの改革をしたいということが背景にあるのではないか。それはアベノミクス以降、強調されるようになってきていることなので、全体としてそういう方向に向かっている中の方策の1つという位置づけになるのではないかと考えております。

　これから行われるであろう 2020 年の改訂でどういう方向に向かうかは、まだ議論が端緒についたばかりですので、どうなるかわからないところもありますけれども、今のところ、外から見ておりますと、方向性に変化はないように感じております。特にイギリスでは、ESG 要素を正面からスチュワードシップコードに取り入れたということが1つの売りになっているわけですけれども、日本では、ここの部分は非常に抑制的であるように思っております。ESG の話は、最初、事務局から紹介された後、途中までは正面から取り上げておらず、途中で議論の対象となったわけですが、その中で、ESG

要素も大事だけれども、あくまで機関投資家の投資戦略にそれが合致している限りにおいて取り入れるべきであるという指摘が一部の委員からなされました。これを受けて、フォローアップ会議の意見書にも下線部を引いた「投資戦略と整合的で」という観点が追加されているわけです。ここからも、ESG自体を正面から追求する方向に向かっているように思えるイギリスとは、大きな違いがあると言うことができるのかなと思っております。

３．シンガポール

　日本の話はその辺にしまして、では、シンガポールはどうだろうかということを少しご紹介したいと思います。

　まず2016年にSingapore Stewardship Principleがまとめられたわけですけれども、そこで目的として掲げられている内容は、イギリスの2012年版コードに非常に近いものであります。最初の1文ですが、Stewardship is about building and growing sustainable businesses to produce long-term benefits for all stakeholdersということで、最終受益者などではなく、いきなりall stakeholdersが来ている。さらにその次の文章で、short-term considerationsだけではいけないということを言っている。昨今short-term viewが強くなってきているので、スチュワードシップを強調することがタイムリーであるということが示唆されておりまして、Kay Reviewに近い認識でつくられた文書ということになるわけです。

　ただ、ここで不思議なのは、イギリスでは機関投資家の圧力が強くて、短期主義ということは現実的な問題として認識されているわけですが、シンガポールではどうかといいますと、シンガポールの上場企業のほとんどにはオーナー一族もしくは国有企業の管理会社であるTemasek Holdingsが支配株主として存在しているために、機関投資家からの圧力は余り強くないと認識されているようです。

　そうしますと、イギリスの企業について指摘されるのは、短期主義はイギリス自体についても本当に問題なのかどうかという問題はありますけれど

も、少なくともシンガポールについてはそれほど問題にはなっていないはずであるし、逆に機関投資家の果たし得る役割というのもそれほど大きくはない可能性があります。そうすると、シンガポールは、なぜこのタイミングでスチュワードシップコードを策定する必要があったのか。イギリスと同じ目的でやったとは思えないということが言えるわけでございます。

　シンガポール版は、そもそもコードとは言わずに、あくまでプリンシプルだということを強調されてもいるのですが、シンガポール版のスチュワードシップ原則がどのようにエンフォースされているかというと、適用するかどうかは完全に任意であり、かつ受入機関のリストもどこにも存在していません。もちろん各機関投資家が、自分たちは署名することを受け入れたということを自分で言うことはできるわけですが、日本の金融庁のように、当局がウェブサイトで署名者のリストを開示してはいませんし、さらに comply or explain も一切必要ないということで、趣旨に賛同するということだけ言って、実は裏で何もやってないということがあったとしても、それを言う必要はないということになっています。

　このことは、シンガポール版をまとめた団体の FAQ の中で、もし Stewardship Principles をサポートすることにしたら何をすればいいのかという質問に対する答えが、absolutely on a voluntary basis ということになっていて、全ては投資家の裁量に委ねられているということになっています。これを FAQ は、box-ticking、チェック・ザ・ボックスはよくないということできれいに説明しているわけですけれども、何のエンフォースもされていない。ただ、割と聞こえのいいように文章をまとめただけというようなところがあるのではないかということを共同研究者である Puchniak さんが評価されているわけです。

　何でこんな形になったのかということですけれども、策定主体がどこかということを見てみますと、それは Singapore Stewardship Principles Working Group という団体になっているのですが、これは Stewardship Asia Centre という団体が組織したものでして、ほかの経済団体なども一緒

に議論はしていますが、Stewardship Asia が主導して、Stewardship Asia Centre のウェブサイトに掲載されているわけです。この Stewardship Asia Centre は、実は Temasek Holdings、シンガポールの国有企業管理会社の出資と支援を受けている非営利団体です。

シンガポールで上場企業の株主保有構造を考えますと、主要企業の大半には Temasek Holdings が支配株主として存在しています。そうすると、外部の機関投資家のモニタリングが厳しくなった場合に、Temasek Holdings は、むしろ支配株主として監視を受ける立場になるわけですので、監視を受ける立場になる側がなぜかスチュワードシップコードをつくっているということで、すごい違和感があるわけです。

これは、うがった見方をしますと、外からそういう声が強くなる前に国際的な動向を自発的にフォローしているというような形をとりつつ、ただ、中身としては非常に緩やかな内容のスチュワードシップコードを策定しておくことでプリエンプションを図ったもの、現在はそれほど機関投資家の圧力が強くなく、Temasek Holdings もそれほど困っているというようには思えないわけですけれども、将来圧力が強くなる可能性もあるので、今のうちに現状維持を図ったものではないかということができるのではないかと考えております。

さらに興味深いのは、最初の原則の策定から 2 年後の 2018 年に、同じ Stewardship Asia Centre が、今度は家族企業のためのスチュワードシップ原則（資料 4－2）という文書をつくりました。これは非上場企業も含む同族企業を対象とするものですので、日本のように上場企業に投資する機関投資家のスチュワードシップとは全く別のものになってくるわけですが、ここでは同族企業のオーナー一族を事業を預かっているという意味で steward と位置づけて、オーナー一族は誰のために経営すべきかというと、一族の利益だけではなくて、企業には多様なステークホルダーがいるのだから、従業員や地域社会、取引先も全部含めた多様なステークホルダーの利益に持続可能な形で貢献できるように経営すべきであるということを言っております。

これは、steward というのが非常に便利な概念であり、全然違った文脈で使うこともできるということを示唆しています。

　また、経営するオーナー一族の利益だけを考えて会社を搾取してはいけないということを言っているわけですけれども、理念をうたっているだけで、エンフォースメントに関する記述は一切なく、comply or explain も、賛同する場合のリストも、全く挙げられておりません。

　では、なぜこれをつくったのか。搾取はよろしくないというのは非常に結構なことだとは思うのですけれども、それをまとめた目的は不明です。アジア諸国にはこういう同族企業が多いわけですけれども、その中でシンガポールはこういうふうにやっていますということを言って、1つの宣伝をしているのではないかという評価もできるのかもしれません。いずれにせよシンガポールでは、日本ともイギリスとも大分違ったものとしてスチュワードシップコードを利用しているということが言えるわけです。

4．小括

　ここまでを簡単にまとめますと、日本版とイギリス版のコードとは、目的は逆方向を向いているわけですが、日本もイギリスも、それぞれの目的を実現するために、スチュワードシップコードによって機関投資家に圧力をかけていくというところでは、割と共通しているように思われます。

　他方で、シンガポールはどうかというと、目的の点では、日本よりもイギリスに類似するようなことを言っておりますが、規制色は、イギリスに比べると、ほぼ皆無に等しいということが言えるわけです。その点で、日本ともイギリスとも違う第三の形というものを持っているように思えるわけです。

Ⅲ．若干の考察

1．コーポレートガバナンスの収斂（convergence）の諸態様

　ここまで見た上で、少しだけ理論的なことを考えてみたのがこの先のお話ですが、まずいわゆる比較コーポレートガバナンスに関する学界の議論の中

では、コーポレートガバナンスの収斂ということが議論されるようになっているわけです。その中で、スタンフォード大学のGilson教授が、収斂には形式的収斂（formal convergence）と機能的収斂（functional convergence）の2つがあるということを大分前の論文で書かれています。

　Gilson教授が言われていたのは、形式的収斂というのは、会社法という制定法を変えることも必要になるので、制度改正に非常にコストがかかるため、なかなか進まないけれども、形式的なルールが違っていても機能的には実は同じようなことが実現できているということがしばしばある。そのため、機能的収斂のほうが先に進むのだということです。

　その例として挙げておられたのが、アメリカでは、例えば会社経営の業績が悪いと、社外取締役の介入によってCEOが交代させられるということがあるけれども、日本では90年代にはそんなことはもちろん起きないわけですが、他方で、業績が悪いと会社内部のメカニズム、幹部従業員からの圧力や前社長の圧力などによって、社長が交代するということがある。結局、経営が悪い場合には、社長がそのうち交代するという点では一緒であるということです。

　これを踏まえたときに、スチュワードシップコードの話がどのように評価できるかということですが、我々といいますのは、私とPuchniakさんとKohさんですけれども、スチュワードシップコードを各国が採択するという意味では、形式的な面ではむしろ収斂が進んでいるのだけれども、イギリスの目的も日本の目的もシンガポールの目的も違っているという意味では、コードの策定で実現しようとした機能は、各国で大きく異なっている。

　これはコロンビア大学のGordon教授が言うdivergence in convergence、収斂の中での多様性というものの1つの例とも言えるわけですが、もう少し言うと、表層的な形式のみが収斂していて機能面は収斂していないという状況です。そこで、このことを、言葉がややきついような気もするのですが、にせのconvergenceではないかということで、faux convergenceとして概念化してみました。これを書いてあるのが8ページの表であります。

Gilson 教授が言っていた formal convergence と functional convergence は、機能面は収斂しているんだけれども、法律レベルでの形式というものが収斂しているかどうかが違っているという分析でした。どちらも収斂していないと、全く convergence がないということも含めてマトリックスを２×２でつくると、左下の部分が faux convergence であって、それが例えばスチュワードシップコードだったのではないかということです。

　Gilson 教授の formal convergence がなかなか起きにくいという指摘は、形式的な収斂には制度改正が必要になり、それにはコストがかかるからということですけれども、スチュワードシップコードは、結局ソフトローであって、formal な立法手続をとる必要がないということになりますので、そのために、制度改正のコストが非常に小さくて済む。そのために、そこだけ真似するということがより簡単に起きるのではないか。これは例えばコーポレートガバナンスコードという中で、独立取締役を要求するということは各国でも行われるようになっているわけですけれども、それも同じようなことがあるのではないかと考えられるわけです。

２．各国のスチュワードシップコードのグルーピング

　共同研究として進めているのは、現在ここまでですが、その上で、スチュワードシップコードで目的がもっと多様なものであるとすると、日英シンガポールの３カ国だけではなくて、もう少し足してみて、それをグルーピングすることはできないだろうかということで、あと韓国と台湾とアメリカの状況も個人的に少し調べてみております。

　まず分類軸としまして、日本とイギリスとシンガポールをまとめますと、日本は最終投資家や株主の利益というものを強調しているのに対して、イギリスと、一応シンガポールも表面上は、公共的な利益を強調しているというところが違っています。この目的のレベルが１つ目の軸になります。あとは、日本とイギリスは、少し語弊がある言い方ですけれども、どちらも規制強化型と言うことができるように思われるのに対して、シンガポールは何も変え

ない、現状を維持しようとしているように見えるという規制の度合いのレベルの軸が2つ目です。

この2つの分類軸でどう言えるかということなんですけれども、まず韓国については、策定経緯が紆余曲折を経ているので、なかなか難しいところがあるのですが、9ページの「コード記載の目的」というところを見ていただくと、日本版をコピーしたような文面がとられております。機関投資家の責任というのは、投資先企業の中長期的な価値の向上を追求することによって、機関投資家の顧客や最終受益者の中長期的な利益を促進することですということで、非常に日本に近い定義になっています。

韓国のスチュワードシップコードの議論が始まったのは、日本のコードができた2014年の終わりごろです。そこから始まっているので、恐らく日本を見ながら議論したということではないかと思われるわけですが、その後、すんなりとはいきませんで、2014年に議論が始まって、2015年3月に起草委員会が設置され、その年の12月に第1次草案ができたわけですけれども、産業界からの反発が強くて成立に至らなかった。FSCというのは韓国の金融庁に当たる組織ですが、そこでの策定ができなかった。

その後、政府がそういうことをやるのは企業経営に対する介入であるという批判があったので、これを受けて、FSCではなくて、韓国証券取引所などが設立していた民間団体であるKorean Corporate Governance Service（KCGS）という組織が起草作業を引き継いで、そこで起草委員会をつくった。2016年11月に第2次草案をつくり、その1カ月後に最終案を公表したということになっているわけですが、その背後に韓国社会ではいろいろな動きがありました。

まず、スチュワードシップコードの議論がまだ始まったばかりだった2015年7月ですが、Samsungのオーナー一族の経営権の承継の過程の中で、李在鎔さん、今の副社長の方に持ち株を引き継ぐということで、その中で、Samsung CTという会社とCheil Industriesという会社を合併することが必要になってきた。

そのときに、Cheil Industries を李ジュニアのほうが支配していまして、Samsung CT は一般上場企業ですけれども、Samsung CT の一般株主に不利な比率での合併議案だったわけです。その中で、Samsung CT の筆頭株主であった韓国の国民年金基金（NPS）は、NPS の議決権行使専門委員会が、この合併はよくないので、反対すべきであるということを勧告していたにもかかわらず、それをどこかの過程で覆して、結局この合併議案に賛成しました。これによって Samsung CT と Cheil Industries が合併することができ、李一族の経営権の承継に寄与したということがあったわけです。この NPS の判断は、韓国の会社法の研究者などによっても批判されていたりするところでございます。

　そういう出来事があった中で、さらに 2016 年 10 月には朴槿恵前大統領のスキャンダルが発覚して、同年 12 月に弾劾決議が可決されることになり、2017 年 5 月の選挙で文在寅氏が当選したわけです。文在寅氏は、公約の中で韓国の財閥改革を掲げるとともに、その中でスチュワードシップコードの導入も 1 つの柱にしていたようでして、さらに就任演説においても財閥改革をするということを宣言しているわけです。

　韓国語の文献を読めているわけではありませんので、全部わかっているわけではないのですけれども、2015 年 7 月の Samsung CT と Cheil Industries の合併の中で国民年金基金が果たした役割に対する批判的な意識から、財閥改革をするためには、韓国内の機関投資家が、もっとしっかりと株主の利益のために行動する必要があるということが指摘されていたのではないかと思われるわけです。さらに、2017 年 12 月には、韓国の財務省に当たる企画財政部が、スチュワードシップコードの導入と、NPS などにもそれを受け入れさせることとを政策として掲げております。NPS は大分後になって、2018 年 7 月にようやくこれを受け入れることを宣言しています。

　ここを見ますと、日本と韓国には似ているところがあります。まず目的の記載のレベルで、最終受益者の利益を韓国も強調しているわけですけれども、その背景には、結局 NPS などが、最終受益者の利益を半ば無視した形で、

財閥のオーナー一族に手心を加えたようなことがあった。それはよくないので、変える必要があるということが意識されていたのではないかということが言えるわけです。

　また、株式保有構造という面では、オーナー一族が多いという点で、韓国の構造はシンガポールに近いわけですけれども、ただ、シンガポールとは違って、政府がコーポレートガバナンス改革のために、機関投資家の圧力を用いようとしているという点では、同様に政府が企業のガバナンスシステムを変えるためにスチュワードシップコードを使っている日本と非常に近いものが見られるわけです。

　さらには、内容のレベルでも、7原則もほとんど日本版コードと同じですが、最初から議決権の行使の個別開示というものが要求されておりますし、KCGSがリストを公表するという意味では、日本と非常に近いモデルがとられているということが言えようかと思います。

　次に台湾ですが、台湾も韓国と似たような株式保有構造になっております。台湾でも同じころにスチュワードシップコードの議論が始まりました。ここでの策定主体は、台湾の金融当局である金融監督管理委員会の指示を受けた台湾証券取引所です。

　「コード記載の目的」は、機関投資家自身が入っているのが不思議なのですが、機関投資家とそのほかの資金提供者の長期的な利益のために行動することが大事ですと言われております。さらに、それによって、投資先企業のガバナンスも改革できるということをうたっているわけですが、その他の国と比べて非常に特徴的なのは、投資先企業の sustainable growth に言及がなく、最終受益者の利益がより強調されている形になっている点です。また、内容面を見ても、原則は6つだけで、日本の原則7、機関投資家は投資先企業への理解と実力を備えていなければいけないという田中さんによって批判された原則7を除いたものであって、ここでも投資家の圧力をより強調するような形になっているわけです。

　ただ、エンフォースメントはどうかといいますと、受入機関のリストはあ

るのですが、各原則の遵守状況について簡単な説明をすればいいということになっておりまして、explain の部分が、不遵守の場合にも、何でそうしているのかということまでは説明を求めていないということで、割と簡単な開示の要求になっています。それに加えて、外国の機関投資家は、母国などで同様の目的のコードや原則を受け入れている場合には、そのことを言えば、それで台湾版コードを受け入れたものと言うことができるとされています。日本、韓国、シンガポールなどで、どれだけ中身が違うかということを余り意識していないのかもしれませんけれども、そういう意味では、エンフォースメントはかなり緩いと言うことができるのかもしれません。

　策定の目的は何なのかということも余りはっきりは書いておりませんで、国際的なトレンドとして機関投資家のスチュワードシップコードが大事なものとなっているということが指摘されるにとどまっています。そうしますと、日本や韓国のように台湾企業のガバナンス改革を何か具体的に変革したいという問題意識があるというよりは、どちらかというと、国際的な動向に合わせることによって、投資家を呼び込もうとしているのではないかということが見えてくるというのが台湾の状況のように思われます。

　最後に、アメリカです。今までの日本、イギリス、シンガポール、韓国、台湾とも、策定主体は、政府もしくは政府機関の意向を受けた取引所などであったわけですが、アメリカでは、策定主体は全くの民間団体である Investor Stewardship Group（ISG）というグループで、大規模な機関投資家や国際的なアセットマネジャーの有志の団体であると自分たちを定義しています。

　「コード記載の目的」は、機関投資家はその資金提供者に対してアカウンタブルであるということを言っております。さらに、この団体が、合わせてガバナンス原則も策定しているわけですけれども、そこでは、取締役会は、今度は株主に対してアカウンタブルであるとされています。さらに、株主には経済的利益の比率に応じて議決権が与えられるべきであるということで、dual class に対して批判的なことを言っているわけです。この二つをあわせ

ると、ISGが言っているのは、取締役会は株主に対して説明責任を負い、株主である機関投資家は最終受益者に説明責任を負うということで、投資先企業の成長云々ということは基本的には言われていないわけです。

では、内容はどうかといいますと、現在アメリカの機関投資家が一般的に行っていると考えられるエンゲージメントを強化するものであるとは思われなくて、どちらかというと、割と緩めの原則になっているように思われます。例えば議決権行使助言機関をそのまま受け入れるのではなくて、それを十分評価した上で使うべきであるとか、機関投資家は、見解の差異がある場合であっても、建設的な態度で企業との対話に臨むべきであるということを言っていますし、集団的エンゲージメント自体を促進するというよりは、みんなで議論をしましょうというようなことで、政策的な議論への参加などを例示するにとどめておりまして、余り介入色は強くないという印象を受けるところでございます。

また、署名した機関投資家のリストがISGのウェブサイトで公表されてはいるのですけれども、原則をどのように運用しているかということは全く各機関投資家に委ねられておりますし、comply or explain も要求されていないという面でも、エンフォースメントは強くない。

そうしますと、「策定の目的」、コードでどう書かれているかというより、その背後にある事情ということですけれども、これは、私の印象では、どちらかというとシンガポール版コードのように現状維持的であると思われます。シンガポールとの違いはどこにあるかというと、投資家・株主の利益を目的としている。それは今現在のアメリカの機関投資家がやっていることかと思いますが、それをそのまま維持したいということです。

これは、イギリスの2010年版スチュワードシップコードの前身であるISCコードに非常に近いものであるように思われるわけです。アメリカのISGがなぜこういうものをつくったのかというのは、まだ十分に探れていないのですけれども、ひょっとしたらイギリス版コードのような機関投資家に社会に対する公益的な責任を負わせようとする政治的な動きがあることへの

対抗策として、我々は最終受益者のためにやっているのだということを宣言しているのかなとも思うところでございます。

改めてグループを分けますと、目的の方向性と規制がどれだけ強いかという２つの軸で、４つのボックスに分けることができるかなと思っています。イギリスと日本及び韓国とは、両方とも規制強化的だけれども、目的の方向性が、イギリスと、日本及び韓国とで違っております。また、シンガポールと、イギリスのISCコード及びアメリカのISGコードとは、現状維持的であるところは似ているわけですけれども、もともとの方向性が違っています。欧米の文献などではスチュワードシップコードが国際的に広まっていると一括してくくられることが多かったりもするのですけれども、実はその中が非常に多様であるということを認識しなければいけないのではないかと思っています。

どういう要素がこの多様性に影響しているのだろうかということを考えますと、１つは、策定主体が政府であるか、投資家の自主的な団体であるか。投資家の団体は、自分たちは今こうやっています、ちゃんとやっているので何も言ってこないでくださいというために文書をまとめる傾向にあり、これがイギリスのISCやアメリカのISGです。他方で、政府がやると、やはりそこには何らかの政策目的があって、それに向けた規制強化の一環として使うことが多い。ただ、シンガポールだけは、政府自体が国有企業の管理会社でありますので、少し特殊なところがあり、現状維持的になっている。目的の方向性がどちらに向いているかということは、これは株主所有構造でその国のガバナンスの問題が何であるかによって変わってくるという印象を持っているところでございます。

特に何の主張も提言もなく、ただ現状がこうなっているように思いますという報告で大変恐縮ですけれども、私からは以上でございます。どうもありがとうございました。

討　議

神作会長　大変貴重なご報告をどうもありがとうございました。英米のみならず、シンガポール、台湾、韓国と多くの国についてご紹介いただき、後藤さんの国際的な人脈や知見を生かしたご報告だったと思います。それでは、どなたからでも結構でございますので、ご質問、ご意見をよろしくお願いいたします。

　なお、いつものように、恐縮でございますけれども、ご発言される前にお名前をおっしゃっていただけると幸いです。どうかよろしくお願いいたします。

河村委員　ありがとうございました。大変勉強になりました。

　何点か確認をさせていただきたいと思うことがあります。

　1つ目は、レジュメで言うと、3ページ目の 2019 年版のイギリスのコード改訂案の「スチュワードシップの目的を修正」というところです。従来のものと比較をすると、企業の持続的な成長の促進という部分が明示的には外れてきていて、先生は揺り戻しとおっしゃっておられましたけれども、受益者の利益というものがむしろ前面に出てきている。これは恐らくスチュワードシップの観点からは、投資した後に、投資先企業にどう関与するかという点だけではなくて、そもそもどの企業に投資をするのかというインベストメント・デシジョン・メイキングのところで、スチュワードシップも重要なんだということで、こういう書きぶりに変わってきているのかなと思っています。

　つまり、先生のご説明にあったように、もともとスチュワードシップコードは金融危機対応の側面があったと思うのですけれども、ただ、金融危機対応という点では、金融機関に関するプルーデンス規制の整備などが進められていて、スチュワードシップコードでその点に対応する必要性が今相対的に小さくなってきているのではないのかなと思いますし、ＥＳＧの観点からのエンゲージメントだけではなくて、そもそもＥＳＧの観点から、どの企業に

投資するのか、あるいはどの企業から撤退するのか、divestment するのか
という話が今広まっていると思いますので、投資した企業に対して、どう関
与していくかだけではなくて、そもそもどこに投資をするのかというところ
も含めて、スチュワードシップというものを考えなくてはいけないんだとい
うことで、こういう書きぶりになってきているのではないでしょうか。

　もう１点つけ加えますと、先ほどのプルーデンス規制の話もそうですけれ
ども、要は、ハードローのほうの状況が変わってきている。つまり、プルー
デンス規制だけではなくて、例えばＥＳＧのうちのＥＳに関して言うと、イ
ギリスの現代奴隷法であるとか、今ＥＵで進められている持続可能な金融制
度に関するさまざまな立法提案、ソフトローも入っていますけれども、ハー
ドローの整備があるので、スチュワードシップコードの中でわざわざそうい
うＥＳの話をしなくても、もうよくなってきているともいえるのではないか。
なので、今もとに戻ってきて、そもそもどこに投資をするのかということも
含めて、スチュワードシップを捉え直そうということではないかと思ってい
ます。これが先生の表現で言うと、揺り戻しということなのかなと思ったの
ですけれども、そういう理解でよいかどうかを確認させていただきたいとい
うのが１点です。

　もう１点は、今の点に関係するのですが、先生はＥＳの話を、どちらかと
いうと、社会的・公益的な要素として捉えておられたように思うのですけれ
ども、今のヨーロッパの状況から言うと、本当にそちらで捉えていいのか。
つまり、企業にとってＥＳの問題というのは、社会的責任というよりも、企
業の価値に直結してくるような話になってきている。つまり、先ほど言った
ようなさまざまな制度整備が進められている。あるいはＥＳに関心を持って
いる市民が増えてきて、ＥＳに配慮していないような企業だということにな
ると、その企業の価値が下がって、最終的には投資家の利益にかかわってく
る。

　ＥＳの問題を、例えば先生の分類で言うと、11 ページの表でイギリスは
public interest のほうに入っているのですけれども、今はむしろＥＳの話を

していても、shareholder とか investor との関係で捉えているのではないか、そちらのほうの感覚が強くなってきているのではないかと思います。もしそうだとすると、11 ページの表の部分も、今動いているのではないかなと思うのですが、そのあたり、いかがでしょうか。

後藤報告者 ご質問とご指摘を、どうもありがとうございました。

まずはイギリスの 2019 年版コードですが、背景を指摘していただきましてどうもありがとうございました。金融機関の話というのは少し後ろに引いたのではないかというのは、確かにおっしゃるとおりかなと思います。それもあって、7 年間も改訂がなかったのかもしれません。アメリカはその観点からショート・ターミズムを余り強調しなくてもよくなったというのもあるかもしれませんし、ヨーロッパでは、むしろ長期主義のほうが大事だという見方の方がメインストリームになっているような感じもします。その意味でも、あえてそれを強調しなくてもということになったのかもしれません。

投資判断レベルのスチュワードシップという考え方は、私は余り気づいておりませんで、非常に参考になりました。ただ、今度は揺り戻しなのかというのは、私はよくわからずにおります。揺り戻しというのが、例えばイギリスの投資家団体である ISC が言っていた、我々はあくまで受益者のためにやっているのであって、社会に対する責任というのは我々は特に負っているわけではありませんというところまで戻ったということは多分ないような気がするのですね。

そうではなくて、むしろ河村先生がおっしゃられたように、ESG も大事だということが前提とされているという意味では、日本と同じになったかというと、日本がどうかというところはご意見があるかもしれませんけれども、やはりまだ違っているのかなという気がします。表現のレベルで、余り強調しなくなったという意味では揺り戻しなのだけれども、ESG にこだわりがあるような気がするという意味では、やはり日本とは違うという気がしているところでございます。

問題のＥＳＧのほうですけれども、おっしゃられるとおり、もちろん社会・

公益だけの話ではなくて、sustainable growth というのは全員にとって大事であり、それはむしろ株主の利益にも資するという話は、日本でも昔からずっとあるわけです。その範囲であれば、それは恐らく日本でもどこでも受け入れられているとは思うのですけれども、ヨーロッパでは、それを超えて、それ以上にやはりＥとＳが大事だという見方が見え隠れをしているような気が私はしています。

　例えばイギリスでスチュワードシップコードを研究している人の論文では、どうしてもＥとＳが大事だということが出てくる。投資先の選択という意味で、ＥとＳを大事にするファンドをつくって、それをみんなが買うということには何の問題もないことだとは思うのですけれども、そうではないファンドというのも世の中にはいっぱいあるわけで、それらにどこまでＥとＳをやらせる必要があるのかというと、それは投資家の資金拠出者への責任という観点からは本来出てこないはずなのだけれども、そこにもやれということを求めているような気がします。

　イギリスでスチュワードシップコードが来年10周年ということで国際会議が今月末にロンドンであって、私は行けないのですけれども、金融庁の井上課長が行かれると伺っています。この会議の主催者と話をしたときも、話が全然かみ合いませんでした。ＥとＳをすごく強調されていて、日本の議論の流れは違うということをさんざん言って、ようやく意図が通じたというところがあるのです。どちらがいいという意味ではなくて、出発点が違うということですが、それは未だに残っていると考えています。

藤田委員　一番最後の整理のところについて、若干の感想です。まず、「規制強化的」、「現状維持的」という目的の方向性で分類されていますが、「規制強化的」という表現は余りよくなくて、現状を変えたいのか、現状を維持するものかということなので、「現状変更型」等にした方がいいと思います。

　そしてここで「影響する要素」が挙げられているんですが、もしこれが原因という意味だとしたら、ちょっと微妙かなと思いました。株式所有構造はまだいいのですけれども、策定主体は原因なのか結果なのかがよくわからな

いです。つまり、現状を変えたいときには政府が乗り出すということなのかもしれないので、政府が乗り出せば現状が変わるという因果関係かどうかがよくわからないのです。ここで、より重要な決め手となる原因は、現状を変更するという政策決定が行われ、受け入れられる原因が何かということのはずなので、そこから現状維持型か否かという話と、そのために適切な主体が選ばれるという話が導かれるという関係ではないかと思います。

　主体についてもう１つ付け加えると、理論的には、政府がかかわると現状変更型になるという関係も見せかけ相関関係の可能性がある。例えば日本のようなところで投資家の利益を代表する民間団体がコードをつくると、現状変更型の内容になりそうです。ただし、それだと無視される可能性があるところを役所などが背後からバックアップするという形をとるとすれば、実質的な策定主体は政府じゃなくても現状変更型になり得ることになります。だから作成主体と現状維持か現状変更かとの関係は、なかなか微妙なところがある。このあたりの理論は、詰めると意外とおもしろいし、同時にきっちり理屈を詰めるのはなかなか難しいという印象を持ちました。

　最後に、現状維持型ですけれども、これもよく考えると、なぜ現状維持型なコードをつくるのかという根本問題があります。お話を聞いている限りだと、大きく２つのパターンがありそうです。一つは、ここに限らずよくある話なのですが、業界団体が自分たちがやっていることを変えたくないときに、外から圧力がかかるのを防ぐために現状をそれほど変えない行為規範を高らかに宣言するというもので、多分イギリスのISCはその性格が非常に強く、アメリカもその性格が強そうだと思います。これに対して、シンガポールはそういう性格ではないかもしれない。これは単純に流行のものを取り入れないとカッコ悪いというふうな動機で作成されているとすれば、現状を維持する、業界をプロテクトするという目的が余り正面に出ていない気がします。アメリカ・イギリスとシンガポールの性格の違いはそこがポイントだとすると、Pro public か Pro shareholder かという軸でコードを分類してしまうと、重要な本質を逃すような気もします。むしろ現状維持型なら、誰が、何のた

31

めの、どういう原動力でコードを作ろうとしているのかをもう少し考えたらいいかなと、理論的にはそういう感想を持ちました。

後藤報告者　いずれもおっしゃるとおりかと思います。

確かに最後の要素は、非常に取ってつけたようなものでして、もう少し深く分析する必要があるところかと思います。また「規制強化的」はちょっと言葉がよくないなと思っていましたので、「現状変更型」にさせていただければと思います。

シンガポールが何なのかということですが、はやりに乗っただけということもあり得るところです。もっとも、Puchniak さんによると、シンガポールが最初に社外取締役が必要だとしたときには、まさにはやりに乗っただけの感じがあるのですが、その後に意味を変えたこともあるというところで、はやりに乗っただけの感じを見せつつ、ひょっとしたら外からの圧力を防ごうとしているのかもしれないという話もあるので、そこは排他的ではないのかもしれません。

また、台湾もはやりに乗っただけという感じがかなりしているんですけれども、台湾とシンガポールは、イギリスの ISC やアメリカの ISG とはちょっと質が違うような気がしましたので同じにはしなかったんですが、どちらも政府がはやりに乗っただけのような感じを見せつつ、少なくとも字面では逆方向のことを言っていますので、なぜその違いが出てきているのかということを考えています。台湾は本当に外からの投資がないと今後国がどうなるかわからない状況にあるとして、シンガポールはその心配は余りないというところがひょっとしたら効いているのかもしれないので、その辺をもう少し深く考えてみたいと思います。

中東委員　貴重かつ興味深いご報告をありがとうございました。

faux convergence というご分析も、後藤先生、Dan W. Puchniak 先生、Alan K. Koh 先生らしいと思って拝聴しました。

株式所有構造との関係で2つお聞きしたいと思います。

分散した株式所有構造をイギリスも日本も持っています。そういう構造に

なると、スチュワードシップコードがコーポレートガバナンスコードにレバレッジをきかせるような感じがいたします。そのあたりが faux convergence にどういう影響を与えたのかを教えていただきたいというのが1点です。

　もう1点は、こういった convergence ができてくると、先日の Business Roundtable の提言をみても、これまでの日本の考え方でよかったのかという点です。例えば、敵対的な企業買収については、防衛買収策がこのところどんどん廃止されていっています。他方でガバナンスコードのほうでは、後継者を育成しなさい、各会社の経営理念や経営戦略を踏まえて十分な時間と資源をかけて計画的に行いなさいとも言っています。このあたりについてダブルコードがどういう影響を与えているのかを教えていただければと思います。

後藤報告者　2点目ですけれども、Business Roundtable が、株主の利益だと言っていたのが、そこにはステークホルダーも入ると言ったことですね。あれが何なのかということですが、先ほどの藤田先生の話でいうと、業界団体が介入しないでくれと言っていることの、まさに典型のような気がします。我々はちゃんとステークホルダーの利益も考えているのです、なぜなら株主の利益もあるんだから、みんなのためにやっているんですと言っていることは、例えばエリザベス・ウォーレンが取締役の3分の1を従業員に選ばせると言い出したことに対して、ちゃんとやっていますからやめてくださいと言っているのだと思います。本音がどう変わったかではなくて、とりあえず話はわかったからあとは任せてくださいということだとすると、それが本当の意味でアメリカがやってきたことを伝統的な日本流にがらっと変えることかというと、多分そこまではいかないんじゃないかという気がしています。

　1点目はよくわからなかったので、もう少し補足していただけますでしょうか。

中東委員　言葉足らずで、失礼しました。コーポレートガバナンスコードでいろいろな comply or explain の項目がありますが、株式が分散保有されていって、スチュワードシップコードがこれらを後押しするようになると、ガ

バナンスコードで決められているデフォルトというか、あるいはスタンダードに、レバレッジがきいた形になるのではないか。それが convergence を後押ししているという気もするんですが、どのようにお考えでしょうか。

後藤報告者 わかりました。まだ消化できているかどうかわからないんですけれども、そのときの convergence が何についての convergence かというお話で、今日お話しさせていただいたのは、スチュワードシップコードを各国が入れるという意味での convergence ということですが、今の話はどちらかというと、例えば社外取締役、独立取締役によるガバナンスという別の側面について、それ自体も convergence があり、独立取締役の存在という形式的な面の話もあれば、独立取締役に何をさせたいかという機能面での話もあるかと思います。独立取締役の存在という形式面だけに着目をするとしても、ガバナンスコードで言われ、さらに日本のスチュワードシップコードの場合には独立取締役が株主の利益のために働くことがいいことだという認識でいて、おっしゃるように両方があることによって同一の方向に向いている、まさにそれが政府がやろうとしたことであり、よく車の両輪と言われるような話に近いのかなとも思います。

　ではイギリスのガバナンスコードで同じことが起きているかというと、イギリスのガバナンスコードはもっと古いわけで、キャドバリーレポートができたのが 1992 年で、その後いろいろあって統合コードになったわけですが、そのときの話は、不祥事も何回かあった中でもっとガバナンスをちゃんとしましょうということで、短期主義は余り正面から言われていなかったようにも思われるわけです。それとはまた別の流れとしてイギリスのスチュワードシップコードの話が出てきたとすると、それは日本と同じように作用するとは限らないのかなという気はします。

　また、シンガポールについて言えば、シンガポールのガバナンスコードも、そもそもオーナーがいる中で外から独立の人を呼んだとしても、どうせオーナーが選んでいるので意味がないという話になって、結局スチュワードシップコードも大して影響は受けないということになるのかもしれません。

ですから、今の印象としては、2つのコードの相互作用のあり方も、結局、国それぞれということになるのかなという気がしております。

中東委員　私がconvergenceとつなげてお尋ねしましたので、わかりにくくなったと思います。2つのコードがどう関係して、どのように相互に作用していくのかをお伺いしたかったので、今教えていただいたことで十分理解できました。どうもありがとうございます。

弥永会長代理　非常に興味深いご報告をありがとうございました。

　ご報告を伺っていて、イギリスが多少Pro public interestであるという見方があることはわかったのですけれども、シンガポールがなぜここに分類されるのかが、目的からはよくわからなかったということを、お聞きできればさいわいです。

　そして、Pro public interestの場合に、なぜ、このようなスチュワードシップコードという手法を使うことに合理性があると考えられるのかという点です。もし公益を実現したいというのだったら、普通はソフトローのレベルで要求するというよりは、法令のレベルなどで要求しそうなものなのに、Pro public interestという類型のスチュワードシップコードを設定するとしたら、どのようなロジックでそのような方法を選ぶのかという点が気になりました。

　その延長上で、シンガポールの場合、ご報告にありましたように全くエンフォースしていない。Pro publicの場合に全くエンフォースしないというのはとても矛盾しているようにみえまして、そのあたりの後藤先生の評価を教えていただければと思います。

後藤報告者　まず、シンガポールがPro public interestかどうかということですが、確かにイギリスほどそっちには行っていないと思います。現状維持的なところに入れたというのは、シンガポールでも機関投資家はゼロではなくて、一定程度存在しており、アクティビズムの形は違うんですけれども、空売りファンドみたいなものが来ており、空売りを仕掛けられた会社の株をTemasekが全部買い上げて撃退したみたいな例があるらしいんですが、そ

ういう意味では、シンガポールも、世界的にお金が余っている状況の中で、いつそういうものが来るかということを恐らく政府として意識していないわけではない。そうすると、外部の資本市場からの圧力が強まることに対して、株主の利益だけではなくてステークホルダーもいるんだからということをカウンターバランスとして出しているという意味での Pro public なのかなという気がしています。ただ、積極的に何かしたいというのではなくて、これ以上資本市場からうるさいことを言われないためにカウンターバランスをとっているだけだとすると、バランスをとっているだけなので、真ん中にいるということかと思います。

　今日の図は４つの箱にしたんですが、最初はもっとグラフのようにしようかと思ったんですけれども、各国をどの辺に置くかが恣意的になってしまいそうな気もするので、大まかな四象限だけにしています。イギリスとシンガポールが同じぐらい左にいっているわけではないので、シンガポールを真ん中辺に置けるかなという気もしたんですけれども、それも言葉のあやになってしまいそうなので、左下に入れさせていただいたところでございます。

　Pro public の意味は、下の段では、イギリスとアメリカの投資家団体は現状が株主寄りなので、現状維持である以上、それをステークホルダーに引き寄らせようとするのはやめてくださいと言っているのに対して、シンガポールは株主側に引っ張られそうになるのをやめたいと言っているというぐらいの趣旨であるとご理解頂ければと思います。

弥永会長代理　Pro public とまでは言えないということですか。

後藤報告者　Pro public だと言いながら現状維持をしているというところでしょうか。

松尾（直）委員　先ほどアメリカの Business Roundtable の話が出ましたけれども、これは事業者団体ですね。ご承知のとおりガバナンスの世界では事業者団体はプレーヤーでありまして、日本では大きな存在感を持っていまして、私は当時、外から観察していました。

　背景として、安倍政権になる前の民主党政権下で会社法改正が行われたわ

けですけれども、社外取締役義務づけが入らなかったということがあって、私の勝手な言い方で申しわけないんですけれども、ガバナンス改革関係者はがっかりしたわけです。

　今調べていたんですけれども、それに対して、第2次安倍政権が2012年12月に発足して、自由民主党の「日本経済再生本部」の会合が2013年1月16日に開催されていまして、5月10日に「中間提言」を出しています。本部長代行に市場重視の塩崎恭久元官房長官が入っています。私は外部から観察していて、当時の金融庁総務企画局長が塩崎先生とタッグを組んで、ガバナンス改革を推進していたのではないかと推察しておりました。日本経済再生本部のヒアリング対象者も、ロバート・フェルドマン氏（第3回）、日本証券取引所社長（第10回）、日本投資顧問業協会会長・理事（第18回）、上村達男教授（第25回）など、市場派のヒアリングが多く、事業者団体（日本経団連・経済同友会・日本商工会議所）のヒアリングは1回だけでした（第14回）。そして、「中間提言」では、「コーポレートガバナンス強化」として、「独立社外取締役の確実な導入」が挙げられていました。このように自民党の日本経済再生本部でガバナンス改革の動きがありました。

　4ページに書かれている、日本型公益資本主義について標榜された方が入った「目指すべき市場経済システムに関する専門調査会」の報告書を当時読んだ記憶がありますが、「『実体経済（real economy）主導』の持続可能な経済社会システム」を目指すべきであるとして、金融への警戒論でありまして、ここでせめぎ合いがあるわけです。推察ですけれども、その背景には日本経団連と経済産業省がいたに違いないと見ていまして、ある意味では妥協ではあります。ただ、官邸が重視していたであろう株価が急上昇していましたから、市場派が強かったので、おかげさまでスチュワードシップコードが導入できて、その後コーポレートガバナンスコードも入れられたので、当時の総務企画局長はさすがだなと思っているわけです。

　先生にお伺いしたいのは、日本では事業者団体とのせめぎ合いが大変で、官邸の力が強かったので事業者団体も文句を言えなかったという構図で、よ

かったよかったと私は思っているんですけれども、イギリスはもともと機関投資家が強いから、そもそもそういう抵抗みたいなものがないのでしょうか。シンガポールは、お話にあった国有企業があるのでどうなのか。韓国は、先生の報告を見ると、むしろ当時の政権は財閥をやっつけたかったということで、事業者あるいは経済界と事業者団体との関係、いろいろな思惑があってやられていると思われます。そういうプレーヤーとして重要となり得る事業者団体ですが、イギリスではどうも存在感を感じられない。

　質問は２つあって、事業者団体も視野に入れた場合、このマトリックスは一体どうなるのでしょうか。もう１つは、イギリスではもう事業者団体、経済界は存在感がないんでしょうか。

後藤報告者　正面からお答えできるかどうかわからないんですけれども、イギリス自体については私はそこまで詳しいわけではないので、むしろ河村先生にお答え頂いた方がいいような気がします。１つ目についてですが、この話は、あくまで機関投資家に政府がこうやれと言ったときに、機関投資家の団体が何をするかという点に着目したものです。Walker Reviewのときには、そもそも金融機関を含めぼろぼろになっている状況で、経営者の団体が何かやるわけではなく、さらにそのときの Walker Review の方向性は市場からの圧力を弱めるものですので、ガバナンスが厳しくなることは当然金融規制として入ってくるわけですけれども、スチュワードシップコードについては、経営者団体が何か言う話ではないので、出てこないのだと思います。

　逆に韓国の場合は、そもそもまだ朴政権だった 2014 年末になぜ韓国の金融庁がこれを始めたのかがわからなくて、そのときの英語の資料がどこにも見つからず、韓国から来た留学生に渡して読んでもらったりしているんですが、ともかく、まだ朴政権のスキャンダルが出る前の 2015 年末に第一次草案をつくったものの、その時には一度産業界からの反発でポシャっています。この時には、恐らく業界団体、経営者団体の圧力があったものと思われます。さらに National Pension Service も大分後になるまで受け入れていないのは、産業界からの抵抗が韓国では強かったということを意味しているのかなと思

います。ただ、韓国の現状でのマトリックスは、このような産業界に対して改革派政権がそれを変えようとするために使っているという意味で、韓国の位置はこれで良いように思っております。

　済みません、横からの回答になってしまったかもしれませんが、貴重な裏情報をありがとうございました。

松尾（直）委員　別に情報はなく、あくまでも私の推測にとどまります。

松井（秀）委員　ご報告を伺いまして、大変頭の整理ができましたし、参考になりました。ありがとうございました。

　3点ほど、コメントとも質問ともつかないようなお話をさせていただきます。

　1点目ですが、今回の後藤先生のご報告を伺っておりまして、このスチュワードシップコードの目的が非常に多様であり、イギリスと日本はそもそも正反対の目的を実現しようとしているということがわかりました。そうだとしますと、スチュワードシップコードというのは単なる「箱」でしかなく、つまり、機関投資家に対する何らかの規律をするための「箱」であって、その概念自体は実質的な意味を失っているという感じもしています。後藤先生の共同研究は、いわば、そういったスチュワードシップコードのベールを剝ぎ取る作業をしているのかなとも思いました。まずは、そもそもこのような理解を出発点としてよいのか、ということをお伺いしたいです。

後藤報告者　まさに全く同じ議論をイギリスの会議の主催者として、余り受けはよくなかったというか、イギリスが発明したこれが世界中に広まったのは、中に何でも入れられる箱を発明したからだよねと言ったら、当たり前ですけれども、余り喜ばれはしないですよね。（笑）ですから、おっしゃるとおりであります。

松井（秀）委員　それをうかがいまして、次の質問につなげられます（笑）。

　そこで2点目なのですが、これはコメントです。メタのレベルで議論をすると、投資先企業に対して、一定のブロックで株を持っていて、この企業に影響力を与え得る株主という存在がいる。そして、この株主に対して何らか

の規律をしたいというときに、どういう手法でこれが実現できるのかというのが課題なのだろう、と。これ自体は、古くからある問題で、たとえば支配株主に対してフィデューシャリーデューティー的なものを負わせたり、あるいはドイツのようにコンツェルン法をつくってしまったり、という手法があるわけです。

　ところが、難しいのは次のレベルです。つまり支配株主ではないけれども、会社に対して何らかの影響力がある。しかも、場合によってはマーケットに影響を及ぼすし、利害関係者の利益を損なう可能性もあるといった例ですと、なかなか規律をするのが難しい。むろん方法がない訳ではなくて、例えばアメリカのエリザ法のように年金基金などに対して、もともと資金の出し手に対する義務を負わせるとか、あるいは古い会社法のようにそもそも大株主の議決権を制限してしまうとか、いろいろな方法がありえます。ここでおもしろいのは、今回のイギリスは、この固まりで保有する株主に対して、私的な利益と公的な利益の両方ともを実現させようとしている。また、その際にハードローではない形で実現させるという方法をとってきた。これは、恐らくイギリスだからできているということがあろうかと思います。もともとパブリックとプライベートの二元論がそんなに強くない国ですし、シティーなどで自治的な規範で解決するという伝統をある程度持っている。多分そういう知恵が、ここにも出ているのかなというのが私の感触です。イギリスのスチュワードシップコードというのが、パブリックであれプライベートであれさまざまな利益をのみ込み、かつ、ハードローではない形で解決するという手法を編み出したがゆえに、まさに後藤先生がおっしゃったように、何でも放り込めるし、各国がすごく使いやすかったということなのかなという感じがしています。

　最後に３点目です。機関投資家に対する何らかの規律が必要であり、かつ、パブリック、プライベートいずれの利益もとりこめるような手法の柔軟性ということが重要だとしたときに、翻って、スチュワードシップコードという名称がついていることの意味は何なのだろうか。イギリスで言うスチュワー

ドシップコードは、ある程度、彼らの明確な目的に基づいてできているのですけれども、ほかの国は手法のところにだけ着目していて、それを導入してスチュワードシップコードという名前をつけてしまっている。これはかえってミスリーディングで、日本はそれをやってしまったわけですけれども、これは果たして妥当なのだろうか。そんな名前をつけたがゆえに——まさに後藤先生の今回のご研究につながるわけですけれども——全然性格の違うもの、全然ベクトルの違うものを取り込んでいってしまって、かえって理解を難しくさせてしまうのではないだろうか。さまざまな国でスチュワードシップコードを入れていると言いながら、よくよく見ると全然中身が違うではないかということがあり、この名前を使うのは結構ミスリーディングなのではないかとも思うわけです。このあたり、後藤先生の感触で結構ですけれども、どう評価されるかを伺いたいと思います。

後藤報告者　まず1点目は先ほどお答えしたとおりで、まさに中身のない箱だと思っているわけでございます。

　イギリスはブロックホルダーをコントロールしたいときに、本当にコントロールしたかったのか。金融危機の後に何かしないと政府がたたかれるから、機関投資家だって悪かったじゃないかと言ってそこに何か圧力をかけようとした。そのときに、機関投資家規制をハードローで入れることももちろんできるはずですけれども、もう既にでき上がっていたコードの前文だけつけかえて中身はそのままという、後から見るとひどいことをやっているなという感じがするわけですけれども、そうやった。確かにパブリック、プライベートの二元論は強くないし、自治的なものも受け入れているからこそ、それを採択するというのは別にイギリスにとってはそんなに変なことではなかったのかもしれないのですが、成功したかどうかというのはまた別の問題です。その手法をとることへの違和感は多分弱かったということはおっしゃるとおりかと思うんですが、そのときイギリスが本当に政策目的としてやりたかったことに役に立ったかというと、よくわからない。ただ、何かやっていますよという感じを出して、その裏で頑張って銀行規制を改革したとすると、時

間稼ぎには多分なったのかもしれません。そういう意味では、イギリスをそんなに褒めてあげる必要もないのかなという気はしています。

　ただ、その副産物としてスチュワードシップコードという便利な箱を生み出した。イギリスは恐らく期せずしてそれを世界中に売ることができた。全く法的な概念ではないスチュワードというものを持ち込んで、広まったということですが、何が良かったかというと、中世のイギリスの王様や貴族の執事の話ですので、何かいい響きがするわけですね。アメリカの人に聞いたら、「アメリカには貴族なんていない」という答えが返ってきたことがあるんですが、シンガポールのファミリーコードがまさにこれかと思うんですけれども、主人のために忠実に働く執事であれば、何でもスチュワードになれるんですね。

　イギリスでも、スチュワードという言葉が最初に出てきたのは、どうやらキャドバリーレポートで、そのときには経営者がスチュワードだと書いてありまして、要は、誰かのものを預かっているということですので、これはエージェンシー理論のエージェントとほぼ変わらない位置づけです。もっとも、エージェントというと、やっぱりどうしても法律的にも経済学的にも意味を持ってしまうので、そこをあえてスチュワードと呼んだ。そこが、Walker Review ではなく ISC コードかもしれませんが、イギリスが賢かったところだと思います。もちろんその結果としてミスリーディングな部分はあり、ミスリーディングなものであるからこそ論文を1本書けたので、私としては非常にありがたかったんですが、（笑）こういう名称だったからこそ、こういう使われ方をした。これがエージェントコードだったら多分こんなにはなっていないかなという気はします。イギリスが生み出したスチュワードシップという概念の特徴は、中身として何でも入れられるというところであり、イギリスの Katelouzou さんに、本家本元である ISC コードに一番近いのは日本で、イギリスはむしろ 2010 年コードで ISC コードをゆがめているんだよ、ミスリーディングなのはイギリスコードだと言っているんですけれども、この経緯はイギリスでは余り触れられることなく議論されているという感じ

で、これはヨーロッパ人にはわかってもらえないところだったりします。

松井（秀）委員　応急措置的だというのは非常におもしろい示唆的な話です
し、すごく経路依存的な話ですね。スチュワードという言葉を使ったがゆえ
に、今度はそれに拘束されていろいろなものが動いている。非常に勉強に
なりました。ありがとうございました。

小出委員　実は今の松井先生のご質問とほぼ同じでして、ご回答もありまし
たので、重複するかもしれませんけれども、後藤先生の資料の8ページにま
た別の四象限がありまして、形式面での収斂はあるけれども、機能面では収
斂しないんじゃないかと。そうなのかと思いながら伺っていたんですけれど
も、なぜ形式面での収斂があるのか。つまり、目的が違うのであれば、なぜ
スチュワードシップコードという形式がこんなにはやったのだろうかという
ことをお聞きしたかったんですけれども、先ほど伺ったように、要するに機
関投資家を規制するための便利な箱だったというご回答だったので、なるほ
どと思いました。ただ、国によってかなり状況が違うということもきょう伺っ
て勉強になったんですけれども、世界中で機関投資家に着目するという流れ
がこの数年の間に随分あるのは、何か理由があるのかなというのが残る質問
の1つです。

　2つ目は、特に韓国などは財閥の改革みたいなものをしたかったという後
藤先生の説明はすごくわかりやすいんですけれども、日本は実は目的がよく
わからない部分もあるかなという気がしています。11ページの図だと、後
藤先生はPro shareholderと書いておられるんですけれども、4ページ、5
ページのあたりですと、公益資本主義、公益というものが言葉として出てき
ている。公益というと、普通に考えればPro publicなのかなという気もし
ていて、日本のいわゆるPro shareholder、あるいは公益資本主義がどうい
う関係にあるのかがよくわからなくて、日本も実は台湾と同じように理由が
よくわからないといえばわからないような気もしたので、その辺を伺わせて
いただければと思います。

後藤報告者　機関投資家がなぜ着目されるようになったのかは、イギリスと

かアメリカではそれぞれ事情は違いますけれども、保有比率がどんどん上がっていってその影響力が強くなってきたというのは日本でもある話でして、それが韓国でも National Pension Service の役割という形で出てきた。その中で、これは投資の呼び込みのような話ですけれども、2016 年ぐらいから急にスチュワードシップコードが各国に受け始めるんですね。これを入れておくとガバナンス改革をしている感じが出て投資してくれるんじゃないかという期待を持ち始めたのが、例えば台湾とか、ケニアがどれだけ真剣にやっているのかよくわからないんですけれども、そういうものなのかなという気がしなくもない。そういう意味では、機関投資家が既に影響力が強いのか、もしくは機関投資家に来てほしいのか。日本でも、ちょっと先ほどお話ししたのと違う観点になるかもしれませんけれども、これがあることによって、機関投資家が最終受益者のために企業経営に口を出してくるのはいいことであると、機関投資家によるモニタリングにお墨つきを与えた側面もあるかと思います。例えば台湾などでは、機関投資家さんがやってくださいと言うことによって、支配株主はいるけれども、呼び込もうとしているという感じはあるのかもしれません。その意味では、現在機関投資家のプレゼンスが低い国でも、それを歓迎するようなメッセージを出したとも言えるのかもしれないとは思います。

　日本の話については、いろんな評価があると思います。先ほど松尾先生からもご指摘があったような話で、結局、政府の議論の中でも、政府は常に一枚岩ではなくて、市場派と市場派じゃない派がある中で、どっちが主導権を握ったか。ガバナンスコードとか会社法改正もそう言えるかもしれませんけれども、どっちかというと株主からの圧力を強める方向の改正が動いている中で、少し前の言葉ですけれども、いわば抵抗勢力的なものとして存在していた甘利経済再生担当大臣が反論してきたので、妥協として一言入れてやるかという形でできたのが公益資本主義から来た「企業の持続的な成長」というフレーズなのかなという気はします。もちろん、これはイギリスのコードにも入っているので、入れないわけにはいかなかったのですが、ドラフティ

ングを見ると、イギリスと全く同じ構文は使っていない。甘利さんとか原さんの公益資本主義的な考え方からすれば、イギリス版コードをそのまま写すのが一番いいはずなのに、あえてそれをひっくり返しているというのは、やはり市場派の方が主導権をとっていたということを意味しているように思います。その上で、「持続的成長」というフレーズもここに入っていますよということで納得してもらったということではないかと思っております。

松井（智）委員　私も最後の表を見ながら考え込んでいて、この表の上のPro public interest とか Pro shareholder/inventor というのが、松井秀征先生の話を聞いていると、左側は年金に公益、私益両方を任意で追求させますよ。だから、場合によっては配当を抑える、年金基金の利益率が下がってもしようがないねという話につながるのに対して、右側は何なのかと思ったときに、韓国の話が出てまいりまして、もっとちゃんとモニタリングをしなさい、もしくは配当をふやせとか、内部留保をするにしてもその使い道をちゃんとコミュニケーションしなさい、ガバナンスが働いていないでしょう、もっと働きなさいというふうに、お尻をたたいているような行動であるような気がいたします。

　そうだとすると、1つ目の質問は、これがあることが本当にいいメッセージになっているのかどうか。要するに、その国の機関投資家は余り機能していませんよというメッセージになりはしないかという危惧が1つありました。

　もう1つは、そうだとすると、イギリスのようなものは年金基金に対して余りおいしくない話を強制するものなので、将来的には強制の方向に行かざるを得ないのに対して、右側の shareholder/investor として強い行動をとるかどうかは、アクティビスト的に、どういう形で投資をするのかということについての経営判断次第で年金の利益にもなり得るものなので、どちらかというと任意でいくのか。そうだとすると、スチュワードシップコードのconvergence という話は、将来的に convert しないんじゃないだろうかという気がしたので、その点についてのご感触を伺えればと思います。

後藤報告者　安易に表はつくるものじゃないなと思っているところです。

　よいメッセージになるかということでは、そもそもよいメッセージとは何かという問題があるのかもしれないですけれども、例えば、日本と韓国はどちらかというと似たようなところがあると思っておりまして、結局、国内の機関投資家が今までちゃんとやっていなかったので、もっとちゃんとやれと。でも、その中身は株主的な目線で、会社にキャッシュが溜まっている場合には、吐き出せるものはもっと吐き出させて、そうでないものはもっとちゃんと使わせるという意味では共通しているかと思います。それが今まで国内機関投資家がちゃんとやっていなかったというふうに受けとめられればもちろん悪いメッセージになってしまうのかもしれないんですけれども、これからはちゃんとやらせるように圧力がかかるんだという意味だとすると、いいメッセージにもなり得るわけで、アベノミクスが始まったときに、国際的な投資家が、日本はこれでガバナンスが変わるかもしれないのでこれから買いだと思った人が多くて株価が上がったんだとすると、どちらかというと後者の状態になっていたんだろうなとは思うんです。

　韓国がそこまで来ているかというと、やはり日本と韓国の違いは株主構成にあって、日本の大きな上場企業では機関投資家の保有比率がかなり大きくなっていて、持ち合いも10％を切ったという報道がありましたけれども、そうすると機関投資家の行動が変わると現実に変わる可能性があるわけです。これに対して、韓国は、やはりオーナー一族がコントロールしている比率がなお高いのだと思います。Samsungの合併の話は、韓国でも特別決議ですので、3分の1さえあれば止められることになり、そうであるとすると、仮に過半数をオーナー側がコントロールできたとしても、機関投資家が3分の1をとることはできるわけですが、会社支配の全体としては変わってこないのだと思います。この意味で、韓国と日本とでは機関投資家の持つ意味合いが違ってきて、日本ではもう少し影響力が強いことになるのかなというふうに思っています。

　これは機関投資家の利益にもなるので、ほっておけば機関投資家がやって

くれるのかということですが、そういう仕組みは確かにあるでしょうし、こ
のコードが入って 2017 年に変わった後に、例えば今年の LIXIL の株主総会
における日本生命の議決権行使とか、大分行動が変わってきているように見
えなくもないところを見ると、やっていいんだということになったらやると
いうところはあるのかもしれません。他方で、アメリカではパッシブファン
ドがやっていないというような議論が多いわけで、機関投資家の投資戦略と
してどこかで限界は来るはずでして、日本の政府の目的が、それ以上に、投
資戦略としては非合理になったとしてもなお介入させることによって企業側
のガバナンスを変えたいという側面は否定できないと思うんですが、そのた
めにはやはり機関投資家に圧力をかけていく側面が出てくるはずです。例え
ば、企業年金にもっとやらせようとしているわけですけれども、そんなキャ
パシティはないところにも何とかやらせようとしていますので、日本でもも
う少し規制的なところが入ってくるのは否定できないのかなと思っています
が、やりたくないことをやらせているという面ではイギリスと共通している
のかなと思います。

加藤委員 ２点、コメントをさせていただきます。

　１点目ですが、ご報告では、国際的にスチュワードシップコードの存在と
いう形式面での収斂が見られることが指摘されていましたが、スチュワード
シップコードの具体的な条項とか規定のレベルでは、収斂は見られないので
しょうか。例えば、韓国のコードについて、「７原則は概ね日本版コードと
同じだが、個別の議決権行使とその理由の開示を要求」と説明されています。
日本のコードの改訂版には個別の議決権行使とその理由の開示に関する規定
が存在しますが、策定当時の日本と韓国のコードに見られたように、コード
の内容について細かい差異が存在するのであれば、そのような差異が生じた
理由に興味を持ちました。何かコメントをいただければと思います。

　２点目は、コーポレートガバナンスコードとスチュワードシップコードと
の関連についてです。日本では、よく２つのコードは車の両輪であると言わ
れます。イギリスは、スチュワードシップコードの改訂の前にコーポレート

47

ガバナンスコードの改訂を行っていたと記憶しています。正確性を欠いているかもしれませんが、最近のイギリスのコーポレートガバナンスに関する規制の改正は、ＥＳＧやＳＤＧ ｓを重視する方向に向っているような気がします。スチュワードシップコードの改訂に際して、コーポレートガバナンスに関する近年の改正がどのように考慮されたのか、果たして２つのコードは両輪として同じ方向を向いているのか、気になりました。この点についても、後藤先生に何かコメントをいただければと思います。

後藤報告者　コードの中身レベルの話はちゃんとやってはいないのですが、例えば台湾は、日本をほぼ完コピしている感じがありまして、最後のところだけ削っています。表現ぶりは違いますが、中身としてはほぼ一緒です。ただ、それをどこまでやろうとしているかというと、日本のほうがよっぽど真剣であり、一方の台湾は、ご紹介もしましたけれども、ほかの国がやっていればそれでいいですよということを言っていて、そのときに、同じような目的のコードと書いているんですが、イギリスと日本は同じ目的だと思っているのか、多分思っているんだろうなという感じがするんですね。そういう意味ではただコピーしただけなのかもしれず、そうすると、その中身の収斂を見ても余り意味がないように思います。

　逆に日本は、イギリスのコードを持ってくるときに、翻訳した上で１つ１つ見て、ここは変える、変えないということをやったという意味では、そこにやりたいことが恐らくあらわれてくる。それは今日お話ししたようなコード策定の目的ということですが、これを見た上で、中身レベルの話をすることはあり得るかと思っています。

　シンガポールのものを見ますと、すごく緩いものができていまして、意識的に日本のことも大分調べられたようですが、表現ぶりも大分変えているという意味では、目的が変われば当然中身も変わるはずだということであると思っています。例えば、Bebchuk の論文などを見ると、機関投資家のパッシブファンドに何をやらせるかという話のときに、スチュワードシップコードはあるけれども、おそらくうまくいかないという文脈で、イギリス、日本、

48

カナダ、イタリアというふうに全部並べられていますので、結局、コードが
あるかないかというところを簡単に見ただけだという気はしております。

　イギリスの Walker Review は分厚くて、全部をしっかり読んではいない
んですけれども、むしろガバナンスの話が本筋で、特に金融機関のガバナン
スについてはリスクばかりとるなという話が入ってきています。そのときの
議論としては金融機関以外についても同じ方向性を向いているはずだと思い
ますが、それがスチュワードシップコード策定後のガバナンスコードにどう
反映されていたかまでは、ちょっと申しわけありませんが、把握はしており
ません。また、元々のガバナンスコードについては、どちらかというと少し
違う話であったように思います。キャドバリーレポートも、たしかどこかの
スキャンダルが契機だったかとは思うんですけれども、公益と言えば公益な
のかもしれませんが、今のＥＳＧの話とはちょっと違う方向なのかなと思っ
ております。

尾崎委員　また最後のページの表のところで、繰り返しになって申しわけな
いのですが、イギリスの ISC が右下に書いてあって、左上にイギリスと出
ていて、右下から何段階かを経てなのかもしれませんが、左上に移行してい
ます。「目的の方向性」のところは、2010 年のコードで目的を含む序文を書
きかえているというのであれば右から左に行ったということはすごくよくわ
かるのですが、下から上に行ったという部分について、2010 年のコードの
段階でも上に行っているという理解でいいのでしょうか。

　それに関連して、イギリスのエンフォースメントの仕組みがどれくらい
コードを守らせる方向、あるいは参加させる方向で働いているのかというの
が、いまいちよくわかりませんでした。例えば、2016 年に開示を強化して、
開示の質に関して最下層のものは排除するというのはエンフォースメントの
強化になるかと思いますが、最下層から排除されるということが各機関投資
家にとってどういう意味合いを持つのかを教えていただければと思います。

後藤報告者　先ほどもお話ししましたけれども、最初はグラフみたいに書い
ていて、下からだんだん上がっていく矢印を書いてみたんですけれども、う

まくいきませんでした。

　イギリスのスチュワードシップコードは、2010年の一回で規制がうまくいったわけではなくて、2010年に入れたときにはほぼ強制力はなかったので、それをだんだん強化しようとしている。現実にできているかどうかはともかくとして、気持ちとしては上がっていっているというところはあるのかなとは思います。

　日本もイギリスも同じように、先ほどの藤田先生の言葉で言えば、現状を変更しようとしている。変更しようと思っている気持ちとしては多分同じだと思うんですが、日本のほうが機関投資家の本来やることに親和的である面で、日本のほうが、コードの影響力が強く出ているんじゃないかと思います。他方で、韓国では、ほかのしがらみなどもまだいろいろあるので、うまくいっていない。

　イギリスは、国内の金融機関であれば渋々サインするというところまでは行っているけれども、それ以上に何かあるかという話では、ティアリングをして、一番下は、あなたはもう署名者とは言えませんといってリストから落とすということです。それは国外の機関投資家であれば痛くも痒くもないという話になってくるので意味はないけれども、国内のアセットマネジャーは署名しなければならないことになっているので、削られてしまうと結局違反していることになるので、そういう人たちに対しては一定の意味を持ってくる。国内の機関投資家であれば、最低限のレベルが少し上がるというぐらいの意味は持ってくるんじゃないかなと思います。本当は署名者のリストを1つ1つ見て、どういう対応をしているか確認すべきなんですけれども、ちょっとそこまではまだ及んでおりません。

神作会長　ほかにご意見はよろしいでしょうか。

　私からもご質問させて下さい。尾崎先生のご意見、ご質問に近いのですが、株主が対象になっているとすると、例えば2010年のイギリスのスチュワードシップコードで公益的なことに言及していると言っても、結局は株主がターゲットで、かつフィデューシャリーデューティーを負っているとすると、

いずれにしてもそれほど株主利益から離れたことはできないと思うんですね。ところが、この点で非常に注目しているのは、2019年の英国のスチュワードシップコード改訂版はエクイティ以外のボンド等に対する資本拠出者も対象に含めていて、スチュワードシップ責任の対象を株式から他のアセットクラスにも拡大しており、何だか世界が変わったなという印象を受けているんですけれども、その点はどのように見ておられるでしょうか。

後藤報告者　本日はご紹介しませんでしたけれども、イギリスのスコープが変わったというのは、イギリスの2019年版の2ページの「Key changes in the 2019 UK Stewardship Code」の2つ目に「Stewardship beyond UK listed equity」というのがあって、これは資金拠出者のほうではなくて、ちょっとうろ覚えですけれども、私が前に読んだところだと、機関投資家は資金拠出者に対してフィデューシャリーデューティーを負っていて、それは日本でもイギリスでもスチュワードシップと呼んでいるわけですけれども、資金を拠出してもらった以上、それをどこに投資するかは関係なくスチュワードシップ、フィデューシャリーデューティーは及ぶはずです。これまでのコードでは、イギリスの上場株を買っている場合にだけスチュワードシップコードがかかってきたわけですけれども、社債を買っていようが国債を買っていようが、投資している以上、資金拠出者に対するフィデューシャリーデューティーはかかってくるはずだという意味では、そこは変わってこないはずだと思います。これも、先ほど揺り戻しかもというふうに言ったところの話で、資金拠出者に対しての責任を急に強調し始めたというところなのかと思っています。

　本来日本でもそうであるべきだと思いますけれども、日本のコードは、そこは余り言っていません。日本は日本で、イギリスとは違う文脈で、上場企業のガバナンス改革に興味があるからということででき上がったものですので、もともとのでき上がり方からしてそういう側面を持っています。

　逆にアメリカであれば、例えばERISAの責任やフィデューシャリーデューティーは何に投資しようがかかってきて、特に株に投資した場合はこういう

ことをやらなきゃいけないということが特別ルールとして入ってくるだけであって、フィデューシャリーデューティーのほうがスコープが広いものです。それがあるので、逆にスチュワードシップコードなんて要らないというのが元々のアメリカの考え方だったかと思いますけれども、そこにある意味近づきつつあるのかもしれません。

　1点目のお話で、フィデューシャリーデューティーがあるので結局公益的なことをやらせようとしてもうまくいかないんじゃないかというのは、私もそのとおりじゃないかというところがありまして、フィデューシャリーデューティーから外れるESGのところまでは本来できないはずです。ただ、長期的にめぐりめぐって資金拠出者の利益になるという裁量の幅は持ってくるでしょうし、逆にSRIファンドなどであれば、それをむしろ売りにして投資を集めていることがフィデューシャリーデューティーに組み込まれてくることになると思います。ですので、SRIファンドであるとはっきりと言えばそうでしょうし、言わなかったらそこまでは行かないということになるのかなと思っています。現状の多くのファンドはそこまでESGを強調して集めているわけではないので、限界があるからこそ、結局ESGをやらせたかったら規制するしかないというイギリスの学説があるのかと思っております。

神作会長　もう1点、お尋ねしたいと思います。スチュワードシップコードの基本的な考え方は、議決権を中心とする株主権をより実効的に行使していきましょうということだと思います。ところが、ボンドの場合には、債権者集会や社債権者集会のような発行会社が危機に陥ったような場合を除き、そういった株主権に対応するような議決権がない。もちろんコベナンツによってはそのような権利を創設することはあり得ますけれども。スチュワードシップコードが考えてきたのは、恐らく最終投資家と投資先企業の間が地理的にもプレーヤーの点でも非常に広がってしまって、すなわちインベストメントチェーンの間に国境を越えたりいろいろな機関が介在したりして、結局コントロールがきかなくなっているというのが、前提となる問題意識であったと思います。これは、議決権を中心とする株主権を念頭に置いた議論だっ

たと思います。ところが、スチュワードシップ責任の対象資産にボンドなど
が入ってきて、従来の考え方と異質なものが入ってきているんじゃないかと
いう感想を持ちました。河村委員が冒頭にご指摘された点にも関連すると思
いますが、スチュワードシップ責任という語感的には管理人の責任というよ
り、投資判断自体の責任が対象に入ってきたという印象があります。

後藤報告者　確かに議決権がないとどうするのかという問題があります。仮
に社債を買った場合、本来だったらもう執行すべきなのに、利益相反がある
ので執行しないということがあるとよくないという話では、同じ発想は出て
き得るとは思うんですが、それは本来債権者としてできる範囲内でというこ
とになってくるかと思いますので、余りよく考えずにこれを追加したという
ところもあるのかもしれません。

河村委員　例えば、グリーンボンドとかがあると思います。つまり、今ヨー
ロッパで進められようとしている改革の中で、適合性原則の中に、顧客のE
SG選好を考慮するというのを定めようとしている。そうすると、お客さん
の意向によってボンドに投資をするときに、ESに考慮したボンドに投資し
てくださいというのが出てくると一番最初に申し上げたように、そもそもど
の企業に投資するかというところでスチュワードシップを果たすことが必要
になってくるので、ボンドにも広げるし、今回みたいな目的の書きかえもし
ている、こういうことじゃないかと理解しています。

神作会長　一番最初の議論に戻りますけれども、スチュワードシップのもと
もとの考え方は、パッシブとかインデックスで議決権をきちんと行使する人
が減ったというところから始まったと思います。デシジョンの段階ではなく
て、持っているものをどう扱うかというのが本来のスチュワードシップの考
え方だったと思いますけれども、もしかしたらそこのところにも変質がある
のかもしれません。

　ほかに何かご質問、ご意見はございますでしょうか。よろしゅうございま
すか。

　もしよろしければ、時間も参りましたので、本日の研究会の質疑はこれで

終了させていただきます。

　後藤先生、どうもありがとうございました。

　次回の研究会は、お手元の議事次第にございますように、11月20日の午後2時から、松尾健一先生より「インデックスファンドとコーポレートガバナンス（仮）」というテーマでご報告いただく予定でございます。会場は、本日と同じく太陽生命日本橋ビルですけれども、12階の証券団体会議室となります。フロアが異なりますので、ご注意いただければと存じます。

　それでは本日の研究会はこれで閉会とさせていただきます。どうもありがとうございました。

2019 年 9 月 10 日
日本証券経済研究所　金融商品取引法研究会

スチュワードシップコードの目的とその多様性

東京大学　後藤　元[1]

I. 問題意識

1. スチュワードシップコードの国際的な流行

イギリス：2010 年に策定、2012 年・2019 年に改訂

日本：2014 年に策定、2017 年に改訂、2020 年に改訂？

アメリカ合衆国（Investor Stewardship Group）：2017 年策定、2018 年発効

その他：カナダ（2010 年）、南アフリカ（2011 年）、オランダ（2011 年）、スイス（2013 年）、イタリア（2013 年・2014 年）、マレーシア（2014 年）、台湾（2016 年）、ブラジル（2016 年）、デンマーク（2016 年）、シンガポール（2016 年）、韓国（2016 年）、オーストラリア（2017 年・2018 年）、香港（2016 年）、ケニア（2017 年）、中国（2018 年改訂 CG コード第 7 章）など

検討中：インド、フィリピン、ベトナム

2. 日英のスチュワードシップコードの違い

● コードの目的、スチュワードシップの定義

> 日本：本コードにおいて、「スチュワードシップ責任」とは、機関投資家が、投資先企業やその事業環境等に関する深い理解に基づく建設的な「目的を持った対話」（エンゲージメント）などを通じて、<u>当該企業の企業価値の向上や持続的成長を促すことにより</u>、「顧客・受益者」（最終受益者を含む。以<u>下同じ。）の中長期的な投資リターンの拡大を図る</u>責任を意味する。

> イギリス（2012 年版）：Stewardship aims <u>to promote the long term success of companies</u> in such a way that <u>the ultimate providers of capital also prosper</u>. Effective stewardship benefits companies, investors and the economy as a whole.

● 日本版（2014 年）の 7 原則のイギリスとの違い：田中亘「日本版スチュワードシップコードの検討」月刊監査役 629 号 66 頁（2014 年）

---

[1] 本報告の一部は、National University of Singapore, Faculty of Law の Dan W. Puchniak 准教授および Nanyang Technological University, Nanyang Business School の Alan K. Koh 助教授との共同研究に基づくものである。また、韓国に関する調査について、東京大学大学院生の高逸薫氏の助力を得た。

> ➤ 柱書における投資先企業の持続的成長の強調

> ➤ エンゲージメントの段階的強化、集団的エンゲージメントへの言及の不存在

> ➤ 「監視」ではなく「適切に把握」

> ➤ 機関投資家の投資先企業に対する理解と実力の要求

3. 各国における株式所有構造の違い

イギリス：分散、機関投資家による保有が大半

日本：株式の持合い等による安定株主の存在

アジア諸国：支配株主（オーナー一族または政府）の存在

II. スチュワードシップコードの目的の多様性

1. イギリス

● Walker Review (2009) と 2010 年版コード

> ➤ 有限責任を享受する株主からの短期的業績へのプレッシャーから金融機関の経営陣が過大なリスクをとったことが金融危機の一因であり、その結果として債権者と納税者が負担を強いられたすることを批判。公益的な観点から、上場企業の経営者による過度のリスクテイクを抑制するために、機関投資家にスチュワードシップ責任を負わせることを主張

> ➤ 投資家団体である Institutional Shareholders' Committee が策定していた ISC Code on the Responsibilities of Institutional Investors を、財務報告評議会（FRC）が公認する形でのスチュワードシップコードの迅速な策定を提言

> ➤ もっとも、ISC コードは、序文において、機関投資家の義務はその顧客と最終受益者に対するものであり、一般社会に対するものではないことを明言

> > ✧ ISC コードの前身となる 2002 年の文書は、年金基金に顧客の利益の観点から議決権行使を義務付けることを提案した Myners Report への業界の自主的対応として作成されたもの

> ➤ FRC は、ISC コードの序文のみを差し替えて、2010 年版コードとして採択

● Kay Review と 2012 年版コード

> ➤ 株式市場の短期主義的傾向を批判し、拡大されたスチュワードシップとして、機関投資家は経営者を単に批判するのではなく信頼するように要求

> ➤ 2012 年版コードでスチュワードシップの目的を規定し、投資先企業の長期的成功に言及

- 2019 年版コード改訂案
  - スチュワードシップの目的を修正（理由の説明なし）
    - Stewardship is the responsible allocation and management of capital across the institutional investment community to create sustainable value for beneficiaries, the economy and society. … This definition identifies the primary purpose of stewardship as looking after the assets of beneficiaries that have been entrusted to the care of others.
  - 他方で、気候変動等の ESG の課題を考慮すべきことを明示

- 学説による批判
  - Cheffins：外国の機関投資家に対する拘束力がないため無意味
  - Chiu & Katelouzou：機関投資家に社会的責任を果たさせるためにはソフトローではなく規制が必要

- エンフォースメント
  - 2010 年版コード
    - 賛同は任意、FRC が署名者のリスト開示
    - comply or explain
  - 2012 年版コード：在英の asset manager には強制適用
  - 2016 年：開示の質による Tiering の導入、最下層の排除
  - 2019 年版コード：Apply and explain への変更、開示項目の追加

2. 日本
- 2014 年版コードの策定経緯
  - 産業競争力会議テーマ別会合（2013 年 3 月 6 日）
    - 「まずはコーポレートガバナンスを始めとして、外から自らを守るという体制から外へ攻められる仕組みづくりをしていくべきではないか。つまり、今はどちらかというと、例えばポイズンピルのように自分の会社を守ることができるような守りの体制の方が強い制度になっているが、むしろ買収なり合併がしやすいような法制度に抜本的に見直すことがまず必要ではないか。また、その中のコーポレートガバナンスについては、まさに英国のスチュワードシップ・コードなどのように、むしろ厳

しく制度を設けて、企業そのものが生産性の高い経営ができるという制度設計も必要なのではないか。」（新浪剛史議員）

✧ 「投資側は、だんだん辛抱がなくなってきて、投資して回収する期間がどんどん短くなっている。例えば内部留保を吐き出すよう求めるアクティビストに関して、長い間株式にあるほうが配当は大きいとか、長く辛抱強く支えた資本のほうが配当は大きくなるような仕組みというのは必要ではないか。積み上げた内部留保を突然来た資本が圧力をかけてかっさらってしまうということが横行した場合には、息の長い資本資金を引っ張ることができない。世の中では投資の視点がどんどん短くなっているが、日本は息の長い資本が来るような環境を整備しないと研究開発型の企業は伸びないのではないか。」（甘利明経済再生担当大臣）

✧ 「実は長期的に見て問題なのは、ROE にしても、長期経営と言っても日本は上がっていないこと。それはなぜかというと、あれだけたくさんの企業があると、集まればバーゲニングパワーになり、収益性も上がる。これは両刃の刃なのだが、実際にはアクティビストもある意味では悪くはない。言いたいことをしっかりこちら側が言って使い道をきちっと示せばいいのだが、そのお金が寝てしまっていると、それが動かないとだめなわけで、ではどうやって使うのかということを圧力をかけていかなければならない。 …企業の価値を上げるというのは、ある意味ではアクティビストみたいなものもある程度必要だと思う。」（新浪議員）

➤ 産業競争力会議（2013 年 3 月 15 日）：「株式市場において、外部からの規律、つまり物言う株主が重要です。アクティビスト的ではなく、中長期に株主として将来を見据えた機関投資家が、企業経営にしっかりと介入し、新陳代謝をすべきです。イギリスのスチュワートシップ・コードの日本版導入も検討し、民に言い訳を言わせない仕組みづくりが必要です。」（新浪議員）

➤ 経済財政諮問会議（2013 年 4 月 18 日）
✧ 公益資本主義を標榜する原丈人氏による「持続的成長を実現する市場経済システムの構築に向けて」の講演
✧ 甘利大臣の提案により、目指すべき市場経済システムに関する専門調査会を設置

➤ 日本再興戦略（2013 年 6 月 14 日）28 頁：「企業の持続的な成長を促す観点から、幅広い範囲の機関投資家が企業との建設的な対話を行い、適切に受託

者責任を果たすための原則について、我が国の市場経済システムに関する経済財政諮問会議の議論も踏まえながら検討を進め、年内に取りまとめる。」
　　✧　日本経済再生本部（2013 年 4 月 2 日）における安倍総理指示も同様
　➢　スチュワードシップコード有識者会議（2013 年 11 月 27 日）
　　✧　目指すべき市場経済システムに関する専門調査会報告書（2013 年 11 月 1日）の紹介（「既に英国において策定されているスチュワードシップ・コードを念頭に置きつつも、機関投資家と企業との建設的なコミュニケーションによって企業の持続的成長を実現することを重視し、日本の実情に応じた日本版スチュワードシップ・コードが策定されることが望まれる。これを契機として、機関投資家と企業のコミュニケーションの質が高まり、信頼関係がより強まり、中長期的な資金確保に重要な役割を果たすことが期待される。」12 頁）
　　✧　田中亘委員の批判に対する佐久間内閣府参事官の応答：「専門調査会が立ち上がった問題意識というのが、ある意味、本調査会の会長代理の原さんが言うところの、公益資本主義的な考え方から出発しているので、そういった問題意識も踏まえて立ち上がっているという経緯もあるので、我々も事務方としても取りまとめに苦労したということで、そういったこともご理解いただければと思っております。」

●　日本版コードの究極的な目的は何か？
　➢　最終受益者の投資リターン＞投資先企業の持続的成長
　　✧　2014 年版コードの「緩さ」への批判（田中）
　　✧　2017 年版コードによる要求強化
　　　●　運用機関の利益相反管理の強化
　　　●　集団的エンゲージメントの有益性への言及
　　　●　議決権行使結果の個別開示
　➢　主たるターゲットは国内機関投資家の態度
　　✧　2017 年版コード
　　✧　銀行・取引先による株式持合いを対象としていないことへの批判（大崎）
　➢　株主利益をベースとしたガバナンス改革＞最終受益者の投資リターン
　　✧　2017 年版コードのパッシブファンドに対するスチュワードシップ活動強化の要求

- 両コードフォローアップ会議の意見書（４）（2019 年 4 月 24 日）
  - ➢ 運用機関による、より充実した情報提供の必要性
  - ➢ 「なお、運用機関がＥＳＧ要素等を<u>含むサステナビリティーを巡る課題</u>に関する対話を行う場合には、<u>投資戦略と整合的で、企業の持続的な成長と中長期的な企業価値向上に結び付くものとなるよう意識する</u>ことが期待される。」（下線部は会議での議論を受けて追加された部分）
  - ➢ 企業年金による受け入れの少なさ
  - ➢ 議決権行使助言会社や運用コンサルタントの体制整備等

3．シンガポール

- Singapore Stewardship Principles for Responsible Investors (November 2016)
  - ➢ 目的として掲げられている内容はイギリスの 2012 年版コードに近い
    - ✧ Stewardship is about building and growing sustainable businesses to produce long-term benefits for all stakeholders, and in the process contributing to the community and economy as a whole. It goes beyond short-term considerations and includes the sustainability of a company's long-term performance. …Coupled with increasingly shorter shareholding tenure, the ownership mentality is arguably being eroded and replaced by a prevalent short-term view of investment and portfolio management. Hence, the emphasis on stewardship is relevant and timely.
    - ✧ もっとも、シンガポールの上場企業のほとんどに支配株主が存在するため、イギリスの企業について指摘されるような短期主義の問題が生じているとは考え難い。また機関投資家が果たしうる役割も大きくないと考えられる。
  - ➢ 適用するかどうかは完全に任意であり、受入機関のリストも存在しない。Comply or explain の要求もない。
    - ✧ What do organisations that support the SSP need to do? - Investors are encouraged to adopt the aim and spirit of the SSP, absolutely on a voluntary basis. The extent to which they practise, articulate and share their stewardship activities, and their level of commitment to the SSP, is to their own discretion and may be adjusted according to their own circumstances. Investors are encouraged to avoid a "box-ticking" approach and to consider instead whether their activities are appropriate to their stewardship orientation. Supporting the

> SSP is not merely about adding one's name to a list. It is an ongoing effort to maintain and improve one's stewardship orientation over the long term. (https://www.stewardshipasia.com.sg/intent#b104)

➢ 策定主体である Singapore Stewardship Principles Working Group は、シンガポールの国有企業管理会社である Temasek Holdings の出資・支援を受けている非営利団体である Stewardship Asia Centre が主導

    ✧ 機関投資家によるモニタリングが厳しくなった場合、Temasek はむしろ支配株主として監視を受ける立場になる。国際的な動向をフォローするように見せつつ、先に緩やかな内容のスチュワードシップコードを策定することにより、現状維持を図ったもの？

● Stewardship Principles for Family Businesses (2018)

➢ 非上場会社を含む同族企業のオーナー一族を steward と位置づけ、一族の利益のみを追求するのではなく、持続可能な形で多様なステークホルダーの利益に貢献すべきと提言

    ✧ Steward 概念の柔軟性・多義性

    ✧ エンフォースメントに関する記述は一切ない

➢ 策定主体は Stewardship Asia Centre

    ✧ 目的は不明。アジアへのシンガポールモデルの輸出？

4. 小括

日本版コードとイギリス版コードは、目的は逆方向だが、規制色の強さは共通
シンガポール版コードは、目的は日本版よりもイギリス版に類似、規制色は皆無

III. 若干の考察

1. コーポレートガバナンスの収斂（convergence）の諸態様

● Gilson の形式的収斂（formal convergence）と機能的収斂（functional convergence）

➢ 形式的収斂には制度改正にコストがかかるので、機能的収斂の方が先に進む

● 表面的な形式のみの収斂（faux convergence）

➢ スチュワードシップコードの存在という形式面での収斂が見られるが、コード策定の目的という機能面は各国で異なっている

    ✧ Cf. Divergence in convergence（Gordon）

> ソフトローの形態をとることによる制度改正のコストの小ささ

    ✧ E.g. コーポレートガバナンスコードによる独立取締役の要求とその多様性（Puchniak & Kim）

	形式面での収斂	
	Yes	No
機能面での収斂　Yes	formal convergence (Gilson)	functional convergence (Gilson)
No	faux convergence (Goto, Koh & Puchniak)	No convergence

2. 各国のスチュワードシップコードのグルーピング

● 分類軸

> 最終投資家・株主の利益　←→　公共的利益

> 規制強化　←→　現状維持

● 韓国

> 策定の経緯

    ✧ 2014 年末：韓国金融監督委員会（FSC）が、「金融業界における消費者の信頼を確立」するための手段の 1 つとして韓国版スチュワードシップコードの策定を挙げる（英語版リリースは 2015/1/29）

    ✧ 2015 年 3 月：FSC による起草委員会設置

    ✧ 2015 年 7 月 17 日：Samsung CT と Cheil Industry の合併議案（出席株主の議決権の 2/3 の賛成必要）が、前者の筆頭株主（11.2%を保有）である韓国国民年金基金（NPS）の賛成により可決。基金の議決権行使専門委員会は反対することを勧告していた。

    ✧ 2015 年 12 月 1 日：FSC 起草委員会による第 1 次草案公表。産業界からの反発強く成立に至らず。

    ✧ 2016 年 8 月：企業経営に対する政府の介入であるとの批判を受け、韓国証券取引所等によって設立された民間団体である Korean Corporate Governance Service が起草作業を引き継ぎ、Korean Stewardship Council を設置

- ❖ 2016 年 10 月：朴槿恵前大統領のスキャンダル発覚
- ❖ 2016 年 11 月 18 日：KCGS による第 2 次草案公表
- ❖ 2016 年 12 月 9 日：朴前大統領に対する弾劾決議可決
- ❖ 2016 年 12 月 16 日：KCGS が最終案を公表
- ❖ 2017 年 5 月 9 日：大統領選挙において、公約の 1 つにスチュワードシップコードの導入を掲げていた文在寅氏当選。翌日の就任演説において財閥改革に言及。
- ❖ 2017 年 12 月 29 日：韓国企画財政部が 2018 年の経済政策の 1 つにスチュワードシップコードの導入と、NPS やその他の機関投資家によるスチュワードシップの促進を掲げる
- ❖ 2018 年 7 月 30 日：NPS が韓国版スチュワードシップコードを受入れ
- ➢ コード記載の目的：The responsibility institutional investors bear …. refers to a sense of responsibility to promote the mid- to long-term interests of their clients and ultimate beneficiaries by pursuing the mid- to long-term value enhancement and sustainable growth of investee companies. Successful implementation of stewardship responsibilities … also supports the sound and substantial growth and development of capital markets and the overall economy.
- ➢ 内容・エンフォースメント
  - ❖ 7 原則は概ね日本版コードと同じだが、個別の議決権行使とその理由の開示を要求（原則 5: disclosure of "voting records and the reasons for each vote"）
  - ❖ 受入機関のリストを KCGS が公表、comply or explain
  - ❖ NPS による受入れは遅く、他の機関投資家による受入れも日本に比べると低調（2018 年 8 月時点）
- ➢ 策定の目的
  - ❖ 2015 年 3 月の作業開始時の目的は不明
  - ❖ 株式保有構造は日本よりもシンガポールに近いが、文政権下で、コーポレートガバナンス改革のために政府が機関投資家の圧力を用いようとしている点で日本に類似
  - ❖ 方向性も、投資家・株主の利益を強調する点でイギリス・シンガポールより日本に近い

- 台湾
  - ➢ 策定主体は金融監督管理委員会の指示を受けた台湾証券取引所
  - ➢ コード記載の目的：The Principles, … are intended to encourage institutional investors to apply their expertise and influence, and fulfill their duties as asset owners or managers, <u>so as to enhance long-term value for themselves and capital providers.</u> The institutional investors, … are also able to improve the quality of corporate governance of the investee companies, thus creating an overall positive effect on the development of industry, economy and society.
  - ➢ 内容：原則 6 つ（日本版の原則 7 を除いたもの）
  - ➢ エンフォースメント
    - ✧ 受入機関のリストを公表
    - ✧ 各原則の遵守状況についての簡単な説明を要求（不遵守の場合の理由の説明までは求められていない）
    - ✧ 外国機関投資家は、同様の目的のコード・原則を受け入れている場合には、そのことに言及すれば台湾版コードの受入機関となることができる
  - ➢ 策定の目的
    - ✧ In observing international trends, the promotion of institutional investors' stewardship is of great importance in cultivating corporate governance in the market.（TWSE ウェブサイト）
    - ✧ 台湾企業のガバナンス改革？
      - 日本や韓国のような具体的問題意識はあるのか？
    - ✧ 国際的な動向に併せることが目的？

- アメリカ
  - ➢ 策定主体の Investor Stewardship Group (ISG)は、大規模な機関投資家および国際的なアセットマネージャーによる民間団体
  - ➢ コード記載の目的：機関投資家は、その資金提供者に対して説明責任を負う（原則 A）。
    - ✧ ISG によって併せて策定された Corporate Governance Principles for US Listed Companies（ISG メンバーである機関投資家の議決権行使・エンゲージメントのガイドラインをまとめたもの）では、取締役会は株主に対して説明責任を負うこと、株主はその経済的利益の比率に応じて議決権を与えられるべきであることなどを規定

> 内容：現在アメリカの機関投資家が一般的に行っていると考えられるエンゲージメントを強化するものではない
  - 議決権行使助言機関を使う場合には、その方針の内容・形成手続・能力・利益相反回避措置を評価すべき（原則 D）
  - 機関投資家は、企業との見解の差異がある場合に建設的かつ現実的な態度で臨むべき（原則 E）
  - 機関投資家は必要な場合には CG 原則とスチュワードシップ原則の採択・実施を奨励するために協働すべきとするが（原則 F）、ガイダンスでは個別企業に対する集団的エンゲージメントではなく、原則自体の改定や政策的な議論への参加が例示されている
> エンフォースメント
  - 署名した機関投資家のリストは ISG のウェブサイトで公表
  - 署名した機関投資家は、その方針・実務を原則の水準以上のものにすることを期待されているが（ISG FAQ）、その運用のあり方は各機関投資家に委ねられており（ISG FAQ）、comply or explain も要求されていない
> 策定の目的
  - シンガポール版コードと同様に現状維持だが、投資家・株主の利益を目的としている点で異なる。同様に投資家団体が作成したイギリス ISC コードと類似。
  - イギリス版コードのような動きへの対抗？

		目的の方向性	
		Pro public interest	Pro shareholder/investor
規制レベル	規制強化的	イギリス	日本 韓国 台湾？
	現状維持的	シンガポール	イギリス ISC アメリカ ISG

- 影響する要素
  > 策定主体が政府（またはその意向を受けた団体）か、投資家の団体か
  > 株式所有構造

資　料

資料 1

Berkeley Business Law Journal

Volume 15 | Issue 2   Article 4

2019

The Logic and Limits of Stewardship Code: The Case of Japan

Gen Goto

Follow this and additional works at: https://scholarship.law.berkeley.edu/bblj

Part of the Law Commons

Recommended Citation

Gen Goto, *The Logic and Limits of Stewardship Code: The Case of Japan*, 15 BERKELEY BUS. L.J. 365 (2019).

Link to publisher version (DOI)

The Logic and Limits of Stewardship Codes: The Case of Japan

Gen Goto[*]

A stewardship code is a set of principles on how institutional investors should act as shareholders of companies in which they invest. Since the first one was adopted by the Financial Reporting Council of the United Kingdom in July 2010, a significant number of countries, including Japan, have followed the lead of the United Kingdom in adopting their own stewardship codes. Although the contents of these codes are not identical, they generally are non-mandatory "comply or explain" rules urging institutional investors to engage more actively with their investee companies by exercising their rights as shareholders.

One might find the trend of jurisdictions adopting stewardship codes unsurprising considering the global increase in the ownership stake held by institutional investors in listed companies, and the growing expectation that these investors will play a role in the corporate governance of investee companies. However, if the goal of adopting stewardship codes is to promote better corporate governance in investee companies, then this uniform approach is rather puzzling since it is widely acknowledged that different countries have different share-ownership structures and often face different corporate governance challenges. It may well be the case that the true intention behind adopting a stewardship code could be highly contextual and, contingent on jurisdiction-specific factor).

From such viewpoint, this article investigates the true intention behind the adoption of stewardship codes in the United Kingdom and Japan by analyzing not only the text of their principles and guidance, but also the contexts in which they were adopted. The main finding is that there is a divergence between the basic goals and orientation of the Japanese and the UK Stewardship Codes that has been largely overlooked in the literature. Although the term "stewardship" suggests that stewardship codes are premised on the logic of

[*] Associate Professor, the University of Tokyo, Graduate Schools for Law and Politics. The research for this article was commenced during the author's stay at the Centre for Asian Legal Studies of the National University of Singapore, the Faculty of Law as a Visiting Associate Professor in the summer of 2017 and was financially supported by JSPS Grant-in-Aid for Scientific Research (C) No.16K03390. The author would like to thank these institutions for their hospitality and generosity. The author would also like to thank Dan W. Puchniak and the participants of the CALS seminar (August 24, 2017), the Comparative Corporate Governance Conference 2018 (January 13-14, 2018 at National University of Singapore) and the Enterprise Law Workshop (March 26, 2018 at Hitotsubashi University) for their valuable comments.

365

fiduciary duties, which compels a fiduciary to forsake its own self-interest and act in the interest of its beneficiary, the goal of the UK Stewardship Code is different. It aims to restrain excessive risk-taking and short-termism by making institutional investors more responsible to the public. In contrast, the Japanese Stewardship Code aims to change the attitude of domestic institutional investors in order to orient Japanese corporate governance towards the interests of shareholders rather than stakeholders. This goal of the Japanese Code is more compatible with the logic of stewardship than that of the UK Code. At the same time, the Japanese Government considers this goal to be in the public interest of Japan.

Another finding of this article is that different stewardship codes have different goals and that this must be taken into consideration when assessing their effectiveness. The success of the Japanese Stewardship Code will primarily depend on how well domestic institutional investors are incentivized to act in the interest of their ultimate beneficiaries and to monitor entrenched management. Conversely, the success of the UK Stewardship Code will likely depend on the extent it can prompt institutional investors to consider the interest of the public and stakeholders other than shareholders. Regulatory interventions might be necessary in both cases, but for different reasons.

The Logic and Limits of Stewardship Codes

PART I: INTRODUCTION: STEWARDSHIP CODES AND THE LOGIC OF "STEWARDSHIP"

A. Stewardship Codes as a Global Trend

A stewardship code is a set of principles on how institutional investors should act as shareholders of companies in which they invest. Since the first was adopted by the Financial Reporting Council of the United Kingdom in July 2010,[1] a significant number of countries, including Japan,[2] have followed the lead of the United Kingdom in adopting their own stewardship codes.[3] Similar measures have also been taken by intergovernmental organizations, such as the Organization for Economic Co-operation and Development (OECD) and the European Union, to promote the concept of stewardship across jurisdictions.[4]

1. The UK Stewardship Code was originally adopted in July 2010 and later revised in November 2012 (hereinafter, "the 2010 UK Code" and "the 2012 Revised UK Code"). Both the original 2010 UK Code (FINANCIAL REPORTING COUNCIL, THE UK STEWARDSHIP CODE (July 2010)) and the 2012 Revised UK Code (FINANCIAL REPORTING COUNCIL, THE UK STEWARDSHIP CODE (September 2012)) are available at https://www.frc.org.uk/investors/uk-stewardship-code/origins-of-the-uk-stewardship-code.

2. The Japanese Stewardship Code was originally adopted in February 2014 and later revised in May 2017 (hereinafter, "the 2014 Japanese Code" and "the 2017 Revised Japanese Code"). The original 2014 Japanese Code (THE COUNCIL OF EXPERTS CONCERNING THE JAPANESE VERSION OF THE STEWARDSHIP CODE, PRINCIPLES FOR RESPONSIBLE INSTITUTIONAL INVESTORS 《JAPAN'S STEWARDSHIP CODE》 TO PROMOTE SUSTAINABLE GROWTH OF COMPANIES THROUGH INVESTMENT AND DIALOGUE (February 26, 2014)) is available at http://www.fsa.go.jp/en/refer/councils/stewardship/20140407.html, and its Japanese version is available at http://www.fsa.go.jp/news/25/singi/20140227-2/04.pdf. The 2017 Revised Japanese Code (the Council of Experts on the Stewardship Code, Principles for Responsible Institutional Investors 《Japan's Stewardship Code》 To Promote Sustainable Growth of Companies through Investment and Dialogue (May 29, 2017)) is available at http://www.fsa.go.jp/en/refer/councils/stewardship/20170529.html and its Japanese version is available at http://www.fsa.go.jp/news/29/singi/20170529/01.pdf.

3. Stewardship codes around the world can be classified into three groups: those adopted by or under auspices of relevant state authorities, those adopted by stock exchanges and industrial organization of finance companies, and those adopted by private groups of institutional investors. JENNIFER G. HILL, GOOD ACTIVIST/BAD ACTIVIST: THE RISE OF INTERNATIONAL STEWARDSHIP CODES, ECGI Law Working Paper No. 368/2017 (2017), at page 11-15 (available at http://ssm.com/abstract=3036357). Among others, the first group includes stewardship codes of the United Kingdom (2010), Japan (2014), Malaysia (2014), Hong Kong (2016), and Taiwan (2016), the second group includes those of South Africa (2011), Singapore (2016) and South Korea (2016), and the third group includes those of Canada (2010), the Netherlands (2011), Switzerland (2013), International Corporate Governance Network (2016), and the United States of America (2017). Some of the stewardship codes in the second group, for example that of Singapore, could be classified in the first group if state authorities were the actual driving force behind the scene. Hill, supra at page 12 note 75. The author believes that this classification is valuable and essential as it is natural to think that the authorities adopting stewardship codes have some policy objectives, which private groups of investors may not necessarily share. In contrast, Professors Fenwick and Vermeulen, who also introduce a similar classification, do not seem to recognize the possible divergence of the goals of state authorities and private groups of investors as they simply compare "which approach is the best option". See MARK FENWICK & ERIK P. M. VERMEULEN, INSTITUTIONAL INVESTOR ENGAGEMENT: HOW TO CREATE A 'STEWARDSHIP CULTURE'. TILEC Discussion Paper DP 2018-006 (2018), at page 37-38 and page 43 (available at http://ssm.com/abstract=3098235).

4. See, G20/OECD Principles of Corporate Governance (September 2015), Part III (available at https://www.oecd.org/daf/ca/Corporate-Governance-Principles-ENG.pdf) and Directive (EU) 2017/828

The Logic and Limits of Stewardship Codes

Although the contents of these codes are not identical, they generally are non-mandatory "comply or explain" rules urging institutional investors to engage more actively with their investee companies by exercising their rights as shareholders.

The trend of jurisdictions adopting stewardship codes is unsurprising when considering the global increase in the ownership stake held by institutional investors in listed companies and the growing expectation that these investors will play a role in the corporate governance of investee companies.[5] However, if the goal of adopting stewardship codes is to promote better corporate governance in investee companies, then this uniform approach is rather puzzling.

It is widely acknowledged that different countries have different share-ownership structures and thus often face different corporate governance challenges.[6] From such a viewpoint, the assertion of two UK law professors that the transplantation of UK-Style stewardship codes "is likely to be driven by the common concerns shared by many jurisdictions" is surprising,[7] as it may well be the case that the true intention behind adopting a stewardship code in a jurisdiction could be highly contextual and contingent upon jurisdiction-specific factors. Indeed, as explained in this article, this is the case in Japan.

B. The Logic of "Stewardship."

Another question arises from the term "stewardship".

A "steward" means a "person employed to manage another's property, especially a large house or estate" or a "person whose responsibility it is to take care of something".[8] In its original historical context, a "steward" was an "officer of the royal household, especially an administrator of Crown estates" in Britain.[9] Without delving much into the British history, it would not be wrong to think of stewards in those days as being responsible to and required to

of the European Parliament and of the Council of 17 May 2017 amending Directive 2007/36/EC as regards the encouragement of long-term shareholder engagement, Chapter Ib (as amended).

5. See for example, G20/OECD Principles of Corporate Governance (September 2015), supra note 4 at 31, and Lucian A. Bebchuk, Alma Cohen & Scott Hirst, The Agency Problems of Institutional Investors, 31 JOURNAL OF ECONOMIC PERSPECTIVES 89, 91-93 (2017). For earlier studies, see for example, Bernard S. Black & John C. Coffee, Jr., Hail Britannia?: Institutional Investor Behavior under Limited Regulation, 92 MICHIGAN LAW REVIEW 1997 (1994).

6. REINIER KRAAKMAN ET AL., THE ANATOMY OF CORPORATE LAW: A COMPARATIVE AND FUNCTIONAL APPROACH, 3rd ed. (Oxford University Press, 2017), at 46. Other factors, such as legal systems, social institutions and culture, may also produce difference of corporate governance issues. While this is an interesting subject of research, it is beyond the scope of this article.

7. Iris H.-Y. Chiu & Dionysia Katelouzou, From Shareholder Stewardship to Shareholder Duties: Is the Time Ripe? in Hanne S. Birkmose (ed.), SHAREHOLDERS' DUTIES (Wolters Kluwer, 2017) at 131, 135. See also ibid. at 133 (arguing that duty of institutional investors regarding stewardship engagement "is relevant to different European jurisdictions despite any differences in the ownership structures").

8. The Oxford Dictionary (online version) https://en.oxforddictionaries.com/definition/steward.

9. Ibid.

demonstrate loyalty to the British royal household, whose estate is entrusted to the stewards.

In the context of modern investment, institutional investors, such as mutual funds, pension funds, insurance companies, and investment advisors, are considered to be "stewards", as they are entrusted with their clients' money for investment purposes. The use of the term "stewardship" suggests that stewardship codes are based on the following logic produced by an analogy with the historical "steward". Institutional investors must be loyal to their clients, who have entrusted their money to the institutions for investment purposes, and should exercise their rights as shareholders of investee companies in order to fulfill their responsibility as "stewards" of their clients.[10]

One would notice that this logic of "stewardship" is essentially that of fiduciary duties, which compels a fiduciary to forsake its own self-interest and act only in the interest of its beneficiary.[11] Indeed, some of the relationships between institutional investors and their clients can be described as a fiduciary relationship. For example, an investment advisor hired by a public pension fund to manage a part of its fund is a fiduciary to the pension fund.[12] By avoiding the use of the term "fiduciary", which is a well-established legal term in the common-law world with a defined scope,[13] stewardship codes have expanded the range of actors they cover, especially those that would not necessarily be considered fiduciaries.[14]

10. Those who are familiar with the UK Stewardship Code might argue that the logic of stewardship stipulated in the text above does not fit the UK Code, which considers institutional investors rather as stewards of investee companies. The author agrees. Indeed, the point of this article is to show that such framing of a stewardship code is UK-specific (or Europe-specific) and is not necessarily universally shared - at least not by the Japanese Stewardship Code. See *infra*, Part I, Section C and Part III, Section C.

11. See for example, Hiroyuki Kansaku, *Kigyoroto gabananasu koryo ni maketa naigai no doko – Suchuwadoshippu kodo wo chushin toshite [Developments towards the Improvement of Corporate Governance in Japan and Other Countries: With Focus on Stewardship Codes]*, 2030 SHOHOMU 11, at 13 (2014).

12. For example, OECD Principles recommends, without using the term "stewardship", that "institutional investors acting in a fiduciary capacity should disclose their corporate governance and voting policies with respect to their investments".

13. For example, the investment advisor in the example above is not in a direct relationship with ultimate beneficiaries of the pension fund and thus may not be considered as a fiduciary in relation to the ultimate beneficiaries. Also, the relationship between a life insurance company and its policyholders is generally considered as that of a contract and not of a fiduciary, although insurance company invests the money paid by the policyholders as premiums out of which insurance proceeds will be paid. The same would apply to the relationship between a proxy advisor and the clients (and their ultimate beneficiaries). See Iris H.-Y. Chiu & Dionysia Katelouzou, *Making a Case for Regulating Institutional Shareholders' Corporate Governance Roles*, 2018 JOURNAL OF BUSINESS LAW 67, at 79-81.

14. See Hiroyuki Kansaku, *Nihon-ban suchuwadoshippu kodo no kihonsei ni tsuite [On the Nature of the Japanese Stewardship Code as a Norm]*, in Etsuro Kuronuma & Tomotaka Fujita (eds.), Kigyoho no shinro – Egashira Kenjiro sensei koki kinen [Future Courses of Enterprise Law - In Celebration of the 70th Birthday of Professor Kenjiro Egashira] (Yuhikaku, 2017), 1005, at page 1014 (in Japanese). Of course, the binding power of stewardship codes taking the "comply or explain" approach is not as strong as that of fiduciary duties imposed by law.

The Logic and Limits of Stewardship Codes

While the above logic of stewardship focuses on the interest of ultimate beneficiaries, scholarly debate on the role of institutional investors focuses on improving corporate governance of investee companies.[15] This difference in focus raises a possibility that stewardship codes are not necessarily based on the logic of stewardship, but rather focus on corporate governance of investee companies.

C. The Japanese Code and the UK Code: Are they the same?

Are stewardship codes about the interests of ultimate beneficiaries, or are they about corporate governance of investee companies? Interestingly, there is an important difference between the Japanese Stewardship Code and the UK Stewardship Code on this point.

The preface of the Japanese Stewardship Code begins with the following definition of "stewardship responsibilities":

In this Code, "stewardship responsibilities" refers to the responsibilities of institutional investors to enhance the medium- to long-term investment return for their clients and beneficiaries (including ultimate beneficiaries; the same shall apply hereafter) by improving and fostering the investee companies' corporate value and sustainable growth through constructive engagement, or purposeful dialogue, based on in-depth knowledge of the companies and their business environment.[16]

In contrast, the preface of the current UK Stewardship Code as revised in 2012 states the aim of stewardship in its first paragraph as follows:

Stewardship aims to promote the long term success of companies in such a way that the ultimate providers of capital also prosper. Effective stewardship benefits companies, investors and the economy as a whole.[17]

These codes are ostensibly alike as they use similar wording on the same two issues. The first is the interest of ultimate beneficiaries ("the medium- to long-term investment return for their clients and beneficiaries" (Japan) or the prosperity of "the ultimate providers of capital" (UK)). The second is the growth of investee companies ("improving and fostering the investee companies' corporate value and sustainable growth" (Japan) or "the long-term success of companies" (UK)).

15. Interestingly, the Financial Services Agency of Japan rather turned to the term "fiduciary duty", which is an imported concept for Japan that does not share the common-law tradition, as a means to change the behavior of sellers of financial instruments, such as banks selling mutual fund or variable life insurance, to disclose more information to their customers. See Nobuko Matsumoto, *Kinyu bunya ni okeru "fiduciary-duyu no yogoho ni tsuite no ichi kosatsu* [A Study on the Terminology of "Fiduciary Duty" in Financial Regulation], in Yoshihisa Nomi, Norio Higuchi & Hideki Kanda (eds.), *Shintaku hosei no shin jidai: Shintaku no gendaiteki tenkai to shorai tenbou* [The New Era of Trust Law: Modern Developments and Future Prospects of Trusts] (Kobundo, 2017) at 223.

16. The 2014 Japanese Code, *supra* note 2 at page 1. The definition of stewardship responsibilities remains unchanged in the 2017 Revised Japanese Code, *supra* note 2 at page 3.

17. The 2012 Revised UK Code, *supra* note 1 at page 1.

The two codes, however, are structured differently and thus seem to emphasize different points. By using the prepositions "to" and "by", the Japanese Code seems to prioritize the enhancement of "the medium- to long-term investment return for [institutional investors'] clients and beneficiaries" as the goal of stewardship responsibility and consider sustainable growth of investee companies as a means to achieve this goal.[18] In contrast, the UK 2012 Code seems to put emphasis on "the long-term success of [investee] companies", which is brought first, and to subordinate the interest of ultimate providers of capital by using the words "in such a way" and "also". Somewhat ironically, Japan seems to demonstrate greater fidelity to the logic of "stewardship", as set out earlier, than the United Kingdom, the motherland of stewardship codes.

D. Research questions

From this divergence, which has been largely overlooked in the literature,[19] a few questions arise. What is, or are, the intended goal(s) of stewardship codes? Why are countries pursuing different goals and trying to use the same measure to achieve them? How compatible are these goals with the logic of stewardship and can they be achieved by adopting stewardship codes?

This Article addresses these questions by drawing on the Japanese experience and by comparing it with the United Kingdom. Briefly stated, there is a divergence between the basic goals and orientation of the Japanese and the UK Stewardship Codes. Although the term "stewardship" suggests that stewardship codes are based on the logic of a fiduciary duty that compels a fiduciary to forsake its own self-interest and act in the interests of its beneficiary, the goal of the UK Stewardship Code is instead to restrain excessive risk-taking and short-termism by making institutional investors more responsible to the public. In contrast, the Japanese Stewardship Code aims to change the attitude of domestic institutional investors so as to make Japanese corporate governance more oriented towards the interests of shareholders rather than stakeholders.

---

18. In response to one of the comments received in the public comment procedure criticizing the inclusion of sustainable growth of investee companies in the scope of stewardship responsibility, the Council of Experts Concerning the Japanese Version of the Stewardship Code admitted that the final goal of institutional investors is to enhance the medium- to long-term investment return for their clients and beneficiaries, while asserting that it is important to improve and foster the investee companies' corporate value and sustainable growth through constructive engagement. See THE COUNCIL OF EXPERTS CONCERNING THE JAPANESE VERSION OF THE STEWARDSHIP CODE, *Wahun ni tuisuru komento no gaiyo oyobi kentokai no kangaekata* [The Summary of the Comments to the Japanese Version of the Draft and the Council's View on Them] (April 22, 2014), available at http://www.fsa.go.jp/news/25/singi/20140422-2/01.pdf), Comment No.2 at page 1.

19. See *infra* note 152-158 and accompanying text.

The Logic and Limits of Stewardship Codes

The remainder of this Article starts with a deeper look at the background and the contents of the UK Stewardship Code with a view to identify its intended goal (Part II). After a similar exercise with the Japanese Stewardship Code (Part III), this Article analyzes whether the intended goals of the UK and Japanese codes are compatible with the logic of stewardship, and whether these codes can achieve their respective goals (Part IV).

PART II: THE ORIGIN OF STEWARDSHIP CODES: THE CASE OF THE UNITED KINGDOM

A. Inconsistency within the 2012 UK Code

As discussed above, the preface to the current 2012 revised version of the UK Stewardship Code, lists two goals of stewardship: (1) "the long term success of companies"; and, (2) the prosperity of "the ultimate providers of capital". However, the first goal appears to have priority over the second. Such a focus on the long-term success of investee companies is also reflected in the second paragraph of the preface, which states that "responsibility for stewardship is shared" in publicly listed companies; that "the primary responsibility rests with the board of the company"; and that investors "also play an important role in holding the board to account for the fulfilment of its responsibilities".[20] If, however, one takes the logic of stewardship discussed in Part I, Section B seriously, it should be institutional investors that bear the primary responsibility to their clients and ultimate beneficiaries.

In contrast, the principles of the 2012 Revised UK Stewardship Code, which are described as "the core of the Code",[21] are stipulated in the following manner:

So as to protect and enhance the value that accrues to the ultimate beneficiary, institutional investors should:

1. publicly disclose their policy on how they will discharge their stewardship responsibilities.
2. have a robust policy on managing conflicts of interest in relation to stewardship which should be publicly disclosed.
3. monitor their investee companies.
4. establish clear guidelines on when and how they will escalate their stewardship activities.
5. be willing to act collectively with other investors where appropriate.
6. have a clear policy on voting and disclosure of voting activity.
7. report periodically on their stewardship and voting activities.[22]

---

20. The 2012 Revised Code, *supra* note 1 at page 1.

21. The 2012 Revised Code, *supra* note 1 at page 4. Each principle is accompanied by detailed guidance. Ibid. at page 6-10.

22. The 2012 Revised UK Code, *supra* note 1 at page 5.

Clearly, the chapeau of these seven principles, which was added by the 2012 revision, emphasizes the interests of ultimate beneficiaries as the goal. It does not even refer to the interest of investee companies. There is thus a clear inconsistency between the preface and the principles of the 2012 Revised UK Stewardship Code on which aspect to emphasize, the interest of investee companies or that of ultimate beneficiaries. Unsurprisingly, the UK Stewardship Code has been criticized as "unclear as to whom shareholders are accountable to".[23] To understand the origin of this inconsistency, the following section will examine the background of the UK Stewardship Code.

B. The Background of the UK Stewardship Code

1. The Walker Review

In November 2009, in the aftermath of the global financial crisis in the preceding years, Sir David Walker submitted a report known as the "Walker Review"[24] commissioned by the UK government. The task, as described by the UK government, was "to review corporate governance in UK banks in light of the experience of critical loss and failure throughout the banking system", on the premise that "serious deficiencies in prudential oversight and financial regulation in the period before the crisis were accompanied by major governance failures within banks" and that these factors "contributed materially to excessive risk taking and to the breadth and depth of the crisis".[25]

In this review, Sir David recommended that the "remit of the FRC [Financial Reporting Council] should be explicitly extended to cover the development and encouragement of adherence to principles of best practice in stewardship by institutional investors and fund managers" and that the "Code on the Responsibilities of Institutional Investors, prepared by the Institutional Shareholders' Committee, should be ratified by the FRC and become the Stewardship Code".[26]

The Walker Report focused on the role of institutional investors since there was " a widespread acquiescence by institutional investors and the market in the gearing up of the balance sheets of banks (and also of many other

---

23.   Arad Reisberg, *The UK Stewardship Code: On the Road to Nowhere?* 15 JOURNAL OF CORPORATE LAW STUDIES 217, 229 (2015). Similar views are expressed by Chiu & Katelouzou, *supra* note 13 at 87 and Paul Davies, *Shareholders in the United Kingdom*, in Jennifer G. Hill & Randall S. Thomas (eds.), RESEARCH HANDBOOK ON SHAREHOLDER POWER (Edward Elgar, 2015) 355, at 373.
24.   Sir David Walker, A Review of Corporate Governance in UK Banks and Other Financial Industry Entities: Final Recommendations (November 26, 2009) (*hereinafter* "the Walker Review"), available at http://webarchive.nationalarchives.gov.uk/+/http://www.hm-treasury.gov.uk/d/walker_review_261109.pdf. Sir David is a prominent British banker and a former officer of the UK Treasury and Bank of England. See https://en.wikipedia.org/wiki/David_Walker_(banker).
25.   The Walker Review, *supra* note 24 at page 9
26.   The Walker Review, *supra* note 24 at Recommendations 16 and 17, at page 17.

The Logic and Limits of Stewardship Codes

companies) as a means of boosting returns on equity".[27] Such an attitude "was not necessarily irrational from the standpoint of the immediate interests of shareholders who, in the leveraged limited liability business of a bank, receive all of the potential upside whereas their downside is limited to their equity stake, however much the bank loses overall in a catastrophe".[28] However, "while shareholders enjoy limited liability in respect of their investee companies, in the case of major banks the taxpayer has been obliged to assume effectively unlimited liability".[29] In another part, the Walker Review criticizes the "increased shareholder pressure on boards to perform in the short term" before the Financial Crisis, and regards "specific short-term initiative[s] such as increased leverage, spin-offs, acquisitions or share buybacks" as "opportunistic behavior" as they brought "a stronger stock price and higher short-term earnings" "at the expense of increased credit risk and potential erosion in credit quality to the detriment of bondholders and other creditors".[30]

In this context the Walker Review emphasizes the importance of discharging the responsibilities of shareholders as owners, and asserts that "those who have significant rights of ownership and enjoy the very material advantage of limited liability should see these as complemented by a duty of stewardship".[31] The Walker Review states that this view "would be shared by the public, as well as those employees and suppliers who are less well-placed than an institutional shareholder to diversify their exposure to the management and performance risk of a limited liability company".[32]

To summarize, the goal of the Walker Review was to make institutional investors who are shareholders of public companies more responsible to the general public and curtail excessive risk taking by monitoring the management of those companies.[33] This goal is understandable given the context of the post-crisis climate.[34]

---

27.   The Walker Review, *supra* note 24 at para.5.10 at page71. See also the Walker Review, *supra* note 24 at para.1.10 at page.26.
28.   The Walker Review, *supra* note 24 at para.5.10 at page71. See also the Walker Review, *supra* note 24 at para.1.8 at page.25.
29.   The Walker Review, *supra* note 24 at page 12.
30.   The Walker Review, *supra* note 24 at para.5.27 at page 78.
31.   The Walker Review, *supra* note 24 at page 12 and para.5.7 at page 70.
32.   The Walker Review, *supra* note 24 at para.5.7 at page 70.
33.   Iris H-Y Chiu, *Institutional Shareholders as Stewards: Toward a New Conception of Corporate Governance*, 6 BROOKLYN JOURNAL OF FINANCIAL AND COMMERCIAL LAW 387, at 396 (2012). It may be worth noting that the Walker Review was not the first policy document to count on institutional investors' monitoring role from the viewpoint of public interest. The Cadbury Report, which was published in 1992 in the wake of financial scandals at Maxwell Communications and Bank of Credit and Commerce International, turned to institutional investors to engage with their investee companies and to make positive use of their voting rights to achieve better corporate governance. Report of the Committee on the Financial Aspects of Corporate Governance (May 1992), para.6.9-6.12, available at http://www.ecgi.org/codes/documents/cadbury.pdf.
34.   Professor Reisberg describes the mood of the period as "Something had to be done quickly and, preferably, visibly". Reisberg, *supra* note 23 at 221.

It is not so clear, however, how the adoption of a stewardship code would help in achieving these public interest goals. While the Walker Review describes the responsibility of shareholders as "a duty of stewardship" without clarifying to whom such a duty is owed and expects that many "ultimate beneficiaries, trustees and other end investors would no doubt wish to be supportive of" it,[35] the above goal would rather contradict with the logic of "stewardship" discussed in Part I, which focuses on maximizing the interests of ultimate beneficiaries of institutional investors.

2. The ISC Code

Interestingly, the Code on the Responsibilities of Institutional Investors (the ISC Code),[36] which was drafted by the Institutional Shareholders' Committee (ISC) and recommended by the Walker Review to the FRC for ratification, did not share the same goal as the Walker Review. In particular, the ISC Code declares that the "duty of institutional investors is to their end-beneficiaries and/or clients and not to the wider public".[37] Also, the paragraph describing the aim of the code places improving "long-term returns to shareholders" ahead of reducing "the risk of catastrophic outcomes due to bad strategic decisions" and "helping with the efficient exercise of governance responsibilities".[38]

As the ISC is not a governmental agency but a private organization formed by trade associations of British institutional investors,[39] it places the interests of clients and ultimate beneficiaries of institutional investors above that of the wider public. This stance, which the ISC has held since at least 2002,[40] however, has apparently been ignored by the Walker Review.[41]

---

35. The Walker Review, *supra* note 24 at para.5.7 at page 70 and para.5.9 at page 71.

36. Institutional Shareholders' Committee, the Code on the Responsibilities of Institutional Investors (November, 2009) (hereinafter "the ISC Code"), available at https://www.theinvestmentassociation.org/assets/components/ima_filesecurity/secure.php?f=industry-guidance/cp-01.pdf. This code is also included in the Annex 8 of the Walker Review.

37. ISC Code, *supra* note 36 at page 2. The declaration in the text was made after stating that the amount of resources of institutional investors should be "sufficient to allow them to fulfill their responsibilities effectively" but be "commensurate with the benefits derived".

38. ISC Code, *supra* note 36 at page 1.

39. The members of the ISC as of 2009 are the Association of British Insurers, the Association of Investment Trust Companies, the National Association of Pension Funds, and the Investment Management Association. ISC Code, *supra* note 36 at page 1, footnote 1.

40. The statement that "(t)he duty of institutional investors is to their end-beneficiaries and/or clients and not to the wider public" appears in "the Responsibilities of Institutional Shareholders and Agents – Statement of Principles" published by the ISC in 2002 and its update in 2007 (available at http://www.ecgi.org/codes/documents/isc_statement_of_principles.pdf and https://www.ivis.co.uk/media/5934/Isc_statement_of_principles_2007_0907.pdf). The 2002 document was the ISC's response to a proposal of the Myers Report to impose a duty on UK-based pension funds to exercise voting rights as shareholders of investee companies on issues that may affect the value of the plan's investment. See Paul Myers, Institutional Investment in the United Kingdom: A Review (March 2001) (hereinafter "the Myers Report") at para.5.89-5.93 at page 92-93 (available at http://webarchive.nationalarchives.gov.uk/20070306151732/http://www.hm-treasury.gov.uk/media/2F9/02/31.pdf) and Brian R. Cheffins, The Stewardship Code's Achilles' Heel, 72

Why did the Walker Review recommend that the FRC ratify the ISC Code and grant it "quasi-official imprimatur"[42] despite fundamental differences in their orientation and philosophy? The Walker Review seems to assume that investors who engage with investee companies "are likely to be relatively long-term holders for whom divestment in potential problem situations comes to be seen as a last rather than first resort" and thus that they would focus on long-term profits and not pursue "specific short-term initiative[s] such as increased leverage, spin-offs, acquisitions or share buybacks" that were seen in the period before the Financial Crisis.[43] It is, however, difficult not to criticize this assumption as "naïve" given the behavior of institutional investors prior to the financial crisis.[44]

3. The 2010 UK Code

In any event, the Financial Reporting Council[45] followed the recommendation of the Walker Review and issued a consultation paper in January 2010 seeking public feedback on whether it should adopt the ISC Code as the UK Stewardship Code.[46]

Although the FRC referred to the responsibility of institutional investors "to ensure that the asset managers act diligently and in the best interest of the ultimate owners",[47] improved governance and performance of investee companies, more efficient operation of capital markets and increased confidence in business were stated as the first potential benefits of more effective engagement.[48] Upon the adoption of the ISC Code as the UK

MODERN LAW REVIEW 1004, 1008-1009 (2010). From the perspective of this article, it is important to note that the Myers Report differs from the Walker Review in focusing on the financial self-interest of institutional investors to serve their clients rather than the governance of investee companies and does not try to make "a public interest argument about shareholder responsibility". The Myers Report, para.5.76 at page 90. See also para.3 of the summary at page 4 ("The review does not seek to argue that the institutions whose investment behaviour it examines have some public interest responsibility to invest in certain ways.")

41. Cf. the Walker Review, *supra* note 24 at para.5.13 at page 72.

42. The Walker Review, *supra* note 24 at para.5.38 at page 82-83.

43. See, the Walker Review, *supra* note 24 at para.5.16 at page 73 and para.5.27-5.29 at page 78-79.

44. Chiu & Katelouzou, *supra* note 13 at 76. See also Reisberg, *supra* note 23 at 233 (describing the attempt to incentivize engagement as "an uphill battle where long-term performance has become less relevant as investors place more value on the ability to mitigate risk and the freedom to detach themselves from an underperforming company.")

45. The Financial Reporting Council is an independent regulator of the United Kingdom, the primary responsibility of which is to oversee auditors, accountants and actuaries to promote transparency and integrity in business. See https://www.frc.org.uk/

46. FINANCIAL REPORTING COUNCIL, CONSULTATION ON A STEWARDSHIP CODE FOR INSTITUTIONAL INVESTORS (January 2010), available at https://www.frc.org.uk/consultation-list/2010/consultation-on-a-stewardship-code-for-institution.

47. FINANCIAL REPORTING COUNCIL, *supra* note 46 at para.1.3 at page 2.

48. FINANCIAL REPORTING COUNCIL, *supra* note 46 at para.1.11 at page 4. As other benefits, the consultation paper states as follows: "Greater clarity in the respective responsibilities of asset managers

Stewardship Code in July 2010, the FRC replaced the introduction of the ISC Code with a new preface and deleted the declaration of the ISC Code that the "duty of institutional investors is to their end-beneficiaries and/or clients and not to the wider public".[49] Taken together, the 2010 UK Code appears to share the same goal as the Walker Review.[50]

This orientation of the 2010 UK Code is obscured, however, because the aim in the newly drafted preface is almost an exact copy of that of the ISC Code, stating that the "Stewardship Code aims to enhance the quality of engagement between institutional investors and companies to help improve long-term returns to shareholders and the efficient exercise of governance responsibilities".[51] The principles and guidance stated in this 2010 UK Code are also essentially the same as those of the ISC Code,[52] as the FRC "decided to adopt the Code in its current form" "with only limited amendments" in order "to build on the momentum generated by the Walker Review, the ISC's initiative, and the debate on engagement stimulated by the changes to the UK Corporate Governance Code and the consultation of this Code".[53]

4. The 2012 Revised UK Code

The FRC made it clear in 2010 that it would revise the UK Stewardship Code as necessary.[54] One of the aims of this revision, which took place in 2012, was to clarify the meaning of the term "stewardship".[55] Consequently, the preface of the Code was substantially redrafted. As mentioned in Part I, Section C above, the 2012 Revised UK Code provides that stewardship "aims

The Logic and Limits of Stewardship Codes

to promote the long term success of companies in such a way that the ultimate providers of capital also prosper".[56] When comparing this statement with the aim of the 2010 Code, which is "to help improve long-term returns to shareholders and the efficient exercise of governance responsibilities", it is clear that the 2012 Revised Code placed more emphasis on "the long-term success of [investee] companies" as its goal over the interest of ultimate beneficiaries.

At the same time, the 2012 Revised UK Code created the inconsistency described in Part II, Section A by emphasizing the interest of ultimate beneficiaries with the phrase "So as to protect and enhance the value to the ultimate beneficiary," in the chapeau of "The Principles of the Code".[57] Similar references to the interest of ultimate beneficiaries are also made in the new guidance to Principles 1 and 2.[58]

Unfortunately, the reason for these amendments is not fully explained in the consultation paper for the 2012 revision. On the subject of revisions to the preface and the guidance to Principle 1, the consultation paper only refers to the existence of "some confusion in the UK market and overseas as to what 'stewardship' means" such as "a perception in some quarters that the Stewardship Code is solely concerned with socially responsible investment".[59] As to the objectives provided in the chapeau of the principles, the consultation paper explains that this phrase was moved from Principle 4 of the original 2010 Code as it "relates to all the principles".[60] but does not explain how it relates to the statement of the aim of the Stewardship Code in the new preface.

5. The Kay Review

The 2012 revision of the UK Stewardship Code seems to be influenced by the position of the Kay Review,[61] the first recommendation of which states that

---

and asset owners and strengthened accountability of institutional shareholders to their clients will also strengthen trust in the financial system. A clear understanding of these responsibilities will also assist beneficial owners in setting the terms of their fund mandates and in holding asset managers accountable".

49. See, FINANCIAL REPORTING COUNCIL, IMPLEMENTATION OF THE UK STEWARDSHIP CODE (July 2010), at para.18 at page 4, available at https://www.frc.org.uk/getattachment/34d5dbd-5c54-412e-9cdb-cb30f21d5074/Implementation-of-Stewardship-Code-July-2010.pdf.

50. Chiu, supra note 33 at 395, 416.

51. The 2010 UK Code, supra note 1 at page 1.

52. The formulation of the chapeau of the principles in the 2010 UK Code, which simply states "institutional investors should", differs from that of the 2012 Revised UK Code cited earlier. See supra note 22 and accompanying text.

53. FINANCIAL REPORTING COUNCIL, IMPLEMENTATION OF THE UK STEWARDSHIP CODE (July 2010), para.7 and 9 at page 2. Some commentators have criticized the FRC for not taking the opportunity to strengthen the standards of the ISC Code. See Lee Roach, The UK Stewardship Code, 11 JOURNAL OF CORPORATE LAW STUDIES 463, 479-493.

54. The 2010 UK Code, supra note 1 at page 3.

55. FINANCIAL REPORTING COUNCIL, REVISIONS TO THE UK STEWARDSHIP CODE CONSULTATION DOCUMENT (April 2, 2012) (available at https://www.frc.org.uk/consultation-list/2012/consultation-document-revisions-to-the-uk-steward), para.6 at page 1. The other aims were to clarify the respective roles and responsibilities of asset owners and managers, to address some issues identified in the initial consultation in 2010, to take into account lessons learned during the initial implementation of the Code and to update the Code to reflect developments in market practice. See ibid, para.6-8 at page 1-2.

56. The 2012 Revised UK, supra note 1 at para.1 at page 1.

57. No change or addition is made to the content of the seven principles itself. FINANCIAL REPORTING COUNCIL, supra note 55 at para.4 at page 1.

58. The 2012 Revised UK Code, supra note 1 at the second paragraph of the guidance to Principle 1 ("The policy should disclose how the institutional investor applies stewardship with the aim of enhancing and protecting the value for the ultimate beneficiary or client.") and the third paragraph of the guidance to Principle 2 ("Institutional investors should put in place, maintain and publicly disclose a policy for identifying and managing conflicts of interest with the aim of taking all reasonable steps to put the interests of their client or beneficiary first.").

59. FINANCIAL REPORTING COUNCIL, supra note 55 at para.5 at page 5.

60. FINANCIAL REPORTING COUNCIL, supra note 55 at para.36 at page 11.

61. THE KAY REVIEW OF UK EQUITY MARKETS AND LONG-TERM DECISION MAKING: FINAL REPORT (July 2012) (hereinafter "the Kay Review Final Report"), available at https://www.gov.uk/government/uploads/system/uploads/attachment_data/file/253454/bis-12-917-kay-review-of-equity-markets-final-report.pdf. To be precise, the Final Report of the Kay Review was published in July 2012 and thus was unable to be taken into consideration by the consultation paper of the FRC, which was published in April of that year. However, the Interim Report of the Kay Review, which was published in February 2012 and is referred to in the consultation paper, had already expressed the views that will be discussed in the following texts. See FINANCIAL REPORTING COUNCIL,

the "Stewardship Code should be developed to incorporate a more expansive form of stewardship, focusing on strategic issues as well as questions of corporate governance". [62]

This "expansive form of stewardship" is premised on the Kay Review's "belief that the investment chain will work best if those who invest funds in equity markets have trust and confidence in the agents with which they place the funds and if the companies which list on equity markets have respect for those who rely on their earnings and cash flow to generate returns on their savings and security in their retirement". [63] In other words, the Kay Review expects institutional investors to "trust" the management of investee companies upon engagement, "which is most commonly positive and supportive, and not merely critical". [64]

The aim of the Kay Review in promoting this "expansive form of stewardship" is, as the official title of the Review suggests, to contribute to "good long-term decision making in British business and finance". [65] To put it differently, the Kay Review's emphasis on stewardship of institutional investors was directed at combating short-termism, which is defined as "a tendency to under-investment, whether in physical assets or in intangibles such

as product development, employee skills and reputation with customers, and as hyperactive behaviour by executives whose corporate strategy focuses on restructuring, financial re-engineering or mergers and acquisitions at the expense of developing the fundamental operational capabilities of the business". [66]

In its foreword, the Kay Review expresses the view that such short-termism is detrimental to the competitive advantages of British companies in global markets and the prosperity of the United Kingdom. [67] Although the Kay Review also refers to the interests of British savers and pension beneficiaries "to benefit from the activity of these businesses through returns to direct and indirect ownership of shares in UK companies", [68] its focus seems to be on the long-term profitability of UK companies rather than on the interest of UK ultimate beneficiaries. [69] Thus, the Kay Review essentially shares the goal of the Walker Review, which is to restrain excessive risk-taking at the cost of stakeholders other than shareholders.

5. Summary: The Goal of the UK Stewardship Code

The above analysis of the background of the UK Stewardship Code illuminates the importance of distinguishing between the UK practice of engagement by traditional institutional investors and the Stewardship Code in conjunction with the Walker and the Kay Reviews. While the UK practice has been carried out for the interest of their beneficiaries as expressed by the ISC, the UK Code and the two Reviews as policy documents focus on public interest by restraining excessive risk-taking and short-termism. [70] The reference to the interest of ultimate beneficiaries in the UK Stewardship Code, especially in the

---

supra note 55 at para.4 at page 1 (referring to the view expressed in the Interim Report of the Kay Review that the 2010 Stewardship Code "should be given time to settle") and THE KAY REVIEW OF UK EQUITY MARKETS AND LONG-TERM DECISION MAKING: INTERIM REPORT (February 2012), available at https://www.gov.uk/government/uploads/system/uploads/attachment_data/file/31544/12-631-kay-review-of-equity-markets-interim-report.pdf (focusing on stewardship and engagement as essential means for equity markets to achieve the ends of "allowing companies to make long term decisions appropriate to their business and . . . allowing savers to make financial plans appropriate to their objectives" (at para.2.15 and 2.16 at page 8, para.2.21 at page 9 and para.2.23 at page 11), observing that asset managers concerned with stewardship "would be expected to engage with, and be committed to, the companies in which they held stock" and "normally be supportive of company management, but would be ready to engage in constructive criticism and, in the extreme cases, to act themselves or in conjunction with others to effect change" (para.2.20 at page 9); acknowledging the concern that "the time horizons adopted by savers . . . to judge their asset managers was significantly shorter than the time horizon over which the saver . . . was looking to maximise a return" and that this "emphasis . . . on short term performance investing influenced the style of asset management in ways that could disadvantage the beneficial owner" by emphasizing "trading rather than investing" (at para.6.32 at page 36); distinguishing asset managers "whose primary focus is on the activities of the company - its business, its strategy, and its likely future earnings and cash flow - and those whose primary focus is on the market for the shares of the company - the flow of by and sell orders, the momentum in the share price, the short term correlations between the prices of different stocks" (para.6.6 at page 31)).

62. The Kay Review: Final Report, supra note 61 at page 13.

63. The Kay Review: Final Report, supra note 61 at para.6.4 at page 45. See also Principle 1, ibid. at page 12.

64. The Kay Review: Final Report, supra note 61 at para.6.3 at page 44-45. It must be noted that the word "trust" may not be used consistently in the Kay Review as para.6.2 refers to the trust on institutional investors by their clients ("The honest steward expects to be rewarded for the discharge of that trust, but on a basis of full disclosure and only on that basis." (emphasis added by the author)).

65. The Kay Review: Final Report, supra note 61 at para.6.27 at page 48. The Kay Review sets out the principles relevant to good long-term decision making so as "to focus the attention of directors on the success of the company in the long-term: to lengthen the time scale of measurement of investment performance by influencing the priorities of asset holders and asset managers: to shorten the time horizon of value discovery by placing greater emphasis on the relationship between the asset manager and the company". The Kay Review: Final Report, supra note 61 at para.6.28 at page 48.

66. The Kay Review: Final Report, supra note 61 at para.vi at para.1.1 and 1.2 at page 14.

67. The Kay Review: Final Report, supra note 61, Foreword at page 5 ("British business must invest and must develop its capacity for innovation, its brands and reputations, and the skills of its workforce. Only in this way can we create and sustain the competitive advantages in global markets which are necessary to maintain our prosperity."). The Kay Review also seems to blame short-term in the UK equity market as one of the reasons that no companies like Amazon, Apple or Google has emerged in Britain "to take the place of the financial institutions which failed in the recent crisis". The Kay Review: Final Report, supra note 61 at para.1.27 at page 20.

68. The Kay Review: Final Report, supra note 61 at page 9. See also the Kay Review: Final Report, supra note 61, Foreword at page 5 ("Through success in world markets, British companies will earn the returns on investment which are necessary to pay our pensions and enable us to achieve our long-term financial goals.").

69. The Kay Review emphasizes the importance of fiduciary duty and standards in investment chain, which "require that the client's interests are put first", but limits the type of the client's interest to be taken into account to long-term and excludes short-term. The Kay Review: Final Report, supra note 61, Principle 5 at page 12, para.7.9 at page 51 and para.9.16 at page 68.

70. The difference between the orientations of the ISC Code and the UK Stewardship Code has been also looked even by British commentators. See for example Chiu & Katelouzou, supra note 7 at 134-135 ("The so-called evolved out of the Institutional Shareholders' Committee's similarly named Code of 2010, and therefore accords with market perceptions of the appropriate role for institutional investors.").

2012 version, should be read restrictively as referring to an interest in long-term returns.

C. Academic Responses in the UK

Legal scholars in the UK generally seem to share the above orientation of the UK Stewardship Code,[71] although commentators have been largely critical of the Code's ability to achieve its intended goal.

For example, after correctly recognizing that the aim of the Walker Review is to impose a duty of stewardship on shareholders who enjoy limited liability,[72] Professor Cheffins questions the effectiveness of the Code as foreign investors who presently own more than 40% of the shares of UK listed companies today are not "under any direct onus to commit to the Code's terms".[73] Professor Davies also observes that "it is difficult to believe that the new regime" envisaged by the Kay Review "will achieve anything of substance in the absence of some amendment of the liberal UK regime for takeovers, which induces corporate management to focus on the current share price and provides episodic but substantial pay-offs to shareholders".[74] In this sense, Professor Davies states that the Kay Review "sits in the mainstream of the UK corporate governance tradition".[75]

Professors Chiu and Katelouzou attempt to depart from this mainstream by pointing out that "even where institutions support shareholder engagement, such engagement is on the basis of a shareholder value ideology that exerts short-termist pressures upon their investee companies and has deleterious effects upon corporate culture, bringing in short-termism and less regard for stakeholders and wider social responsibility".[76] They criticize the UK Stewardship Code as "ideologically perplexed" for conceptualizing "investor-led governance within a public-interest framing" while continuing "to make overly optimistic assumptions about the motivations of different types of institutions and their alignment with socially beneficial effects in the long-

---

71.   See however Arad Reisberg, *The Role of Institutional Shareholders: Stewardship and the Long-/Short-Termism Debate*, in Iris H-Y Chiu (ed.), THE LAW ON CORPORATE GOVERNANCE IN BANKS (Edward Elgar, 2015), 99, 124-126 (introducing views of mainly US and European scholars critical of the Kay Review).

72.   Cheffins, *supra* note 40 at 1011.

73.   Cheffins, *supra* note 40 at 1018, 1023-1024. See also Lee Roach, *The UK Stewardship Code*, 11 JOURNAL OF CORPORATE LAW STUDIES 463, 469-471 (2011); Konstantinos Sergakis, *The UK Stewardship Code: Bridging the Gap between Companies and Institutional Investors*, 47 REVUE JURIDIQUE THÉMIS DE L'UNIVERSITÉ DE MONTRÉAL 109, at 133-134 (2013) and Reisberg, *supra* note 23 at 236-247.

74.   Paul Davies, Shareholders in the United Kingdom, in Jennifer G. Hill & Randall S. Thomas (eds), Research Handbook on Shareholder Power (Edward Elgar, 2015) 355, at 375.

75.   *Ibid.*

76.   Chiu & Katelouzou, *supra* note 12 at 73-74.

The Logic and Limits of Stewardship Codes

term".[77] At the same time, "the Code, being soft law, does not provide adequately for the accountability and governance mechanisms that would check and balance shareholders' enhanced engagement roles and powers".[78] From such a viewpoint, Professors Chiu and Katelouzou propose imposing mandatory disclosure requirements on institutional investors regarding their engagement intentions, plans and outcomes to the public, and regulatory standards of conduct focusing on "the long-term well-being of the company taking into account of other shareholders' and stakeholders' interest" via securities and investment regulation.[79] In contrast, Professor Reisberg suggests providing financial incentives through weighted dividends or tax benefits to reward worthy stewardship by long-term investors.[80]

Professors Chiu and Katelouzou go on to assert that other countries including Japan have adopted stewardship codes from "the common concern" about "minority shareholder activism, especially of the offensive variant" "especially due to its perceived short-term nature and is likely negative impact on corporate wealth in general".[81] To ascertain whether this statement is correct, this Article next analyzes the text and the backgrounds of the Japanese Stewardship Code.

PART III: THE TRANSPLANT OF STEWARDSHIP CODES: THE CASE OF JAPAN

A. How is the Japanese Stewardship Code Different from the UK Code?

Japan adopted its stewardship code in February 2014, and later revised it in May 2017. The framework of the Japanese Stewardship Code is heavily influenced by the UK Stewardship Code. It takes the form of soft law; it is not mandatory for institutional investors to sign up to the code. If an institutional investor chooses to sign up, it is only required to comply with the principles

---

77.   Chiu & Katelouzou, *supra* note 12 at 87

78.   Chiu & Katelouzou, *supra* note 12 at 88

79.   Chiu & Katelouzou, *supra* note 12 at 90-92, 94-96. See also Chiu & Katelouzou, *supra* note 7 at 151-152 (discussing the then-proposed Shareholder Rights Directive of the European Union and calling for complete "hardening" of the soft law of shareholder stewardship" while pointing out that "policy-makers need to be more honest and open about the regulatory objectives and premises underlying such legalisation of institutional shareholder duties."). For similar arguments in the United States, see Usha Rodrigues, *Corporate Governance in an Age of Separation of Ownership from Ownership*, 95 MINNESOTA LAW REVIEW 1822 (2011) (asserting that shareholder empowerment and disclosure requirements introduced by the Dodd-Frank Act cannot solve the issue of short-termism and that substantive governmental regulation such as limitation on executive compensation is a better choice).

80.   Reisberg, *supra* note 23 at 249-250. See also, Sergakis, *supra* note 73 at 146-147.

81.   Chiu & Katelouzou, *supra* note 7 at 135, 138. See also ibid. at 139 (stating that stewardship codes have been "further internationalised to address the need for constructive engagement by institutional investors for the purposes of supporting a long-term wealth-creating corporate sector and mitigating short-termism and trading-focused investment management, and the need to define the terms of engagement in order to rein in opportunistic activist behavior.").

---

and guidance of the Code, or to explain why it does not do so.[82] The seven principles of the Japanese Code were also drafted by first translating those of the UK Code into Japanese and then considering one by one whether any modifications or additions were necessary to meet the circumstances in Japan.[83]

1. The Principles

The content of the Japanese Stewardship Code, however, is not identical to that of the UK Code. The principles of the Japanese Code are as follows:[84]

So as to promote sustainable growth of the investee company and enhance the medium- and long-term investment return of clients and beneficiaries,

1. Institutional investors should have a clear policy on how they fulfill their stewardship responsibilities, and publicly disclose it.
2. Institutional investors should have a clear policy on how they manage conflicts of interest in fulfilling their stewardship responsibilities and publicly disclose it.
3. Institutional investors should monitor investee companies so that they can appropriately fulfill their stewardship responsibilities with an orientation towards the sustainable growth of the companies.
4. Institutional investors should seek to arrive at an understanding in common with investee companies and work to solve problems through constructive engagement with investee companies.
5. Institutional investors should have a clear policy on voting and disclosure of voting activity. The policy on voting should not be comprised only of a mechanical checklist; it should be designed to contribute to the sustainable growth of investee companies.
6. Institutional investors in principle should report periodically on how they fulfill their stewardship responsibilities, including their voting responsibilities, to their clients and beneficiaries.
7. To contribute positively to the sustainable growth of investee companies, institutional investors should have in-depth knowledge of the investee companies and their business environment and skills and resources needed to appropriately engage with the companies and make proper judgments in fulfilling their stewardship activities.

Principles 1, 2 and 6 of the Japanese Stewardship Code are substantially the same as Principles 1, 2 and 7 of the UK Code. However, the other parts of the Japanese Stewardship Code differ from the UK Code in that they appear to apply less investors' pressure on investee companies.[85]

82. The 2017 Revised Japanese Code, *supra* note 2 at para 11-12 at page 6.
83. See Document No.3 of the Third Meeting of the Council of Experts Concerning the Japanese Version of the Stewardship Code, submitted by the Secretariat (available at https://www.fsa.go.jp/en/refer/councils/stewardship/material/20131018_1.pdf).
84. The 2017 Revised Japanese Code, *supra* note 2, the Principles of the Code at page 8. The principles remain unchanged from the original 2014 version. See the 2014 Japanese Code, *supra* note 2 at page 6.
85. The following paragraphs are based on the analysis of Wataru Tanaka, *Nihon-ban suchuwadoshippu codo no kento. Kikan-toshika no yakuwari nitsuite no ambivarento na mikata* [An Analysis of the Japanese Stewardship Code: An Ambivalent View on the Role of Institutional Investors], 629 KANSAYAKU 66 at 68-69 (2014).

To begin with, the chapeau of the Japanese principles puts sustainable growth of the investee company ahead of the enhancement of the medium- and long-term investment return of clients and beneficiaries; whereas the UK Code only refers to the interest of the ultimate beneficiaries.

Secondly, while Principles 4 and 5 of the UK Code refer to the possibility of escalating stewardship activities when necessary, and recommend that institutional investors act collectively with other investors, no such reference can be found in the Japanese principles.[86] Instead, Principle 4 of the Japanese Code requests institutional investors to arrive at a common understanding with investee companies, and to work with them in solving problems. It must be noted that the FSA admitted that sometimes it would be necessary to take more aggressive measures than merely asking for explanation and such measures are not excluded as a way of giving Japanese companies room to argue that institutional investors requesting certain actions, such as an increase in payouts, are not making sufficient efforts to reach such a common understanding. In a similar vein, Principle 7 calls on institutional investors to have in-depth knowledge of investee companies and their business environment, as well as skills and resources necessary for appropriate engagement – again in order to contribute to the sustainable growth of investee companies.

Further, while Principle 3 of the English version of the Japanese Code requests institutional investors to "monitor" investee companies, as does that of the UK Code, the original Japanese document does not use the literal Japanese translation of the term "monitor"; instead it requests investors to "properly

86. At the second meeting of the Council of Experts Concerning the Japanese Version of the Stewardship Code, Mr. Muneaki Tokunari of Mitsubishi UFJ Trust and Banking Corporation, as the representative of trust banks that are often in charge of management of private pension funds, stated that in the then-current practice his bank asks investee companies for more explanation on certain occasions but does not have a concrete guideline on escalating the level of stewardship activities and that the banks does not participate in collective engagement. Mr. Toshinao Matsushima of Daiwa Asset Management, as the representative of the mutual funds industry, also made a similar statement. See the Minutes of the 2nd Council of Experts Concerning the Japanese Version of the Stewardship Code, at pages 12-13 and 15-16 (available at http://www.fsa.go.jp/en/refer/councils/stewardship/material/20130918_1.pdf). Based on these presentations, FSA proposed to deviate from the UK Code in this regard. See the Minutes of the 3rd Council of Experts Concerning the Japanese Version of the Stewardship Code, at page 13 (available at http://www.fsa.go.jp/en/refer/councils/stewardship/material/20131018_2.pdf).While there was some support for making no reference to the possibility of escalating the level of stewardship activities as it would not fit the Japanese practice (ibid at page 18), a few members of the Council expressed positive views on collective engagement and criticized the FSA's proposal (ibid at page 19-20). It must be noted that, as a partial response, FSA issued a document on its interpretation of the legal ambiguities that may hinder collective engagement. FINANCIAL SERVICES AGENCY, CLARIFICATION OF LEGAL ISSUES RELATED TO THE DEVELOPMENT OF THE JAPAN'S STEWARDSHIP CODE (February 26, 2014, available at http://www.fsa.go.jp/en/refer/councils/stewardship/20140226.pdf). For the 2017 revision of the Japanese Stewardship Code that added some reference to collective engagement in the guidance section, see *infra* note 130 and accompanying text.
87. The COUNCIL OF EXPERTS CONCERNING THE JAPANESE VERSION OF THE STEWARDSHIP CODE, *supra* note 18 at Comment no.15 at page 4.

grasp the circumstances of investee companies".[88] Together with the reference to "the sustainable growth of investee companies" in the same principle, the Japanese wording is milder and more nuanced – not encouraging institutional investors to take a tough stance against investee companies.

Overall, the Japanese principles can be described as being much friendlier to investee companies as compared to the UK principles.[89] This divergence from the UK Code has been criticized by some academics,[90] but welcomed by industries as reflecting the reality of Japanese corporate governance system,[91] which traditionally focused on the interest of stakeholders, especially employees.[92]

2. The Preface

Unlike the UK Code, the preface to the Japanese Stewardship Code prioritizes the enhancement of "the medium- to long-term investment return for

---

[88] This change in phrasing has been influenced by a remark at the 3rd meeting of the Council by Mr. Takaaki Eguchi, who had been involved in engagement and voting at large foreign institutional investors, stating that the term "monitoring" is not appropriate here as it suggest a "one-way surveillance" while the focus of the Council is promotion of "the long-term growth of investee companies, thereby building a win-win relationship between institutional investors and their investee companies". See the Minutes of the 3rd Council of Experts Concerning the Japanese Version of the Stewardship Code, *supra* note 86 at page 17.

[89] Principle 5 of the Japanese Code also differs from Principle 6 of the UK Code as the second sentence of the former explicitly discourages the use of a mechanical checklist as a voting policy, which is accompanied by a paragraph in the guidance section stating that when "institutional investors use the service of proxy advisors, they should not mechanically depend on the advisors' recommendations". The 2014 Japanese Code, *supra* note 2, Paragraph 5-4 at page 11. However, this may not be so large a difference from the UK Code as the fourth paragraph of the Guidance to Principle 6, which was added by the 2012 revision, also requires that institutional investors to "disclose the use use made, if any, of proxy voting or other voting advisory services" and "describe the scope of such services, identify the provider/s and disclose the extent to which they follow, rely upon or use recommendations made by such services".

[90] See for example, Wataru Tanaka, *Koporeto gobananasu no kanten kara mita nihonban suchuwadoshippu kodo – Eikoku kodo tono sui ni chakumoku shite* [The Japanese Stewardship Code from the Perspective of Corporate Governance: With Focus on the Differences between the UK Code], 1 SHINTAKU FŌRAMU 35, at 38 (2014) (criticizing the emphasis of the sustainable growth of investee companies in the principles of the Japanese Stewardship Code as such idea would sometimes contradict with the interest of clients and ultimate beneficiaries).

[91] See for example, Jun'ichi Kawada, *Kigyo saido no taio – JX Horudhingusu no haui* [Reactions of Companies to the Japanese Stewardship Code: The Case of JX Holdings], KIGYO KAIKEI Vol.66, No.8 (2014), 33 at 34-35. Mr. Kawada was a member of the Council of Experts Concerning the Japanese Version of the Stewardship Code and a director and senior vice president of JX Holdings, Inc. On the other hand, some academics have criticized the Japanese Code on this point. See for example, Tanaka, *supra* note 85 at 69 (asserting that the Japanese Code obscures, possibly intentionally, the fact that the interest of ultimate beneficiaries could conflict with that of investee companies, which could occur in a scenario such as when the company does not have an investment opportunity with returns exceeding investors' cost of capital).

[92] For detailed description of the traditional Japanese corporate governance system, see Zenichi Shishido, *Japanese Corporate Governance: The Hidden Problems of Corporate Law and Their Solutions*, 25 DELAWARE JOURNAL OF CORPORATE LAW 189 (2000) and Gregory Jackson & Hideaki Miyajima, *Introduction: The Diversity and Change of Corporate Governance in Japan*, in Masahiko Aoki, Gregory Jackson & Hideaki Miyajima (eds.), CORPORATE GOVERNANCE IN JAPAN: INSTITUTIONAL CHANGE AND ORGANIZATIONAL DIVERSITY (Oxford University Press, 2007), at 1, 3-6.

The Logic and Limits of Stewardship Codes

their clients and beneficiaries" as the goal of stewardship responsibility and regards sustainable growth of investee companies as its metric, as mentioned earlier in Part I, Section C. Thus, the Japanese Stewardship Code also harbors some inconsistency between its preface and principles, albeit in a different manner from the UK Code, the preface of which emphasizes the long-term success of investee companies to the contrary.

The question arising from this difference is, why the Japanese Stewardship Code is structured differently from the UK Code despite their apparent similarity. Let us now turn to the background of the Japanese Stewardship Code to examine its intended goal.

B. Background

1. Japan Revitalization Strategy: June 2013

As the background of establishing the Council of Experts Concerning the Japanese Version of the Stewardship Code, the preface of the Japanese Stewardship Code cites a document titled "the Japan Revitalization Strategy".[93]

This document was prepared by the Headquarters for Japan's Economic Revitalization[94] as part of the Abe administration's policies aimed at economic growth in the 2013 fiscal year. It claims that bold investment by private sector is necessary to promote innovation and that better corporate governance is required to support such "aggressive" management.[95] The adoption of a Japanese version of a stewardship code is listed as one of the representative measures that needs to be implemented swiftly.[96] In particular, the Japan Revitalization Strategy states as follows:

> With the aim of promoting sustainable growth of companies, discuss and establish the principles for a wide range of institutional investors to appropriately discharge their stewardship responsibilities through constructive dialogues with invested companies by the end of this year while considering discussion of the Council on Economic and Fiscal Policy concerning the market economy system in Japan.[97]

It should be noted that the phrase "sustainable growth of companies" had already appeared at this stage as "the aim" for adopting a stewardship code. The document itself, however, does not provide any explanation on the reason

---

[93] The 2014 Japanese Code, *supra* note 2, paragraphs 2-3 at page 1-2. No change is made to these paragraphs in the 2017 version.

[94] The Headquarters for Japan's Economic Revitalization (*Nihon Keizai Saisei Honbu*) is a body established by the Abe administration by a cabinet decision on December 26, 2012, and consists of all ministers with the Prime Minister as its chief. Its mandate is to plan and to coordinate economic policies of the government as a whole. See, http://japan.kantei.go.jp/96_abe/decisions/2012/1226saiseihonbu_e.html.

[95] JAPAN REVITALIZATION STRATEGY – JAPAN IS BACK (June 14, 2013) (available at https://www.kantei.go.jp/jp/singi/keizaisaisei/pdf/en_saikou_jpn_hon.pdf) at page 36-37.

[96] JAPAN REVITALIZATION STRATEGY, *supra* note 95 at 14, 16.

[97] JAPAN REVITALIZATION STRATEGY, *supra* note 95 at 37.

for such a mandate.[98] On the other hand, the adoption of a stewardship code is listed together with other measures such as the promotion of appointment of independent directors and the creation of a new stock index consisting of high-profile companies in terms of profitability and management,[99] making it difficult to ascertain the orientation of the document. The same problem applies to the order made by Prime Minister Abe on April 2, 2013 at the sixth meeting of the Headquarters for Japan's Economic Revitalization. It calls on the Minister for Financial Services to "coordinate with other relevant ministers and consider, with the aim of promoting the sustainable growth of companies, principles for a wide range of institutional investors to appropriately discharge their stewardship responsibilities".[100]

2. Industrial Competitiveness Council: March 2013

Interestingly, discussions held a few months earlier at the Industrial Competitiveness Council,[101] which is mentioned in the preface of the Japanese Stewardship Code as the basis of the order by Prime Minister Abe cited above,[102] were a little different.

On March 15, 2013, at the fourth meeting of the Industrial Competitiveness Council, the introduction of a Japanese version of the UK Stewardship Code was proposed by members of the Council from the private sector as one of the measures to promote the replacement of obsolete industries and businesses by new ones.[103] Here, the stewardship code was described as a mechanism to compel institutional investors to play an active role – but no additional details about its goals were provided (e.g., such as promoting sustainable growth of investee companies).[104]

98. The same problem applies to the order made by Prime Minister Abe at the 6th meeting of the Headquarters for Japan's Economic Revitalization, which is also cited in the preface of the Japanese Stewardship Code. See the 2014 Japanese Code, paragraph 1 at page 1.

99. JAPAN REVITALIZATION STRATEGY, *supra* note 95 at 37-38.

100. As cited by the 2014 Japanese Code, *supra* note 2 at paragraph 1 at page 1.

101. The Industrial Competitiveness Council (*Sangyo Kyosoryoku Kaigi*) was established by the Headquarters for Japan's Economic Revitalization on January 8, 2013 to consider specific measures for economic growth and consisted of the Prime Minister, the Vice Prime Minister, the Minister for Economic and Fiscal Policy, the Cabinet Secretary, the Minister of Economy, Trade and Industry, and members appointed from the industry and academics. See https://www.kantei.go.jp/jp/singi/keizaisaisei/skkkaigi/konkyo.html.

102. The 2014 Japanese Code, *supra* note 2 at paragraph 1 at page 1.

103. See Document No.1 of the Fourth Meeting of the Industrial Competitiveness Council, submitted by Mr. Masahiro Sakane as the chair of the subgroup on the promotion of replacement of outdated industries and businesses, at page 2 (available in Japanese at https://www.kantei.go.jp/jp/singi/keizaisaisei/skkkaigi/dai4/siryou1.pdf).

104. Document No. 3 of the Sixth Meeting of the Headquarters for Japan's Economic Revitalization, The Issues Raised by at the Fourth and the Fifth Meetings of the Industrial Competitiveness Council by Members from the Private Sector (available in Japanese at https://www.kantei.go.jp/jp/singi/keizaisaisei/dai6/siryou03.pdf), at page 1.

The Logic and Limits of Stewardship Codes

On the contrary, Mr. Takeshi Niinami, the then-CEO of a major convenience store chain Lawson, emphasized the necessity of interventions by institutional investors. In particular, he stated as follows:

Mr. Niinami: It is important to have external discipline of the management by the stock market, namely by outspoken shareholders.[105] Non-activist institutional investors as shareholders with a mid- to long-term perspective should properly intervene in management of companies to promote replacement of outdated industries and businesses by new ones. In this regard, the government should consider introducing a Japanese version of the UK's Stewardship Code so that the private sector cannot make excuses for failing to act.[106]

The ministers at the meeting did not object to Mr. Niinami's statement on the role of institutional investors.[107] However, at a subgroup meeting of the Industrial Competitiveness Council held earlier on March 6, 2013, where Mr. Niinami proposed the introduction of a stewardship code for the first time, Mr. Akira Amari, then the Minister for Economic and Fiscal Policy and the Minister for Economic Revitalization disagreed with Mr. Niinami.[108]

Minister Amari: Investors have gradually become less patient and the period from their investment to exit is getting shorter and shorter. To respond to requests from activist shareholders to payout retained earnings, companies should, for example, be permitted to pay more dividends to shareholders that have held shares for a longer period of time. It would be impossible to attract long-term investment when investors that had only recently bought shares can easily pressure companies and make off with retained earnings that have been accrued over time. Although investors are becoming more and more short-termed oriented across the world, Japan should establish a system that attracts long-term investment. Otherwise, R&D-intensive firms cannot prosper.[109]

Mr. Niinami responded with the assertion that return on equity of Japanese companies had not increased in the long term despite their allegedly long-term management approach, and that activist shareholders are necessary to some extent to improve corporate value by exerting pressure on companies to give

105. The term "outspoken shareholders" is the literal English translation of the Japanese term used in Mr. Niinami's remark, "*mono iu kabunushi*." This term, which is often used in Japanese media, is usually translated as "shareholder activist," but the author chose the term "outspoken shareholder" as the second sentence of Mr. Niinami's remark seems to differentiate institutional investors from activists.

106. The Minutes of the Fourth Meeting of the Industrial Competitiveness Council (March 15, 2013), at page 5 (available in Japanese at https://www.kantei.go.jp/jp/singi/keizaisaisei/skkkaigi/dai4/gijiroku.pdf).

107. See, the Minutes of the Fourth Meeting of the Industrial Competitiveness Council, *supra* note 106 at page 5-10. In contrast, Professor Heizo Takenaka expressed his support for Mr. Niinami (*ibid.* at page 11).

108. The Summary of the Discussions at the Meeting on March 6, 2013 of the Subgroup of the Industrial Competitiveness Council on Specific Topics, at page 3 (available in Japanese at https://www.kantei.go.jp/jp/singi/keizaisaisei/kaigou/pdf/h250306_gijyousi.pdf) (Mr. Niinami arguing that "it is necessary to make rigorous systems, such as the UK Stewardship Code, in order to achieve higher productivity of firms" and to have "institutional investors such as Government Pension Investment Fund monitor corporate governance," if convert, as a practice of General Electric that it "only pursues segments in which they can become the leader or the second in that market within a few years").

109. The Summary of the Discussions at the Meeting on March 6, 2013 of the Subgroup of the Industrial Competitiveness Council on Specific Topics, *supra* note 108 at page 5-6.

reasonable explanations for the usage of cash they are hoarding.[110] This view of Mr. Niinami, however, substantially differs from the basic orientation of the UK Stewardship Code, which focuses on public interest by restraining excessive risk-taking and short-termism.[111] In contrast, Mr. Amari's views appears to be largely congruent with the UK Code.

This interesting exchange suggests the following two points. First, Mr. Niinami's true intention seems not to be in favor of adopting the UK Stewardship Code as such, but rather in importing the UK practice of engagement by institutional shareholders for effective discipline of management. Second, Minister Amari's anti-activist view seems to be the background of the insertion of the phrase "with the aim of promoting sustainable growth of companies" into the Japan Revitalization Strategy.

3. Council on Economic and Fiscal Policy: April 2013

Minister Amari's anti-activist orientation is also reflected in the role he played in the Council on Economic Fiscal Policy.[112] On April 18, 2013, about one month after the fourth meeting of the Industrial Competitiveness Council, Mr. Jyoji (George) Hara was invited to the eighth meeting of the Council on Economic Fiscal Policy to make a presentation on establishing "a market economy system that enables sustainable growth".[113] He criticized US-style corporate governance as focusing only on the interests of shareholders and management, and advocated that companies should be evaluated not by return on equity, but by its sustainability, distributive fairness and improvements in its business.[114] He also made various proposals, such as the restriction of stock-

110. The Summary of the Discussions at the Meeting on March 6, 2013 of the Subgroup of the Industrial Competitiveness Council on Specific Topics, *supra* note 108 at page 6. Mr. Yasuchika Hasegawa, then the president of Takeda Pharmaceutical Co., Ltd., also expressed a similar view that the management of a company is responsible to explain to its shareholders why the company is holding retained earnings. Ibid.

111. See Part II, Section B.

112. The Council on Economic and Fiscal Policy (*Keizai Zaisei Shimon Kaigi*) was originally established in 2001 pursuant to Article 18, paragraph 1 of the Act for Establishment of Cabinet Office (Act. No.89 of 1999). The core mission of this council is to discuss important issues regarding economic and fiscal policy as consulted by the Prime Minister or the Minister on Economic and Fiscal Policy. Article 19, paragraph 1, no.1 and paragraph 2, Act for Establishment of Cabinet Office. The Minister on Economic and Fiscal Policy is an *ex officio* member of the Council and is to chair the meeting of the Council when the Prime Minister is absent. Article 21, paragraph 4 and Article 22, paragraph 1, no.2, Act for Establishment of Cabinet Office.

113. Mr. Jyoji (George) Hara is a venture capitalist based in the United States and the chairman of the board of directors of a non-governmental organization Alliance Forum Foundation, which criticizes shareholder primacy advocates an idea named "public interest capitalism". See http://www.allianceforum.org/en/profile/?cat=cnt_01 and http://www.allianceforum.org/en/capitalism/?cat=cnt_01.

114. The Minutes of the 8th Meeting of 2013 of the Council on Economic and Fiscal Policy, at page 5–6 (available in Japanese at http://www5.cao.go.jp/keizai-shimon/kaigi/minutes/2013/0418/gijiroku.pdf).

---

based compensation and share repurchases, together with the introduction of preferential treatment of mid- to long-term shareholders.[115]

Following the lines of Mr. Hara's presentation, Minister Amari then proposed establishing an expert group under the Council to conduct research on a "desirable market economy system" that "enables sustainable growth through appropriate allocation of capital and distribution of profits".[116] Accordingly, the Expert Committee on Desirable Market Economy System (*Mezasubeki shijyo keizai shisutemu ni kansuru senmon chosakai*) was established,[117] and the Japan Revitalization Strategy explicitly directed that the discussions of this committee must be taken into consideration when drafting the Japanese Stewardship Code.[118]

The final report of the Expert Committee, which was published on November 1, 2013, emphasizes that "corporate governance prioritizing adjustments of the interests of various stakeholders" is necessary in order to "improve the overall corporate value from a medium- and long-term perspective".[119] It also asserts that institutional investors should "fulfill fiduciary responsibility by taking into account improvement of the overall corporate value in the medium and long terms, instead of leaning excessively toward maximization of short-term shareholder returns".[120] From such a perspective, this report calls for the adoption of the Japanese Stewardship Code based on "the circumstances in Japan, with a focus placed on the achievement of sustainable growth of companies through constructive communications between institutional investors and companies".[121]

When the Council of Experts Concerning the Japanese Version of the Stewardship Code heard this final report at its fourth meeting held on November 27, 2013, Professor Wataru Tanaka criticized the Final Report for not supporting its arguments with factual evidence necessary to convince "readers who may view such arguments as a means to give an excuse for the

115. The Minutes of the 8th Meeting of 2013 of the Council on Economic and Fiscal Policy, *supra* note 114 at page 8.

116. Document No.2 of the 8th Meeting of 2013 of the Council on Economic and Fiscal Policy, submitted by the Minister on Economic and Fiscal Policy (available in Japanese at http://www5.cao.go.jp/keizai-shimon/kaigi/minutes/2013/0418/shiryo_02.pdf).

117. Summary of discussions and documents of the Experts Committee on Desirable Market Economy System are available in Japanese at http://www5.cao.go.jp/keizai-shimon/kaigi/special/market/index.html.

118. See *supra* note 97 and accompanying text.

119. Report by the Expert Committee on Desirable Market Economy System (November 1, 2013), at page 12 (available at http://www5.cao.go.jp/keizai-shimon/kaigi/special/market/report.pdf).

120. *Ibid.* The overall corporate value is defined as "a broad concept that does not merely refer to ordinary monetary value (so-called shareholder value) but also includes elements difficult to measure in numerical terms, such as value arising from external economies and diseconomies whose monetary value cannot be evaluated immediately (reduction of environmental burden, etc.) and value relating to uncertain future sustainability (measures concerning exhaustible resources, etc.)". *Ibid.* at page 9-10.

121. *Ibid.* at page 14.

currently stagnant profitability".[122] Mr. Masaya Sakuma, the Director of Economic, Fiscal and Social Structure of the Cabinet Office in charge of the secretariat of the Expert Committee on Desirable Market Economy System, responded that the report "does not intend to criticize short-term investment at all" as it also "refers to the need to maintain 'liquidity' in transactions'" in the market, and that it is not the intention of the report "to use our argument about short-termism and the lack of medium to long-term funding as an excuse for the stagnant state of profitability".[123]

At the end of his remarks, however, Mr. Sakuma also stated that the "Committee was in a sense initiated by a concept similar to Public Interest Capitalism as noted by Mr. Hara, Deputy Chairman of the committee. In view of such background, I would appreciate your understanding as to the difficulty we faced in putting ideas together as the secretariat to the CEFP Committee."[124] This statement of Mr. Sakuma arguably suggests that the orientation of the Final Report was already determined by a political initiative of Minister Amari to promote Mr. Hara's view from the Expert Committee's inception, and thus that it was impossible to alter the final outcome of the discussions, even though the government officials in charge might not have been completely convinced.

4. Other Corporate Governance Reforms Around the Same Period

The above analysis depicts the existence of two camps with different views on the role of pressure from shareholders (i.e., one represented by Mr. Niinami and the other by Minister Amari) that led to the adoption of the Japanese Stewardship Code. This sub-section analyzes other corporate governance reforms around the same period as a way to illuminate which camp was ultimately more influential.[125] To state the conclusion upfront, it appears from the recent corporate governance reforms that the camp promoting more shareholder pressure to discipline management has prevailed[126] – supporting Mr. Niinami's, not Minister Amari's, point of view.

122. See the Minutes of the Fourth Meeting of the Council of Experts on the Stewardship Code, at page 5 (available at http://www.fsa.go.jp/en/refer/councils/stewardship/minutes/20131127.pdf).

123. The Minutes of the Fourth Meeting of the Council of Experts on the Stewardship Code, *supra* note 122 at page 5.

124. *Ibid*

125. See Kansaku, *supra* note 14 at 1012-1013 (stating that the Japanese Stewardship Code was adopted as part of the so-called "growth strategy" of the Abe administration which aims to improve corporate governance and to promote corporate value).

126. An earlier report published in 2009 by a study group established for the Financial Services Agency also emphasized the importance of exercise of voting rights based on fiduciary duty of institutional investors and disclosure of their voting results. At this time, there was no mention to the sustainable growth of investee companies. See, REPORT BY THE FINANCIAL SYSTEMS COUNCIL'S STUDY GROUP ON THE INTERNATIONALIZATION OF JAPANESE FINANCIAL AND CAPITAL MARKETS – TOWARD STRONGER CORPORATE GOVERNANCE OF PUBLICLY LISTED COMPANIES (June 17, 2009) at 15-16, available at https://www.fsa.go.jp/en/news/2009/20090618-1/01.pdf.

The Logic and Limits of Stewardship Codes

First, it has been clarified through the public comment process that the Japanese Stewardship Code does not prohibit institutional investors from requesting investee companies to increase dividends.[127] Institutional investors are expected to consider whether such a request fits within their overall stewardship responsibilities in the particular context. Further, the Japanese Stewardship Code was revised in 2017,[128] placing more emphasis on the pressure of institutional investors on investee companies.[129] For example, a paragraph on collective engagement, to which no reference was made in the original 2014 text, is added in the guidance section to Principle 4, stating that "it would be beneficial for" institutional investors "to engage with investee companies in collaboration with other institutional investors (collective engagement) as necessary".[130] Under the 2017 Revised Code, institutional investors are also required to disclose how they have voted on each agenda item at shareholders' meetings of individual investee companies.[131] In addition, the revision emphasizes the role of asset owners such as pension funds in stewardship activities,[132] calls for effective control of conflicts of interest of asset managers, especially those belonging to financial conglomerates,[133] and requires institutional investors which have a passive governance strategy to participate in engagement and voting more actively.[134]

Second, the Japanese government has succeeded in nudging Japanese listed companies to appoint at least one or two outside/independent directors through measures such as the 2014 Reform of the Companies Act and the 2015 Japanese Corporate Governance Code, which introduced "comply or explain" rules regarding appointment of one outside director or two independent directors, respectively.[135] One of the roles expected to be performed by these

127. The Council of Experts Concerning the Japanese Version of the Stewardship Code, *supra* note 18, Comment No.3 at page 1.

128. For the 2017 revision of the Japanese Stewardship Code, see generally, Yasumasa Tahara, Hiroshi Someya & Keita Yasui, *Suchuwadoshippu codo kaitei no kaisetsu* [*Commentaries on the Revision of the Stewardship Code*], 2138 SHOJI HOMU 15 (2017) (in Japanese).

129. The 2017 revision has added "opportunities arising from social and environmental matters" as one of the factors that institutional investors should "monitor" or "grasp" at Guidance 3-3. In the author's view, however, this amendment is not so meaningful as the original 2014 text already listed "risks arising from social and environmental matters" in the same paragraph.

130. The 2017 Revised Japanese Code, *supra* note 2, Guidance 4-4, at page 13.

131. The 2017 Revised Japanese Code, *supra* note 2, Guidance 5-3, at page 15. This individual disclosure requirement was not included in the original 2014 version due to the objections from the industry and some investors. Kansaku, *supra* note 11 at 19. The revised code, however, decided to override such objections and to introduce this requirement in order to enhance the transparency of the stewardship activities of asset managers and to eliminate concerns on conflicts of interest of asset managers who belong to financial conglomerates. See, the 2017 Revised Japanese Stewardship Code, at page 15, note 15.

132. The 2017 Revised Japanese Code, *supra* note 2,Guidance 1-3, 1-4 & 1-5 at page 9-10.

133. The 2017 Revised Japanese Code, *supra* note 2,Guidance 2-2, 2-3, & 2-4 at page 11.

134. The 2017 Revised Japanese Code, *supra* note 2,Guidance 4-2 at page 13.

135. For details of the recent Japanese reforms on board independence, see Gen Goto, Manabu Matsunaka & Souichirou Kozuka, *Japan's Gradual Reception of Independent Directors: An Empirical*

outside and/or independent directors is to represent the interests of shareholders in the boardroom and to function as a barrier insulating the management from the interests of core employees.[136]

Third, the Japanese government has also been trying to tackle the issue of "cross-shareholdings".[137] One characteristic of traditional Japanese listed companies is that a large proportion of their shares, often the majority, was held by "stable shareholders", which consisted of the company's banks and friendly business partners.[138] Since such shareholders have an incentive to support the management of the company in order to maintain good business relationships, this ownership structure effectively insulated managers from the pressure of capital markets. Seeing such phenomenon as problematic as it arguably leads to inefficiency and managerial slack, the 2015 Japanese Corporate Governance Code provides that Japanese listed companies shall disclose their policy on cross-shareholding, and provide an annual detailed explanation on the objective and rationale behind major cross-shareholdings after examining their mid- to long-term economic rationale.[139] The 2018 revision of the Japanese Corporate Governance Code further seeks to accelerate the reduction of cross-shareholdings by adding a supplementary principle calling on companies not to discourage their shareholders from divesting their shareholding by, for example, suggesting that such divestments would result in reduction of business transactions with them.[140]

It is also worth noting that the so-called "Ito Review", a report commissioned by the Ministry of Economy, Trade and Industry to Professor Kunio Ito under inspiration from the Kay Review,[141] rather emphasizes the importance of Japanese companies achieving a level of return on equity that exceeds the cost of capital required by global investors, so that the Japanese

and Political-Economic Analysis, in Dan W. Puchniak, Harald Baum & Luke Nottage (eds.), INDEPENDENT DIRECTORS IN ASIA (Cambridge University Press, 2017) at 135 and Gen Goto, Recent Boardroom Reforms in Japan and the Roles of Outside/Independent Directors, in Hiroshi Oda (ed.), COMPARATIVE CORPORATE GOVERNANCE: THE CASE OF JAPAN, Journal of Japanese Law, Special Issue No.12 (Carl Heymanns/Wolters Kluwer, 2018) at 33.

136. Goto, supra note 135 at 50-51. See also, Franz Waldenberger, 'Growth Oriented Corporate Governance Reform – Can It Solve Japan's Performance Puzzle?, 29 JAPAN FORUM 354, 366-369 (2017) (describing the disadvantages of the predominance of in-house careers in Japanese companies).

137. For the effect and the current state of cross-shareholdings in Japan, see Gen Goto, Legally "Strong" Shareholders of Japan, 3 MICHIGAN JOURNAL OF PRIVATE EQUITY AND VENTURE CAPITAL LAW 125 142-146, 149-152 (2014).

138. This situation is also called "cross-shareholding", as such a relationship is often mutual.

139. Principle 1-4, Japanese Corporate Governance Code.

140. Supplementary Principle 1.4.1, the Revised Japanese Corporate Governance Code, at page 7, available at https://www.jpx.co.jp/english/news/1020/b5b4p00000yst-att/20180602_en.pdf.

141. See an interview with Prof. Kunio Ito by MARR Online, available at https://www.marr.jp/etc/hot_interview/entry/4793 (stating that the launch of the "Ito Review" project on July 2013 was greatly inspired by the Kay Review published one year before).

market can attract capital to support investment for long-term innovation.[142] Such an emphasis on return on equity clearly differs from Mr. Hara's stakeholder-oriented view.[143]

5. Summary: The Goal of the Japanese Stewardship Code

The above analysis shows that the adoption of the Japanese Stewardship Code was part of a recent trend of corporate governance reforms in Japan aimed at a more effective discipline of management for the purpose of meeting shareholders' interests – in line with Mr. Niinami's initial rationale for proposing the code. In this context, it appears clear that the insertion of the phrase "with the aim of promoting sustainable growth of companies" was not the driving force behind the Code. Rather it was a compromise to appease those who resisted the trend towards a more shareholder-oriented system of corporate governance.

From this perspective, the goal of the Japanese Stewardship Code is to change the behavior of domestic institutional investors, in particular life insurance companies and some investment trust management companies which have been criticized for their reluctance to take a tough stance against management due to their business relationships with investee companies.[144] In contrast, foreign institutional investors, who are often viewed in Japan as being free from conflict of interests and being unreluctant to exert pressure on the management of investee companies when necessary,[145] are not the main target

142. The ITO REVIEW OF COMPETITIVENESS AND INCENTIVES FOR SUSTAINABLE GROWTH – BUILDING FAVORABLE RELATIONSHIPS BETWEEN COMPANIES AND INVESTORS– FINAL REPORT (August 2014), at page 7-9 (available at http://www.meti.go.jp/english/press/2014/pdf/0806_04b.pdf).

143. See supra note 113-114 and accompanying texts.

144. For example, Professor Kenjiro Egashira lists the inactivity of domestic institutional investors as one of the basic foundations of traditional Japanese corporate governance system and claims that the 2014 Reform of the Companies Act introducing the "comply or explain" rule on appointment of at least one outside director would fail to change the behavior of Japanese listed companies as long as domestic institutional investors stay the same. See Kenjiro Egashira, Kaishaho no kaisei to yotte nihon no kaisha ha kawaranai [Japanese Companies Would Not Change Regardless of the Companies Act Reform], Vol.86, No.11 HORITSU JIHO 59, at 60 (2014). One recent empirical study reports that the ratio of shareholding by domestic institutional investors has a positive effect on the probability of hedge fund activism internationally, but a negative effect in Japan (both effects were statistically significant), Marco Becht, Julian Franks, Jeremy Grant & Hannes F. Wagner, Returns to Hedge Fund Activism: An International Study, 30 REVIEW OF FINANCIAL STUDIES 2933, at 2946-2948 (2017). It must be noted, however, that the unwillingness of investment managers to take actions that are disfavored by corporate managers is not unique to Japan. See Bebchuk, Cohen & Hirst, supra note 5 at 21-23 (describing the similar attitude of investment managers in the United States).

145. Professor Hideaki Miyajima and his colleagues report that, after controlling for reverse causality, higher shareholding by foreign investors in Japanese companies facilitates appointment of independent directors, affects corporate policy on investment, capital structure and payout, and has positive impact on ROA and Tobin's Q of investee companies. See Hideaki Miyajima, Takaaki Hoda & Ryo Ogawa, Does Ownership Really Matter? The Role of Foreign Investors in Corporate Governance in Japan (2015, available at https://www.rieti.go.jp/jp/publications/dp/15e078.pdf) and Hideaki Miyajima & Ryo Ogawa, Convergence or Emerging Diversity? Understanding the Impact of Foreign Investors on Corporate Governance in Japan (2016, available at

of the Japanese Stewardship Code. Stated differently, the Japanese Stewardship Code aims to make domestic institutional investors act like foreign institutional investors. Reflecting such an orientation, the Japanese Stewardship Code has been criticized for not covering cross-shareholdings by banks and non-financial companies,[146] whereas the UK Stewardship Code was criticized by Professor Cheffins for not including foreign investors in its scope.[147]

C. The True Difference between the Japanese and the UK Codes

In summary, although the Japanese Stewardship Code and the UK Stewardship Code may bear superficial resemblance due to their broad focus on the same two core concepts, their fundamental policy rationales are almost diametrically opposed. The UK Stewardship Code aims to restrain excessive risk-taking and short-termism by making institutional investors more responsible to the public. Conversely, the Japanese Stewardship Code intends to champion shareholders' interests by making domestic institutional investors more active shareholders who would exert pressure on entrenched management.[148]

It is worth emphasizing, however, that the Japanese Stewardship Code "primarily targets institutional investors investing in Japanese listed shares".[149] This focus, which is similar to the UK Code's, suggests that the Japanese Government's objective in adopting the Stewardship Code was to improve the corporate governance of Japanese listed companies, rather than to promote the

https://www.rieti.go.jp/jp/publications/dp/16e053.pdf). For international research with similar findings, see also, Stuart Gillan & Laura T. Starks, *Corporate Governance, Corporate Ownership, and the Role of Institutional Investors: A Global Perspective*, 13 JOURNAL OF APPLIED FINANCE 4 (2003) and Jan Bena, Miguel A. Ferreira, Pedro P. Matos & Pedro Pires, *Are Foreign Investors Locusts? The Long-Term Effects of Foreign Institutional Ownership*, 126 JOURNAL OF FINANCIAL ECONOMICS 122 (2017).

146. Sadakazu Osaki, *Nihon-ban kōdo seido no jōken* [*The Japanese Code's Condition for Success*], Vol.66, No.5 KIYOU KAIKEI 48, at 51-52 (2014); Ryōhei Nakagawa, *Shareholding Characteristics and Imperfect Coverage of the Stewardship Code in Japan*, 29 JAPAN FORUM 338, at 346 (2017). See also *supra* note 137-140 and accompanying text (discussing the principles of the Japanese Corporate Governance Code on cross-shareholdings).

147. See *supra* note 73 and accompanying text.

148. It must be noted that at the third meeting of the Council of Experts Concerning the Japanese Version of the Stewardship Code, the Financial Services Agency as the secretariat of the Council described that the statement of the Japan Revitalization Strategy referring to "the aim of promoting the sustainable growth of companies" and the language in the preface to the 2012 Revised UK Stewardship Code aiming to "promote the long-term success of companies in such a way that the ultimate providers of capital (managed by institutional investors) also prosper" "do not contradict each other". See, Document No.3 of the Third Meeting of the Council of Experts Concerning the Japanese Version of the Stewardship Code, submitted by the Secretariat (available at https://www.fsa.go.jp/en/refer/councils/stewardship/material/20131018_1.pdf) at page 1. While this description does not conform perfectly with the view explained in the text, it does not preclude the possibility that the secretariat deliberately avoided pointing out the divergence between the UK Code and the Japan Revitalization Strategy, which might have provoked controversies over the goal to be aimed at.

149. The 2017 Revised Japanese Code, *supra* note 2, para.8 at page 5 (unchanged from the 2014 original Code)

The Logic and Limits of Stewardship Codes

interests of Japan's ultimate beneficiaries.[150] This may sound superficially similar to the goal of the UK Code. Nevertheless, this goal of the Japanese Stewardship Code is still different than that of the UK Code, as the former aims to prioritize the interests of shareholders over other stakeholders, especially employees.[151]

This difference in the basic orientations of the Japanese and the UK Stewardship Codes has been largely overlooked,[152] even by Professor Hiroyuki Kansaku, who chaired the Council of Experts Concerning the Japanese Version of the Stewardship Code.[153] Also, Professor Wataru Tanaka, who was a member of the Council, focused only on the principles of the Japanese and the UK Codes, and erroneously states that the concept of the sustainable growth of investee companies does not exist in the UK Code.[154] In a similar vein, in the international discourse, Professors Bebchuk, Cohen and Hirst portrayed the

150. If the goal of the Japanese Stewardship Code were to promote the interests of Japanese ultimate beneficiaries, then it should target institutional investors funded by Japanese interest investing in non-Japanese listed shares as well.

151. In a separate piece on recent Japanese reforms on board independence, the author discusses that one of the various roles expected to be performed by outside/independent directors is to represent the interests of shareholders in the boardroom and to function as a barrier insulating the management from the interests of core employees who may oppose decisions such as divestment of non-core businesses. See Goto, *supra* note 135 at 50-51.

152. See for example, Yoko Manzawa, *Suchwuadoshippu sekinin to jyutakusha sekinin – Eibei ni okeru kangaekata no hikaku no kokoromi* [*Stewardship Responsibility and Fiduciary Duty: A Comparison with the Anglo-American Way of Thinking*], 2070 SHOJIHOMU 23, at 24, 32 note 6 (2015) (stating that the Japanese Code and the UK Code are the same as both codes require institutional investors to promote the growth of investee companies and the interest of their beneficiaries, although there is a slight difference in the wording) and Nakagawa, *supra* note at 349 (stating that making institutional investors less speculative is "the whole intention of deploying the stewardship rules").

A notable exception is the view of Mr. Sadakazu Osaki of Nomura Research Institute, who briefly but correctly observes the difference of the goals of the two stewardship codes. See Sadakazu Osaki, *The New Stewardship Code in Japan. Comparison with the UK Code and its Implementation*, in Hiroshi Oda (ed.), COMPARATIVE CORPORATE GOVERNANCE: THE CASE OF JAPAN, Journal of Japanese Law Special Issue No.12 (Carl Heymanns/Wolters Kluwer, 2018) at 101, 102-103. Professor Mika Takahashi also states that "the Japanese Stewardship Code is not based on a radical criticism against the short-termism as in the United Kingdom" and "puts itself in line with fiduciary duty" as it aims to "enlarge the mid- to long-term investment return to the clients and beneficiaries of institutional investors". Professor Takahashi, however, does not provide the background for such a difference between Japan and the UK. See Mika Takahashi, *Jyutakusha no chui gimu to suchwuadoshippu sekinin* [*Fiduciary's Duty of Care and Stewardship Responsibility*], 2 SHINTAKU FORAMU 45, at 49 (2014).

In the international discourse, Professor Jennifer Hill correctly notes that while the UK Stewardship Code seeks to meet "the need for effective risk control in the post-crisis era", the Japanese Stewardship Code focuses "on arresting declining profitability, unlocking value and increasing investor returns" and deliberately creates "a warmer climate" for foreign investors and shareholder activists". Hill, *supra* note 3 at 20-22. She, however, fails to explain the whole picture underlying the Japanese Code as she views the reference to the concepts of "sustainable growth" and "medium to long-term corporate value" is a reflection of the above goal of the Japanese Code, and does not explain why the Japanese Code envisages relatively gentle kind of shareholder engagement. *Ibid* at 22, 23. As noted earlier, these concepts and the relatively gentle stance were included in the Japanese Code rather as a compromise to appease those who resisted shareholder-oriented system. See *supra* Part III, Section B.5.

153. See Kansaku, *supra* note 11 at 18-20 (listing characteristics of the Japanese Code in comparison with the UK Code).

154. Tanaka, *supra* note 85 at 69.

stewardship codes of the United Kingdom, Japan, and Canada as attempts to solve the agency problem of institutional investors,[155] a conclusion that is correct in Japan's case but not for the UK.

In contrast, Professor Chiu provides a UK-biased view[156] by stating that the Japanese Stewardship Code "could be seen as providing an ex ante form of defence against more unpredictable forms of shareholder activism", despite her recognition that the Japanese Code "is purportedly introduced as part of a package of measures to revitalize the Japanese economy and to improve the investment appeal of its listed sector".[157] Also, Professors Fenwick and Vermeulen, who have recently conducted a survey on the regulatory environment of engagement by institutional investors in various countries, state that "shareholders, particularly institutional investors, must be viewed as 'stewards' of the *company*" and observe that stewardship codes in general "attempt to create more responsible and purposeful investor engagement" and that the "Japanese Stewardship Code is modeled after the UK code".[158] The finding of this Article shows that the value of studies such as Fenwick and Vermeulen's would be diminished unless enough attention is paid to the context behind the adoption of stewardship codes in each country.

PART IV: THE EFFECTS AND THE LIMITS OF STEWARDSHIP CODES

A. The Effects and the Limits of Stewardship Codes

1. Different Goals, Different Effects and Limits

When the goals of stewardship codes differ, as seen in the case of the UK Code and the Japanese Code, their effectiveness and limits could also differ. Thus, the effectiveness of each stewardship code must be evaluated individually, taking into consideration possible differences in the goals of each.

In the United Kingdom, the goal of a stewardship code is to advance the public interest by restraining excessive risk-taking and investor short-termism. There, the problem is that institutional investors acting as loyal "stewards" of

---

155.   Bebchuk, Cohen & Hirst, *supra* note 5 at 108.
156.   In the same vein, the view of this article could be criticized as Japan-biased. The author's point is not to discuss which one of the two is more appropriate or authentic but to emphasize the importance of recognizing a possible home-country bias of an observer.
157.   Iris H-Y Chiu, *Learning from the UK in the Proposed Shareholder Rights Directive 2014?* *European Corporate Governance Regulation from a UK Perspective*, 114 ZEITSCHRIFT FÜR VERGLEICHENDE RECHTSWISSENSCHAFT 121, at 150-151 (2015).
158.   Fenwick & Vermeulen, *supra* note 3 at 10, 36 (emphasis added by the author). It is also worth noting that Professors Fenwick and Vermeulen summarize the goal of the Japanese Stewardship Code somewhat roughly as "(1) to discharge its responsibility to facilitate the continuous growth of the invested company and (2) to try to increase the medium-term or long-term return of the beneficial owners and clients of the institutional investor" thereby ignoring the priority provided in the preface of the Japanese Code. See *ibid.* at 36 and *supra* note 18 and accompanying text.

The Logic and Limits of Stewardship Codes

their clients and ultimate beneficiaries would not act in furtherance of such public interest when doing so does not coincide with the interest of their clients and ultimate beneficiaries. In other words, this goal is incompatible with the logic of stewardship that requires institutional investors to be loyal to the interests of their ultimate beneficiaries.

It is from such a viewpoint that Professors Chiu and Katelouzou propose imposing disclosure requirements and regulatory standards of conduct on institutional investors instead of introducing a stewardship code; in similar vein, Professor Reisberg proposes to provide weighted dividends or tax benefits to long-term shareholders.[159] While the desirability of some of these proposals remain debatable, they seem to be at least more consistent with their goal of restraining excessive risk-taking and investor short-termism when compared with the UK Stewardship Code.

In contrast, the goal of the Japanese Stewardship Code is more effective discipline of management from the viewpoint of shareholders' interests by urging domestic institutional investors to act for the benefit of the ultimate beneficiaries. This goal is compatible with the logic of stewardship where institutional investors are the fiduciaries of ultimate beneficiaries. In this context, the key issue becomes the effective enforcement of fiduciary duties, in particular, the duties of loyalty and care.[160] After taking a brief look at the current status of the adoption of the Japanese Stewardship Code by institutional investors, the remainder of this part will analyze the effect and limits of the Code from this perspective.

2. Signatories to the Japanese Stewardship Code

The Japanese Stewardship Code requests institutional investors who have adopted the Code to notify the Financial Services Agency (FSA) accordingly, and the FSA to publicize the list of such institutional investors ("signatories" to the Code).[161] Table 1 below shows the composition of these signatories as of April 5, 2018.[162]

Table 1: Signatories to the Japanese Stewardship Code as of April 5, 2018

---

159.   See *supra* note 76-80 and accompanying texts.
160.   The Kay Review states that the "core fiduciary duties are those of loyalty and prudence" and that "effective stewardship is possible only if … the steward proceeds on the basis of obligations of loyalty and prudence". The Kay Review: Final Report, *supra* note , para.9.6-9.8 at 66. See also, the Myners Report, *supra* note 40 at 92-93 (asserting that all pension fund trustees and the UK law should incorporate the principle of the US Department of Labor's Interpretive Bulletin, which states that the "fiduciary obligations of prudence and loyalty to plan participants and beneficiaries require the responsible fiduciary to vote proxies on issues that may affect the value of the plan's investment".).
161.   The 2014 Japanese Code, *supra* note 2, para.14 at page 4, and the 2017 Revised Japanese Code, *supra* note 2, para.13 at page 6-7.
162.   FINANCIAL SERVICES AGENCY, LIST OF INSTITUTIONAL INVESTORS SIGNING UP TO "PRINCIPLES FOR RESPONSIBLE INSTITUTIONAL INVESTORS" «JAPAN'S STEWARDSHIP CODE» (April 5, 2018), available at https://www.fsa.go.jp/en/refer/councils/stewardship/20180405/en_list_01.pdf.

Types of signatories	Number of signatories
Trust banks	6
Investment managers (mutual funds and investment advisors)	162
Pension funds	30
Insurance companies	22
Other institutions (including proxy advisors)	7
Total	227

These signatories include most of Japan's major domestic trust banks and insurance companies, whereas adoption by Japan's private pension funds is limited.[163]

Out of the 162 investment managers (mutual funds and investment advisors), 48 are foreign institutions.[164] Among them are several activist hedge funds including Brandes Investment Partners, Dalton Investments, Effissimo Capital Management, and Oasis Management Company. Some Japanese activists, such as SPARX Asset Management Co. and Strategic Capital, also have signed up. In addition, there are four foreign pension funds, namely, CalPERS, Fourth Swedish National Pension Fund, UK Railway Pension Trustee Company Limited, and the University of California.

While the number of signatories itself does not guarantee the effectiveness of the Stewardship Code in improving the quality of institutional investors' engagement,[165] it is still noteworthy that foreign institutional investors, especially activist hedge funds, took the trouble of signing up to the Japanese Stewardship Code, which features rather investee company-friendly principles and guidance.[166] One possible reason for this move is that by signing up, these investors are trying to portray themselves as long-term investors supportive of the "sustainable growth of investee companies" and to dilute their image as hostile activists.[167] This tactics, however, may not be that effective as

---

163. Ryoko Ueda, *Nihonban suchuwadoshippu kodo no kaitei – Kikantoshika no yakuwari to jikkosei no kyoka* [The Revision of the Japanese Stewardship Code: The Role of Institutional Investors and Strengthening of Its Effectiveness], 382 SHOJI HOMU 26 at 30 (2017). For private pension funds, see also *infra* note 196-205 and accompanying texts.
164. This is judged by their lack of corporate numbers assigned to legal persons established under Japanese law. Corporate numbers of signatories are only shown in the Japanese version of the list of signatories. See https://www.fsa.go.jp/sing/stewardship/list/20180405/list_01.pdf.
165. Reisberg, *supra* note 23 at 224-226. See also, Sergakis, *supra* note 73 at 136.
166. See *supra* note 84-89 and accompanying texts.
167. See Tanaka, *supra* note 90 at 37-38 (suggesting that, if the Japanese Stewardship Code had taken more adversarial stance, Japanese domestic institutions would have been more reluctant to sign up to the Code).

The Logic and Limits of Stewardship Codes

companies are unlikely to be so naïve as to believe in a declaration of this sort that is not supported by formal sanctions.

B. Duty of Loyalty and Conflicts of Interest

1. Institutional Investors and Conflicts of Interest

Turning back to the analysis of the effects and limits of the Japanese Stewardship Code, the essence of the duty of loyalty of fiduciaries is that fiduciaries must put the interests of their beneficiaries ahead of their own.[168] Thus, the core issue for a stewardship code from the duty-of-loyalty perspective is managing the effect of conflicts of interest between institutional investors and their ultimate beneficiaries. Accordingly, Principle 2 of the Japanese Stewardship Code, in conformity with Principle 2 of the UK Code, requests institutional investors to "have a clear policy on how they manage conflicts of interest in fulfilling their stewardship responsibilities and publicly disclose it".

A conflict of interest is particularly likely to occur when an institutional investor offers financial services to its investee companies, or when it is affiliated with companies that offer financial services to investee companies.[169] For example, a life insurance company may undertake management of an investee company's pension fund, or an investment advisor could be a subsidiary of a bank making a loan to its subsidiary's investee company. In such cases, institutional investors might face pressure not to vote against the management of investee companies so as to avoid losing valuable contracts for themselves or their affiliated companies' other businesses.

On the assumption that institutional investors have not done enough to manage conflicts of interest, the 2017 revision of the Japanese Stewardship Code has added a few sentences to the Guidance to Principle 2 requesting institutional investors to make their policies on conflict of interest more specific and to establish governance structures to prevent conflict of interest, such as independent committees on voting of shares.[170]

2. Disclosure of Voting Records on Individual Agenda of Each Investee Company

As voting of shares is an important aspect of stewardship activities by institutional investors, the Japanese Stewardship Code has a separate principle

---

168. See Guidance 2-1, the 2017 Revised Japanese Code, *supra* note 2 (stating that "institutional investors should put the interest of their client and beneficiary first"and Guidance to Principle 2, the 2012 Revised UK Code, *supra* note 1 ("An institutional investor's duty is to act in the interest of its clients and/or beneficiaries.").
169. Black & Coffee, *supra* note 5 at 2059-2061.
170. The 2017 Revised Japanese Code, *supra* note 2, Guidance 2-2 and 2-3. See also, Tahara et al., *supra* note 128 at 18-19.

on this issue, requesting institutional investors to "have a clear policy on voting and disclosure of voting activity",[171] again in line with the UK Code.[172]

One of the most controversial issues that arose in the process of the 2017 revision was whether institutional investors should disclose how they have voted on the individual agenda of each investee company, or whether it is sufficient to disclose their voting records on an aggregate basis. In the end, disclosure of voting results on the level of individual agenda was adopted as Guidance 5-3 to address conflicts of interest in the Japanese market,[173] overriding oppositions from some institutional investors and listed companies arguing that such individual disclosure may encourage institutional investors to follow formalistic voting standards, which in turn may hinder meaningful dialogue between institutional investors and investee companies.[174]

Major domestic trust banks and investment managers belonging to large financial conglomerates quickly accepted the request of Guidance 5-3 on individual disclosure, presumably in response to the criticism on the high-likelihood of conflict of interest in financial conglomerates.[175] In contrast, two of the four largest life insurance companies have not decided to disclose individual voting results as of April 2018.[176] In lieu of individual disclosure, Nippon Life Insurance, the largest life insurer in Japan, has established an independent advisory council on stewardship activities, which is comprised of one independent director, two academics, and one lawyer, to oversee the voting process and how the company should vote on important cases.[177] Such an independent committee is one possible solution for issues of conflicts of

171. The 2017 Revised Japanese Code, *supra* note 2, Principle 5.
172. The 2012 Revised UK Code, *supra* note 1, Principle 6, the 2012 UK Stewardship Code.
173. The 2017 Revised Japanese Code, *supra* note 2, note 15 at page 15; Tahara et al., *supra* note 128 at 21. The UK Stewardship Code does not explicitly require disclosure of voting records on individual agenda, but it is reported that major institutional investors in the United Kingdom do so for the sake of better accountability and management of conflict of interest. *Ibid.*
174. The 2017 Revised Japanese Code, *supra* note 2, note 15 at page 15 at page 15, Hiroki Sanpe, *Giketsuken koshi kekka no kaiji* [Disclosure of Voting Results], 1515 JURISTO 22, at 26 (2018).
175. Osamu Hamada, *Giketsuken koshi kekka no kobetsu kaiji no meguru giron to kikan toshika no taio jyokyo* [Discussions on the Disclosure of Individual Voting Results and the Responses of Institutional Investors], 2145 SHOJI HOMU 37, at 40-41 (2017); Naoyoshi Ema, *Kikan toshika ni yoru giketsuken koshi no jyokyo—2017-nen no kabunushi sokai wo furikaette* [The Current State of Voting of Shares by Institutional Investors: Looking Back at Shareholders' Meetings in 2017], 2150 SHOJI HOMU 13, at 14 (2017), Sanpe, *supra* note 174 at 23.
176. It might be worth noting that these two life insurance companies, namely Nippon Life Insurance and Meiji Yasuda Life Insurance, take the form of mutual insurance company instead of stock corporation. In this case, profits of insurance company through services offered to investee companies substantially belong to insurance policyholders as the equity holders of a mutual insurance company. Thus, conflicts of interest between beneficiaries and insurance company would not be as strong as in the case of insurance companies taking the form of a stock corporation.
177. Nihon Seimei Sogo Gaisha, *Suchuwadoshippu shimon iinkai" no shinsetsu oyobi kongo no kadai* ["Establishment of "the Advisory Council on Stewardship" and Future Action Plans toward Improvement of Stewardship Activities], March 30, 2009, available at https://www.nissay.co.jp/news/2016pdf/20170330pdf.

interest;[178] whether it works effectively will in turn depend on whether the committee is adequately monitoring.

What then is the effect of the individual disclosure requirement by the 2017 revision? Although there is no systematic empirical study on this issue to the best of the author's knowledge as of April 2018,[179] there is some anecdotal evidence suggesting that such disclosure matters.[180] For example, Mitsubishi UFJ Trust Bank disclosed that it had voted against the reelection of directors of Mitsubishi Motors in December 2016, which was surprising as both companies belong to Mitsubishi group, one of the six largest *keiretsu* known for its strong group unity.[181] Also, in June 2017, Mizuho Trust Bank supported a shareholder's proposal that was opposed by the management of its parent company, Mizuho Financial Group.[182]

C. Duty of Care and Business Models of Investors

The duty of care requires institutional investors as fiduciaries to exercise reasonable care when they perform their task. The core task is of course to invest the fund they manage, and the investment strategy of institutional investors differ depending on their "business model".

In the same vein, stewardship activities of these investors would also differ rationally depending of their business model and investment strategy.[183] For

178. Simon CY Wong, *How Conflicts of Interest Thwart Institutional Investor Stewardship*, BUTTERWORTHS JOURNAL OF INTERNATIONAL BANKING AND FINANCIAL LAW, September 2011, 481, at 482.
179. See Hamada, *supra* note 175 at 42, 43 note 22 (citing a descriptive statistic reporting that at shareholders' meetings held of companies comprising Nikkei 225 index in June 2017, the amount of decrease of the average ratio of votes supporting proposals made by the management, except for those on anti-takeover measures, was less than one percentage point). See also, Yasutomo Tsukioka, *The Impact of Japan's Stewardship Code on Shareholder Voting* (2017), available at https://ssrn.com/abstract=3013999) (studying the effects of the original Japanese Stewardship Code using data of investee companies from 2010 to 2016 on the ratio of votes for and against for agenda on appointment of directors).
180. Hamada, *supra* note 175 at 41.
181. Nihon Keizai Shinbun, *Mitsubishi UFJ Shintaku, Mitsubishi Jidosha no jinjian ni "no"* Toshi no ronri zenmenni [Mitsubishi UFJ Trust votes against the nomination of directors in Mitsubishi Motors: The Logic of Investment Comes to Front], 2017/5/31 22:30JST. While the shareholders' meeting in question was held before the revision of the Japanese Stewardship Code, disclosure of individual voting records had been already proposed by another council at the Financial Services Agency on November 30, 2016. See, the Council of Experts Concerning the Follow-up of Japan's Stewardship Code and Japan's Corporate Governance Code Opinion Statement No. 3, *Effective Stewardship Activities of Institutional Investors - To Enhance Constructive Dialogue toward Sustainable Corporate Growth*, page 3-4 (November 30, 2016, available at https://www.fsa.go.jp/en/refer/councils/follow-up/statements_3.pdf).
182. Nihon Keizai Shimbun, *Giketsuken koshi de oyagaisha ni "hanki" Asemane One nado* [Rising in "Revolt" against the Parent Company in Voting of Shares: Asset Management One and Others], 2017/8/30 19:59 JST (https://www.nikkei.com/article/DGXLASGD30H5H_Q7A830C1EE9000/).
183. Serdar Celik & Mats Isaakson, *Institutional Investors as Owners: Who Are They and What Do They Do?*, OECD Corporate Governance Working Papers, No.11 (2013, available at http://dx.doi.org/10.1787/5k3v1dvmfk42-en), at 5, 22-27, John C. Coates IV, *Thirty Years of Evolution*

example, investors with a concentrated portfolio would actively engage with the management to raise the firm value of their investee companies.[184] However, active engagement is not a rational choice for a passive fund aiming to fully replicate a certain market index, the business model of which is to provide diversified investment at a low cost.[185]

As long as there is no conflict of interest, and as long as clients of institutional investors have entrusted their funds knowing the latter's business model, such diversity of type and intensity is not problematic from the viewpoint of the interest of ultimate beneficiaries. In other words, the type and intensity of stewardship activities could and should be left to the discretion of each institutional investor as part of their business model and investment strategy, as long as conflict of interest is effectively managed.

However, from the perspective of the Japanese Government, whose aim is to make Japanese companies to prioritize the interest of shareholders over that of stakeholders by utilizing the pressure from institutional investors,[186] passivity on stewardship activity of some institutional investors would be problematic. Thus, the 2017 revision of the Japanese Stewardship Code has added a new paragraph requesting passive funds "to actively take charge of the engagement and voting,"[187] although such active engagement might not be in the best interest of clients of such funds. In other words, the goal of the Japanese Stewardship Code is not perfectly compatible with the logic of stewardship as fiduciaries of ultimate beneficiaries.[188]

in the Roles of Institutional Investors in Corporate Governance, in Jennifer G. Hill & Randall S. Thomas (eds.), RESEARCH HANDBOOK ON SHAREHOLDER POWER (Edward Elgar, 2015), 79, at 85-86.

184   Takaaki Eguchi, Tayo na toshika, tayo na gabunanmu koka – Passibu unyo no kakudai ga imisuru mono [Diverse Investors, Diverse Governance Effects: The Meaning of the Expansion of Passive Investment], in Hiroyuki Kansaku (ed.), KIGYO HOSEI NO SHORAI TENBO – SHIHON SHIJYO SEIDO NO KAKAKU HENO TENKIN – 2018-NENDO BAN [Future Prospects of Enterprise Law: Proposals on Reforms of the Capital Market System, 2018 edition] [Shihon Shijyo Kenkyukai], 415, at 422-423.

185   See Ronald J. Gilson & Jeffrey N. Gordon, The Agency Cost of Agency Capitalism: Activist Investors and the Revaluation of Governance Rights, 113 COLUMBIA LAW REVIEW 863, 866, 868-869, 889-895, Bebchuk, Cohen & Hirst, supra note 5 at 97-98, 100-101, 108 and Curtis J. Milhaupt, Evaluating Abe's Third Arrow: How Significant Are Japan's Recent Corporate Governance Reforms?, in Hiroshi Oda (ed.), COMPARATIVE CORPORATE GOVERNANCE: THE CASE OF JAPAN, Journal of Japanese Law, Special Issue No.12 (Carl Heymanns/Wolters Kluwer, 2018) at 65, 74 For a similar view in Japan, see Takahito Kato, Suchiwadoshippu kodo no rironteki konsatsu – Kikan toshika no mienhibu koco no kanten kara [A Theoretical Analysis of the Stewardship Code: From the Perspective of the Incentive Structure of Institutional Investors], 1515 JURISUTO 16, 18-21 (2018).

186   See supra Part III, Section C

187   The 2017 Revised Japanese Code, supra note 2, Guidance 4-2. See also Tahara et al., supra note 128 at 20.

188   See also Celik & Isaakson, supra note 183 at 21 ("Before we discuss these different determinants of shareholder engagement it is important to remind ourselves why the degree of ownership engagement is a public policy concern. Why should policy makers care? From a public policy perspective, ownership engagement is not a moral issue. Nor can it be seen as a general obligation or fiduciary duty that would override other objectives, such as maximizing the return to the institution's ultimate beneficiary. What is primarily matters for public policy is the role that ownership engagement plays for effective capital allocation and the informed monitoring of corporate performance.")

Would then the Japanese Stewardship Code be effective? On one hand, there is a possibility that the Stewardship Code may be entirely ignored[189] or result only in formalistic engagement that does not produce value.[190] On the other hand, the Stewardship Code could "serve as a focal point for changing the norms about asset management and capital productivity in Japan".[191] While it is still too early to have definitive empirical evidence, the anecdotal evidence described in the previous section on voting behavior by large trust banks show that the latter effect may be more than a pipe dream.

D. Monitoring and Enforcement

The Japanese Stewardship Code takes the form of "comply or explain". As signing up to the code does not guarantee either compliance or meaningful explanation, monitoring and enforcement from the viewpoint of ultimate beneficiaries is essential for the Stewardship Code to be effective.[192] In particular, whether an institutional investor who declares compliance does comply, and whether an institutional investor who chooses to explain provides a persuasive explanation must be monitored.[193]

The question is who would provide such monitoring. In this regard, the Japanese Stewardship Code follows the UK Code that divides institutional investors into two categories: asset managers, who are entrusted with the day-to-day management of funds provided by the other group; and asset owners such as pension funds and life insurance companies.[194] Both codes expect asset

189   Milhaupt, supra note 185 at 9 (noting that the Stewardship Code would be "practically useless" as many institutional investors "rationally do not engage").

190   Takaaki Eguchi, Engejimento no jidai ni okeru kikan toshika no yakuwari – Nihon ni okeru atarasii toshikazo kochiku wo mezashite [The Role of Institutional Investors in an Era of Engagement: Toward Building of a New Image of Investors in Japan], 2109 SHOJI HOMU 24, at 27 (2016).

191   Milhaupt, supra note 185 at 9. See also Wataru Tanaka, Nihonban suchiwadoshippu kodo no kaitei [The Revision of the Japanese Stewardship Code], 398 SIRYOBAN SHOJI HOMU 6, at 12 (2017) (asserting that by officially acknowledging the value of stewardship activities, the Stewardship Code might make coordination among institutional investors easier and thus solve the collective action problem).

192   One of the major concerns in Japan has been the weakness of the enforcement due to the Stewardship Code's "comply or explain" approach and the lack of a specific enforcement mechanism. See Kansaku, supra note 14 at 1018-1019, Mayumi Takahashi, Sofuto ro to shiteno koporeto gabanansu kodo to suchuwadoshippu kodo [The Corporate Governance Code and the Stewardship Code as Soft Law], JIYU TO SEIGI, Vol.67, No.7, 41, at 45 (2016).

193   While the data of the Financial Services Agency as of December 2016 shows that the ratio of "compliance" by signatories exceeds 90% for all seven principles, more specific requests in the guidance section may have a lower compliance rate. See Document No.3 of the First Meeting of the Council of Experts on the Stewardship Code submitted by the Financial Services Agency, Status of the Stewardship Code and Opinion Statement of the Follow-up Council (January 31, 2017), at page 6 and 19, available at https://www.fsa.go.jp/en/refer/councils/stewardship/material/20170131_3.pdf.

194   The 2017 Revised UK Code, supra note 1, para.6 at page 1, the 2017 Revised Japanese Code, supra note 2, para.7 at page 5.

owners to monitor stewardship activities of asset managers as their direct clients.[195]

It has been observed, however, that private pension funds, have tended not to sign up to the Japanese Stewardship Code.[196] As of April 5, 2018, there are 30 pension-fund signatories, which comprise of 12 public pensions, 14 private pensions, and 4 foreign pension funds.[197] Out of the 14 private pension funds, 8 are of companies are under the supervision of the FSA, such as banks and insurance companies, and 3 are associations of private pension funds.[198] This leaves only 3 signatories that are pension funds of individual companies, out of a total of 774 private pension funds as of April 1, 2018.[199]

The reason for the low adoption rate by pension funds seems to be threefold. First, most of the private pension funds are small in size, holding less than 10 billion Yen, and cannot afford to hire sufficient staffs for stewardship activities.[200] Second, as the beneficiaries of private pension funds are employees they cannot monitor such funds effectively due to collective action problems. And third, unlike trust banks or investment managers, private pension funds are not supervised by the Financial Services Agency and thus do not face regulatory pressure to sign up, except for those of financial companies which are regulated by the Agency.[201]

Actually, the 2017 revision did take this issue into consideration, and added a few paragraphs in the guidance section to promote stewardship activities by

---

195. The 2012 Revised UK Code, *supra* note 1, para.7 at page 2 ("Since asset owners are the primary audience of asset managers' public statements as well as client reports on stewardship, asset owners should seek to hold their managers to account for their stewardship activities. In so doing, they better fulfil their duty to their beneficiaries to exercise stewardship over their assets."), the 2017 Revised Japanese Code, *supra* note 2, Guidance 1-3, 1-4 and 1-5. See also Reinberg, *supra* note 23 at 241.

196. Tahara et al., *supra* note 128 at 18. In contrast, public pension funds, in particular the Government Pension Investment Fund (GPIF), are very active on stewardship. See for example, GPIF, STEWARDSHIP PRINCIPLES & PROXY VOTING PRINCIPLES (June 1, 2017), available at http://www.gpif.go.jp/en/stewardship_and_esg/pdf/stewardship_principles_and_proxy_voting_principle s.pdf.

197. For the list of signatories, see Financial Services Agency, *supra* note 162.

198. One of such association is the Pension Fund Association, which has been active in stewardship activities since early 2000s. See Bruce E. Aronson, *A Japanese CalPERS or a New Model for Institutional Investor Activism? Japan's Pension Fund Association and the Emergence of Shareholder Activism in Japan*, 7 NYU JOURNAL OF LAW & BUSINESS 571 (2011).

199. The three signatories are the pension funds of Eisai, Panasonic and Secom. The total number of private pension funds (774) is derived from adding the 32 employees' pension funds (*kosei nenkin kikin*) to the 742 fund-type defined-benefit corporate pensions (*kikin-gata kakutei kyufu kigyo nenkin*) which is 742. See Kigyo Nenkin Rengokai (Pension Fund Association), *Kigyo nenkin no gensho* (*Heisei 30-nen 4 gatsu 1 nichi genzai*) [The Current State of Corporate Pensions (as of April 1, 2018)] (April 9 2018), available at https://www.pfa.or.jp/activity/tokei/nenkin/files/genkyo.pdf.

200. Ryoko Ueda, *Nihonban suchuwadoshippu kodo no kaitei – Kikantoshika no yakuwari to jikkosei no kyoka* [The Revision of the Japanese Stewardship Code: The Role of Institutional Investors and Strengthening of Its Effectiveness], 382 SHOKEN 26 at 30 (2017).

201. Naoya Ariyoshi, *Suchuwadoshippu kodo kaitei heno jitsumu taio* [Practical Issues in Response to the Revision of the Stewardship Code], 2141 SHOJI HOMU 84, at 91 (2017).

The Logic and Limits of Stewardship Codes

asset owners.[202] The number of pension fund signatories after the revision, however, did not increase by much,[203] suggesting that the Revised Code is unlikely to address such collective action problems. To urge private pension funds to be more active, encouragement from their regulator, the Ministry of Health, Labor and Welfare,[204] is crucial.[205] This may call for additional regulations, but for a reason that is completely different from that in the UK.[206]

PART V: CONCLUSION

This article has demonstrated that there is a divergence between the basic goals and orientation of the Japanese and the UK Stewardship Codes, which has been largely overlooked in the literature. Although the term "stewardship" suggests that stewardship codes are based on the logic of a fiduciary duty compelling a fiduciary to act in the interest of its beneficiary, the goal of the UK Stewardship Code is instead to restrain excessive risk-taking and short-termism by making institutional investors more responsible to the public.

In contrast, the Japanese Stewardship Code aims to change the attitude of domestic institutional investors in order to make Japanese corporate governance more oriented towards the interests of shareholders rather than those of stakeholders. This goal of the Japanese Code is more compatible with the logic of stewardship than that of the UK Code. At the same time, the Japanese Government considers this goal to be in the public interest of Japan.

Another finding of this article is that different stewardship codes have different goals and that this must be taken into consideration when assessing their effectiveness. The success of the Japanese Stewardship Code will primarily depend on how well domestic institutional investors are incentivized to act in the interest of their ultimate beneficiaries and to monitor entrenched management. Conversely, the success of the UK Stewardship Code will likely depend on how well it can make institutional investors consider the interests of the public and of stakeholders other than shareholders. Regulatory interventions might be necessary in both cases, but for different reasons.

---

202. Tahara et al., *supra* note 128 at 17-18.

203. The number of pension-fund signatories as of December 27, 2016, the year before the 2017 revision, was 26.

204. The Ministry of Health, Labor and Welfare, in collaboration with the Pension Fund Association, has issued a report to foster adoption of the Stewardship Code by private pension funds. Suchuwadoshippu Kentokai (The Study Group on Stewardship), *Kigyo nenkin to nihonban suchuwadoshippu kodo* [Corporate Pensions and the Japanese Stewardship Code] (March 17, 2017), available at https://www.pfa.or.jp/kanyu/shiryo/stewardship/boukoku/files/all.pdf.

205. See also Ariyoshi, *supra* note 201 at 91 (asserting that it is not enough to rely on spontaneous adoption by private pension funds and suggesting that fiduciary duties of directors of such funds would call for adequate stewardship activities).

206. See *supra* note 159 and accompanying texts.

The diversity in the goals and measures of effectiveness of stewardship codes is the consequence of the variety in the systems and primary issues of corporate governance in each jurisdiction. This suggests that, although stewardship codes are proliferating around the world, what seems like a move towards convergence may actually be an evidence of continued divergence – with "stewardship" having different meanings in different jurisdictions. Thus, inter-jurisdictional comparisons of stewardship codes must be undertaken with caution, with a comparison of the text of the principles and guidance being only the starting point – and not the end - of any analysis. Ultimately, the policies driving the adoption of such codes and the specific corporate governance context into which a stewardship code is implemented appear to be critical. As such, multiple jurisdiction-specific lenses are necessary when examining stewardship codes in a comparative context.

資料２

改訂前からの変更点

「責任ある機関投資家」の諸原則

《日本版スチュワードシップ・コード》

～投資と対話を通じて企業の持続的成長を促すために～

スチュワードシップ・コードに関する有識者検討会

平成 29 年 5 月 29 日

平成 29 年 5 月 29 日
スチュワードシップ・コードに関する有識者検討会

スチュワードシップ・コード改訂に当たって

1. 平成 26 年 2 月 26 日、「日本版スチュワードシップ・コードに関する有識者検討会」によりスチュワードシップ・コードが策定されてから約 3 年が経過した。この間、スチュワードシップ・コードの受入れを表明した機関投資家は 200 を超えるに至り、また、平成 27 年 6 月には、上場企業に対し、コーポレートガバナンス・コードの運用が開始された。両コードの下で、コーポレートガバナンス改革には一定の進捗が見られるものの、いまだに形式的な対応にとどまっているのではないかとの指摘もなされている。

2. こうした中、平成 28 年 11 月 30 日、金融庁・東京証券取引所に設置された「スチュワードシップ・コード及びコーポレートガバナンス・コードのフォローアップ会議」において、「機関投資家による実効的なスチュワードシップ活動のあり方」と題する意見書（以下「意見書」という。）が公表された。意見書においては、コーポレートガバナンス改革を「形式」から「実質」へと深化させていくことが必要であるとされ、機関投資家が企業との間で深度ある「建設的な対話」を行っていくことは、スチュワードシップ・コードの改訂が必要であるとされ、スチュワードシップ・コードの改訂が提言された。

3. 意見書を受け、金融庁において、平成 29 年 1 月から計 3 回にわたり、「スチュワードシップ・コードに関する有識者検討会」（以下、前出の「日本版スチュワードシップ・コードに関する有識者検討会」と併せ、「本検討会」という。）を開催し、コード改訂に向けた議論を重ねてきた。こうした議論を踏まえ、今般、本検討会は改訂版のスチュワードシップ・コード（以下「本コード」という。）を取りまとめた。

4. 意見書においては、
   ・ アセットオーナーによる実効的なチェック
   ・ 運用機関のガバナンス・利益相反管理等
   ・ パッシブ運用における対話等
   ・ 議決権行使結果の公表の充実
   ・ 運用機関の自己評価
について提言がなされており、本検討会は、これらの内容について議論を行い、新たに本コードに盛り込むこととした。

5. さらに、検討の過程では、意見書にある論点以外についても、以下のような指摘がなされた。

経緯及び背景

1. 平成24年12月、我が国経済の再生に向けて、円高・デフレから脱却し強い経済を取り戻すため、政府一体となって、必要な経済対策を講じるとともに成長戦略を実現するため、内閣に「日本経済再生本部」が設置された。また、平成25年1月、同本部の下に、我が国産業の競争力強化や国際展開に向けた成長戦略の具現化について調査審議するため、日本経済再生本部に「産業競争力会議」が設置された。
   同会議における議論を踏まえ、日本経済再生本部において、本部長である内閣総理大臣より、「内閣府特命担当大臣(金融)は、関係大臣と連携し、企業の持続的な成長を促す観点から、幅広い範囲の機関投資家が適切に受託責任を果たすための原則のあり方について検討すること。」との指示がなされた[1]。

2. 以上の経緯を経て、平成25年6月、いわゆる「第三の矢」としての成長戦略を定める「日本再興戦略」において、機関投資家が、対話を通じて企業の中長期的な成長を促すなど、「受託者責任を果たすための原則(日本版スチュワードシップコード)」について検討し、幅広い観点から企業の持続的な成長を促す、幅広い対話を行い、適切に受託責任を果たすための原則」について検討を進め、年内に取りまとめることが閣議決定された。

3. 前記の総理指示及び閣議決定を踏まえた検討の場として、平成25年8月、金融庁において「日本版スチュワードシップ・コードに関する有識者検討会」(以下「本検討会」という。)が設置された。本検討会は、同年8月から計6回にわたり議論を重ね、今般平成26年2月26日、「「責任ある機関投資家」の諸原則《日

[1] 日本経済再生本部 第6回会合(平成25年4月2日)

・ 現在のコードにおいても、議決権行使助言会社に当てはまる旨は示されているが、議決権行使助言会社自身が、十分な経営資源を投入した上でサービスを提供することが重要であり、また、自らの取組みについて公表を求めることが考えられるのではないか。

・ 複数の機関投資家が協働して企業と対話を行うこと(集団的エンゲージメント)について、企業との間で対話を行う際の選択肢として考えられることを、コードにも盛り込むべきではないか。他方で、集団的エンゲージメントを行う際には、対話が形式的にならないよう、十分留意する必要があるのではないか。

・ ESG(環境・社会・ガバナンス)要素のうち、投資先企業の状況を踏まえた重要と考えられるものは、事業におけるリスク・収益機会の両面で、中長期的な企業価値を及ぼす事項について、関連する企業リンについて、今回の改訂に当たって盛り込んだところである。

6. 本コードの取りまとめに当たっては、策定時と同様に、和英両文によるパブリッククコメントについては18の個人・団体から、英訳版については11の個人・団体から意見が寄せられた。本検討会においては、これらについても検討を行い、本コードの取りまとめに反映させていきたい。

7. 本検討会は、現在のコードを受け入れている機関投資家に対して、改訂版コード公表の遅くとも6ヶ月後(平成29年11月末)までに、改訂内容に対応した公表項目の更新(及び更新を行った旨の公表又は金融庁への通知)を行うことを期待する。

本版スチュワードシップ・コード》（以下「本コード」という。）を策定した。
なお、「本コード」の取りまとめに当たっては、和英両文によるパブリックコメントを実施し、和文については26の個人・団体から、英文版については19の個人・団体から意見が寄せられた。本検討会は、これらについても議論を行い、「本コード」の取りまとめに反映させていただいた。

本コードの目的

4. 冒頭に掲げたように、本コードにおいて、「スチュワードシップ責任」とは、機関投資家が、投資先の日本企業やその事業環境等に関する深い理解に基づく建設的な「目的を持った対話」（エンゲージメント）などを通じて、当該企業の企業価値の向上や持続的成長を促すことにより、顧客・受益者（最終受益者を含む。以下同じ。）の中長期的な投資リターンの拡大を図る責任を意味する。本コードは、機関投資家が、顧客・受益者と投資先企業の双方を視野に入れ、「責任ある機関投資家」として当該「スチュワードシップ責任」を果たすに当たり有用と考えられる諸原則を定めるものである。

5. 一方で、企業の側において、コーポレートガバナンス・コード（平成27年6月1日適用開始）に示されているように、経営の基本方針や業務執行に関する意思決定を行う取締役会が、経営陣による業務執行を適切に監督しつつ、適切なガバナンス機能を発揮することにより、企業価値の向上を図る責務を有している。こうした責務と本コードに定める機関投資家の責務とは、いわば「車の両輪」であり、両者が適切に相まって質の高いコーポレートガバナンスが実現され、企業の持続的な成長と顧客・受益者の中長期的な投資リターンの確保が図られていくことが期待される。本コードは、こうした観点から、機関投資家と投資先企業との間で建設的な「目的を持った対話」（エンゲージメント）が行われることを促すことを意図するものであり、機関投資家が投資先企業の経営の細部にまで介入することを意図するものではない²。

6. また、スチュワードシップ責任を果たすための機関投資家の活動（以下「スチュワードシップ活動」という。）において、議決権の行使は重要な要素ではあるものの、当該活動は単に議決権の行使のみを意味するものではない。スチュワードシップ活動は、機関投資家が、投資先企業の持続的成長に向けてスチュワードシップ責任を適切に果たすため、当該企業の状況を適切に把握することや、これらを踏まえて当該企業と建設的な「目的を持った対話」（エンゲージメント）を行うことなどを含む、幅広い活動を指すものである³。

2 （http://www.fsa.go.jp/singi/stewardship/legalissue.pdf）

3 金融庁において、平成26年2月、機関投資家に係る法的論点について「スチュワードシップ責任と法的論点に係る考え方の整理」を公表し、最低有価報告書や公開買付制度等について、可能な限り法律面・評価の明確化を図っている

7. 本コードにおいて、機関投資家は、資金の運用等を受託し自ら企業への投資を担う者（投資運用会社など以下「運用機関」という。）である場合と、当該資金の出し手を含む「資産保有者としての機関投資家」（年金基金や保険会社など以下「アセットオーナー」という。）である場合とに大別される。

このうち、「資産運用者としての機関投資家・運用機関」には、投資先企業との日々の建設的な対話等を通じて、当該企業の企業価値の向上に寄与することが期待される。

また、「資産保有者としての機関投資家・アセットオーナー」には、スチュワードシップ責任を果たす上での基本的な方針を示した上で、自ら、あるいは委託先である「資産運用者としての機関投資家・運用機関」の行動を通じて、投資先企業の企業価値の向上に寄与することが期待される。
「資産運用者としての機関投資家・運用機関」は、「資産保有者としての機関投資家・アセットオーナー」の期待するサービスを提供できるよう、その意向の適切な把握などに努めるべきであり、また、「資産保有者としての機関投資家・アセットオーナー」は、「資産運用者としての機関投資家・運用機関」に求める事項やサービスを明確にし、これを適切に評価するよう努めるべきである。
機関投資家による実効性のある適切なスチュワードシップ活動は、最終的には顧客・受益者の中長期的な投資リターンの拡大を目指すものである。したがって、スチュワードシップ活動の実施に伴う適正なコストは、投資に必要なコストであるという意識を、機関投資家と顧客・受益者の双方において共有すべきである。

8. 本コードの対象とする機関投資家は、基本的に、日本の上場株式に投資する機関投資家を念頭に置いている。また、本コードは、機関投資家から業務の委託を受け議決権行使助言会社等に対しても当てはまるものである。

「プリンシプルベース・アプローチ」及び「コンプライ・オア・エクスプレイン」

9. 本コードに定める各原則の適用の仕方は、各機関投資家が自らの置かれた状況に応じてエ夫すべきものである。本コードに定める機関投資家の態様は、例えば、機関投資家の規模や運用方針（長期運用であるか短期運用であるか、アクティブ運用であるかパッシブ運用であるか等）などによって様々になり得る。

10. こうした点に鑑み、本コードは、機関投資家が取るべき行動について詳細に規定する

ることが望ましい。（金融庁では別紙一覧表など形で公表している（http://www.fsa.go.jp/singi/stewardship/legalissue.pdf）。本コードの策定を踏まえ、「日本版スチュワードシップ・コードの実効性を高める法的論点に係る考え方の整理」を公表し、解釈の明確化を図っている（http://www.fsa.go.jp/singi/stewardship/legalissue.pdf）。）

― 「コードを受け入れる旨」（受入れ表明）及び
― スチュワードシップ責任を果たすための方針など「コードの各原則」（指針を含む）に基づく公表項目」

① スチュワードシップ責任を果たすための方針（指針を含む）において公表が求められている具体的な項目
② 実施しない原則（指針を含む）がある場合には、その理由の説明を含む

当該公表項目について、毎年、見直し・更新を行うこと（更新を行った場合には、その旨も公表すること）。

・ 当該公表を行ったウェブサイトのアドレス（URL）を金融庁に通知すること
を期待する。

また、本検討会は、当該通知を受けた金融庁に対して、当該公表を行った機関投資家について、一覧性のある形で公表を行うことを期待する。

15・14. 本検討会は、機関投資家の動向等を踏まえ、本コードの実施状況や国際的な議論の動向も踏まえ、本コードの内容の更なる改善が図られていくことを期待する。このため、本検討会は、金融庁において、おおむね3年毎を目途として、本コードの定期的な見直しを検討するなど、適切な対応をとることにより、機関投資家やその顧客・受益者において、機関投資家に対する認識が一層深まり、本コードが我が国において更に広く定着していく効果が期待できるものと考えられる。

----

1 指針の中には、一定の事項が「重要である」とするなど、必ずしも一定の行動を取るべき・取るべきでない」旨が明示されていないものがあり、こうした指針については、必ずしも、実施しない理由を説明することを求めるものではない。

する「ルールベース・アプローチ」（細則主義）ではなく、機関投資家が各々の置かれた状況に応じて、自らのスチュワードシップ責任を実効的に果たすことができるよう、いわゆる「プリンシプルベース・アプローチ」（原則主義）を採用している。

「プリンシプルベース・アプローチ」の意義は、我が国では、いまだ馴染みの薄い面があると考えられるため、その意義を、一見、抽象的で大掴みな原則（プリンシプル）について、関係者がその趣旨・精神を共有し、互いに受け止めて、各自、自らの活動が、形式的な文言・記載ではなく、その趣旨・精神に照らして真に適切か否かを判断することにあることにある。機関投資家が本コードを踏まえて行動するに当たっては、こうした「プリンシプルベース・アプローチ」の意義を十分に踏まえることが望まれる。

11. 本コードは、法令とは異なり、法的拘束力を有する規範ではない。本検討会は、本コードの趣旨に賛同しこれを受け入れる用意がある機関投資家が、これを受け入れることを期待する。

12. その上で、本コードは、いわゆる「コンプライ・オア・エクスプレイン」（原則を実施するか、実施しない場合には、その理由を説明するか）の手法を採用する。すなわち、本コードの原則の中に、自らの個別事情に照らして実施することが適切でないと考える原則があれば、それを「実施しない理由」を十分に説明することにより、一部の原則を実施しないことも想定している。したがって、前記の受入れ表明を行った機関投資家であっても、全ての原則を一律に実施しなければならない訳ではなく、例えば、当然のこととして、機関投資家が、顧客・受益者の理解が十分に得られるよう工夫すべきである。

13. こうしたコンプライ・オア・エクスプレインの手法も、我が国では、いまだ馴染みの薄い面があると考えられる。機関投資家のみならず、顧客・受益者においても、当該手法の趣旨を理解し、本コードの受入れを表明した機関投資家の個別の状況に応じ、その全てを実施していないことをもって、機械的に評価することは適切ではない。その一部を実施していないことをもって、機械的に評価することは適切ではない。なお、原則を実施しつつ、併せて自らの具体的な取組みについて説明を行うことも、顧客・受益者から十分な理解を得る観点からは、有益であると考えられる。

14・13. 機関投資家が本コードの受入れ状況を可視化するため、本コードを受け入れる場合には、以下を自らのウェブサイトで公表すること。

・ 以下を自らのウェブサイトで公表すること

93

原則1 機関投資家は、スチュワードシップ責任を果たすための明確な方針を策定し、これを公表すべきである。

指針

1−1. 機関投資家は、投資先企業やその事業環境等に関する深い理解に基づく建設的な「目的を持った対話」[5](エンゲージメント)などを通じて、当該企業の中長期的な企業価値の向上やその持続的成長を促し、顧客・受益者の中長期的な投資リターンの拡大を図るべきである。

1−2. 機関投資家は、こうした認識の下、スチュワードシップ責任を果たすための方針、すなわち、スチュワードシップ責任をどのように考え、その考えに則って当該責任をどのように果たしていくのか、また、顧客・受益者から投資先企業へと向かう投資資金の流れ(インベストメント・チェーン)の中での自らの置かれた位置を踏まえ、どのような役割を果たすのかについての明確な方針を策定し、これを公表すべきである[6]。

1−3. アセットオーナーは、最終受益者の利益の確保のため、可能な限り、自らスチュワードシップ活動に取り組むべきである。また、自ら直接的に議決権行使を含むスチュワードシップ活動を行わない場合には、運用機関に、実効的なスチュワードシップ活動を行うよう求めるべきである。

1−4. アセットオーナーは、運用機関による実効的なスチュワードシップ活動が行われるよう、運用機関の選定や運用委託契約の締結に際して、議決権行使を含むスチュワードシップ活動に関して運用機関に求める事項や原則を明確に示すべきである。特に大規模なアセットオーナーにおいては、インベストメント・チェーンの中での自らの置かれている位置・役割を踏まえ、運用機関の方針を検証し(単に確認するのではなく)、自ら主体的に検討を行った上で、スチュワードシップ責任を果たす観点から、自らのスチュワードシップ活動に関して求める事項や原則を明確に示すべきである。

---

[5] 「目的を持った対話」とは、「中長期的視点から投資先企業の企業価値及び資本効率を高め、その持続的成長を促すことを目的とした対話」を指す(原則4の指針4−1参照)。

[6] 当該方針の内容は、各機関投資家の業務の違いにより、例えば、主として資産運用を行っている機関投資家と、主として資産保有者としてのアセットオーナーとでは、自ずと異なり得る。

本コードの原則

投資先企業の持続的成長を促し、顧客・受益者の中長期的な投資リターンの拡大を図るために、

1. 機関投資家は、スチュワードシップ責任を果たすための明確な方針を策定し、これを公表すべきである。

2. 機関投資家は、スチュワードシップ責任を果たす上で管理すべき利益相反について、明確な方針を策定し、これを公表すべきである。

3. 機関投資家は、投資先企業の持続的成長に向けてスチュワードシップ責任を果たすため、当該企業の状況を的確に把握すべきである。

4. 機関投資家は、投資先企業との建設的な「目的を持った対話」を通じて、投資先企業と認識の共有を図るとともに、問題の改善に努めるべきである。

5. 機関投資家は、議決権の行使と行使結果の公表について明確な方針を持つとともに、議決権行使の方針については、単に形式的な判断基準にとどまるのではなく、投資先企業の持続的成長に資するものとなるよう工夫すべきである。

6. 機関投資家は、議決権の行使も含め、スチュワードシップ責任をどのように果たしているのかについて、原則として、顧客・受益者に対して定期的に報告を行うべきである。

7. 機関投資家は、投資先企業の持続的成長に資するよう、投資先企業やその事業環境等に関する深い理解に基づき、当該企業との対話やスチュワードシップ活動に伴う判断を適切に行うための実力を備えるべきである。

1-5. アセットオーナーは、運用機関のスチュワードシップ活動が自らの方針と整合的なものとなっているかについて、運用機関の自己評価なども活用しながら、実効的に運用機関に対するモニタリングを行うべきである。このモニタリングに際しては、運用機関と投資先企業との間の対話の「質」に重点を置くべきであり、運用機関と投資先企業との面談時間や回数、面談時間等の形式的な確認に終始すべきではない。

原則2　機関投資家は、スチュワードシップ責任を果たす上で管理すべき利益相反について、明確な方針を策定し、これを公表すべきである。

指針

2-1. 機関投資家は顧客・受益者の利益を第一として行動すべきである。一方で、スチュワードシップ活動を行うに当たっては、自らが所属する企業グループと顧客・受益者の双方に影響を及ぼす事項について議決権を行使する場合など、利益相反の発生が避けられない場合がある。機関投資家は、こうした利益相反を適切に管理することが重要である。

2-2. 機関投資家は、こうした認識の下、あらかじめ想定し得る利益相反の主な類型について、これをどのように実効的に管理するのかについての明確な方針を策定し、これを公表すべきである。
特に、運用機関は、議決権行使や対話に重要な影響を及ぼす利益相反が生じ得る局面を具体的に特定し、それぞれの利益相反を回避し、その影響を実効的に排除するなど、顧客・受益者の利益を確保するための措置について具体的な方針を策定し、これを公表すべきである。

2-3. 運用機関は、顧客・受益者の利益の確保や利益相反防止のため、例えば、独立した取締役会や議決権行使の意思決定や監督のための第三者委員会などのガバナンス体制を整備すべきである。

2-4. 運用機関の経営陣は、自らが運用機関のガバナンス強化・利益相反管理に関して重要な役割・責務を担っていることを認識し、これらに関する課題に対する取組みを推進すべきである。

原則 4 機関投資家は、投資先企業との建設的な「目的を持った対話」を通じて、投資先企業と認識の共有を図るとともに、問題の改善に努めるべきである。

指針

4-1. 機関投資家は、中長期的視点から投資先企業の企業価値及び資本効率を高め、その持続的成長に向けて投資先企業との間で建設的に行うことを目的とした対話[8]を、当該企業との共有を図るよう努めるべきである。

なお、投資先企業の状況や当該企業との対話の内容等を踏まえ、当該企業の企業価値が毀損されるおそれがあると考えられる場合には、より十分な説明を求めるなど、投資先企業と更なる認識の共有を図るとともに、問題の改善に努めるべきである[10]。

4-2. パッシブ運用は、投資先企業の株式を売却する選択肢が限られ、中長期的な企業価値の向上を促す必要性が高いことから、機関投資家は、パッシブ運用を行うに当たって、より積極的に中長期的視点に立った対話や議決権行使に取り組むべきである。

4-2-3. 機関投資家は、実際に起こり得る様々な局面に応じ、投資先企業との間でどのように対話を行うのかなどについて、あらかじめ明確な方針を持つべきである[11]。

4-4. 機関投資家が投資先企業との間で対話を行うに当たっては、単独でこうした対話を行うほか、必要に応じ、他の機関投資家と協働して対話を行うこと(集団的エンゲージメント)が有益な場合もあり得る[12]。

[8] その際、対話を行うこと自体が目的であるかのような「形式主義」に陥ることのないよう留意すべきことに加え、機関投資家と投資先企業との間で意見が一致しない場合においても、一致の理由やお互いの意見の背景について理解を深めていくことにも考えられる。

[9] 当該企業との対話の内容等を踏まえ、更に深い対話を行うよう選択することにも考えられる。

[10] 当該方針の内容は、主として資産保有者であるアセットオーナーとしての機関投資家とでは、自ずと異なり得る。

[11] 当該方針の内容は、例えば、主として資産保有者であるアセットオーナーとしての機関投資家と、主として資産運用者であるアセットマネージャーとしての機関投資家とでは、自ずと異なり得る。

[12] この点に関しては、平成26年2月に公表された金融庁の「日本版スチュワードシップ・コードの策定を踏まえた論点の整理」(http://www.fsa.go.jp/singi/stewardship/legalissue.pdf)(再掲)は、具体的にどのような場合に大量保有報告制度における「共同保有者」及び公開買付制度における「特別関係者」に該当するかについて、解釈の明確化を図っている。

原則 3 機関投資家は、投資先企業の持続的成長に向けてスチュワードシップ責任を適切に果たすため、当該企業の状況を的確に把握すべきである。

指針

3-1. 機関投資家は、中長期的視点から投資先企業の企業価値及び資本効率を高め、その持続的成長に向けてスチュワードシップ責任を果たすため、当該企業の状況を的確に把握することが必要である。

3-2. 機関投資家は、こうした投資先企業の状況の把握を継続的に行うべきであり、また、実効的な把握ができているかについて適切に確認すべきである。

3-3. 把握する内容としては、例えば、投資先企業のガバナンス、企業戦略、業績、資本構造、事業におけるリスク・収益機会(社会・環境問題への対応など、非財務面の事項を含む)及びそうしたリスクへの対応など、特にどのような事項に着目すべきかについては、機関投資家ごとに運用方針には違いがあり、また、投資先企業ごとに把握すべき事項の重要性も異なることから、機関投資家は、自らのスチュワードシップ責任に照らし、自ら判断を行うべきである。その際、投資先企業の企業価値を毀損するおそれのある事項については、これを早期に把握することができるよう努めるべきである。

[7] 「ガバナンス」と共に、ESG要素と呼ばれる。

原則5 機関投資家は、議決権の行使と行使結果の公表について明確な方針を持つとともに、議決権行使の方針については、単に形式的な判断基準にとどまるのではなく、投資先企業の持続的成長に資するものとなるよう工夫すべきである。

指針

5-1. 機関投資家は、すべての保有株式について議決権を行使するよう努めるべきであり、議決権の行使については、投資先企業の状況や当該企業との対話の内容等を踏まえた上で、議案に対する賛否を判断すべきである。

5-2. 機関投資家は、議決権の行使について明確な方針を策定し、これを公表すべきである[14]。当該方針は、できる限り明確なものとすべきであるが、単に形式的な判断基準にとどまるのではなく、投資先企業の持続的成長に資するものとなるよう工夫すべきである。

5-3. 機関投資家は、議決権の行使結果を、少なくとも議案の主な種類ごとに整理・集計して公表すべきである。

こうした公表に加え、また、機関投資家がスチュワードシップ責任を果たすための方針に沿って適切に議決権を行使しているか否かについての可視性をさらに高める観点から、機関投資家は、議決権の行使結果を、個別の投資先企業及び議案ごとに公表すべきである[15]。それぞれの機関投資家の置かれた状況により、個別の投資先企業及び議案ごとに公表することが必ずしも適切でないと考えられる場合には、その理由を積極的に説明すべきである。

議決権の行使結果を公表する際、機関投資家が議決権行使の賛否の理由について対外的に明確に説明することも、可視性を高めることに資すると考えられる。

ただし、スチュワードシップ責任を果たすための活動に重点を置くべきとかは、自らのスチュワードシップ責任を果たすための方針・運用方針...

---

14 なお、投資先企業の議決権の行使をまたぐ貸株取引を行うことを想定している場合には、当該方針において、こうした貸株取引についての方針を記載すべきである。

15 個別の議決権行使結果を公表するのではないかとの懸念が指摘されている。
しかし、運用機関は、自らが運用する資産の最終受益者に向けて、活動の透明性を高めていくことが重要である。さらに、我が国では、金融グループ系列の運用機関が多く見られるところ、こうした運用機関において、議決権行使をめぐる親子上場等の利益相反への懸念が生じかねない状況が見られる。個別の議決権行使結果を公表することは、こうした懸念を払拭することにもつながると考えられ、個別の議決権行使結果を公表することが重要である。

4-3-5. 一般に、機関投資家は、未公表の重要事実を受領することなく、公表された情報をもとに、投資先企業との建設的な「目的を持った対話」を行うことが可能である。また、「G20/OECDコーポレート・ガバナンス原則」や、これを踏まえて策定された東京証券取引所の「上場会社コーポレート・ガバナンス・コード」は、企業の未公表の重要事実の取扱いについて、株主間の平等を図ることを基本としている。投資先企業と対話を行う機関投資家は、企業がこうした基本原則の下に置かれていることを踏まえ、当該対話において未公表の重要事実を受領することについては、基本的には慎重に考えるべきである[13]。

---

13 その上で、投資先企業との特別な関係等に基づく未公表の重要事実を受領する場合には、当該企業の株式の売買を停止するなど、インサイダー取引規制に抵触することを防止するための措置を講じた上で、当該企業との対話に臨むべきである。

原則6 機関投資家は、議決権の行使も含め、スチュワードシップ責任をどのように果たしているのかについて、原則として、顧客・受益者に対して定期的に報告を行うべきである。

指針

6-1. 「資産運用者としての機関投資家」は、顧客・受益者に対して、スチュワードシップ活動を通じてスチュワードシップ責任をどのように果たしているのかについて、定期的に報告を行うべきである。[16]

6-2. 「資産保有者としての機関投資家」「アセットオーナー」は、受益者に対して、スチュワードシップ責任を果たすための方針と、当該方針の実施状況について、原則として、少なくとも年に1度、報告を行うべきである。[16]

6-3. 機関投資家は、顧客・受益者への報告の具体的な様式や内容については、顧客・受益者との合意や、顧客・受益者のニーズ、コストなども考慮して決めるべきであり、効果的かつ効率的な報告を行うよう工夫すべきである。[17]

6-4. なお、機関投資家は、議決権の行使活動を含むスチュワードシップ活動について、スチュワードシップ責任を果たすために必要な範囲において記録に残すべきである。

---

16 ただし、当該報告の相手方自身が個別報告は不要との意思を示しているようような場合には、この限りではない。また、顧客・受益者に対する個別報告が事実上困難な場合などには、当該報告に代えて、一般に公開可能な情報を公表することも考えられる。
17 なお、当該報告において、資産運用上の秘密等を明かすことを求めるものではない。

顧客・受益者の特性等により様々に異なり得るものであるため、こうした点に照らし、前記の集計結果を公表により他に代わる他の方法により議決権の行使結果を公表する方が、自らのスチュワードシップ活動全体についてより的確な理解を得られると考えられる場合には、その理由を説明しつつ、当該他の方法により議決権行使結果の公表を行うことも考えられる。

5-4. 機関投資家は、議決権行使助言会社のサービスを利用する場合であっても、議決権行使助言会社の助言に機械的に依拠するのではなく、投資先企業の状況や当該企業との対話の内容等を踏まえ、自らの責任と判断の下で議決権を行使すべきである。仮に、議決権行使助言会社のサービスを利用している場合には、議決権行使助言会社の名称及び当該サービスをどのように活用したのかについても公表すべきである。

5-5. 議決権行使助言会社は、企業の状況の的確な把握等のために十分な経営資源を投入し、また、本コードの各原則（指針を含む）が自らに当てはまることに留意して、適切にサービスを提供すべきである。
また、議決権行使助言会社は、業務の体制や利益相反管理、助言の策定プロセスに関し、自らの取組みを公表すべきである。

原則7 機関投資家は、投資先企業の持続的成長に資するよう、投資先企業やその事業環境等に関する深い理解に基づき、当該企業との対話やスチュワードシップ活動に伴う判断を適切に行うための実力を備えるべきである。

指針

7-1. 機関投資家は、投資先との対話を建設的なものとし、かつ、当該企業の持続的成長に資する有益なものとしていく観点から、投資先企業やその事業環境等に関する深い理解に基づき、当該企業との対話やスチュワードシップ活動に伴う判断を適切に行うための実力を備えていることが重要である。

7-2. このため、機関投資家は、こうした対話や判断を適切に行うために必要な体制の整備を行うべきである。

7-2. 特に、機関投資家の経営陣はスチュワードシップ責任を実効的に果たすための適切な能力・経験を備えているべきであり、系列の金融グループ内部の論理などに基づいて構成されるべきではない。
また、機関投資家の経営陣は、自らが対話の充実等のスチュワードシップ活動の実行とそのための組織構築・人材育成に関して重要な役割・責務を担っているとことを認識し、これらに関する取組みを推進すべきである。

7-3. こうした対話や判断を適切に行うための一助として、必要に応じ、機関投資家が、他の投資家との意見交換を行うことやそのための場を設けることとも有益であると考えられる。

7-4. また、機関投資家は、過去に行った投資先企業との対話やスチュワードシップ活動に伴う判断の機会（指針を含む）について、これらが適切であったか否かやホームコードの各原則（指針を含む）の実施状況を適宜の時期に省みることにより、スチュワードシップ責任を果たすための方針や議決権行使の方針など、将来のスチュワードシップ活動がより適切なものとなるよう努めるべきである。
特に、運用機関は、持続的な自らのガバナンス体制・利益相反管理や、自らのスチュワードシップ活動の改善に向けて、ホームコードの各原則（指針を含む）の実施状況を定期的に自己評価し、結果を公表すべきである[18]。

[18] こうした自己評価の結果の公表は、アセットオーナーが運用機関の選定や評価を行うことにも資すると考えられる。

– 18 –

INSTITUTIONAL SHAREHOLDERS' COMMITTEE

CODE ON THE RESPONSIBILITIES OF INSTITUTIONAL INVESTORS

Introduction & Scope

This Code has been drawn up by the Institutional Shareholders' Committee[1] and covers the activities of both institutional shareholders and those that invest as agents, including reporting by the latter to their clients.

The Code aims to enhance the quality of the dialogue of institutional investors with companies to help improve long-term returns to shareholders, reduce the risk of catastrophic outcomes due to bad strategic decisions, and help with the efficient exercise of governance responsibilities.

The Code sets out best practice for institutional investors that choose to engage with the companies in which they invest. The Code does not constitute an obligation to micro-manage the affairs of investee companies or preclude a decision to sell a holding, where this is considered the most effective response to concerns.

In the Code the term "institutional investor" includes institutional shareholders such as pension funds, insurance companies, and investment trusts and other collective investment vehicles and any agents appointed to act on their behalf.

Institutional shareholders' mandates given to fund managers or agents should specify the policy on stewardship, if any, that is to be followed.

Institutional shareholders are free to choose whether or not to engage but their choice should be a considered one, based on their investment objectives. Their managers or agents are then responsible for ensuring that they comply with the terms of the mandate as agreed[2].

The Code applies to institutional investors on a comply-or-explain basis. Institutional investors that do not wish to engage should state publicly that the Code is not relevant to them and explain why.

---

[1] ISC members are: the Association of British Insurers; the Association of Investment Trust Companies; the National Association of Pension Funds; and the Investment Management Association.

[2] In the case of pension funds best practice is set out in the 2008 Myners' Principles under Principle 5:
- * Trustees should adopt, or ensure their investment managers adopt, the Institutional Shareholders' Committee Statement of Principles on the responsibilities of shareholders and agents.
- A statement of the scheme's policy on responsible ownership should be included in the Statement of Investment Principles.
- Trustees should report periodically to members on the discharge of such responsibilities.

Institutional investors that elect to engage should provide a statement on how they implement the Principles in practice. Institutional investors that apply the Code will be listed on the ISC's website (www.institutionalshareholderscommittee.org.uk). This statement should contain information on what steps have been or will be taken in respect of verification.

Fulfilling fiduciary obligations to end-beneficiaries in accordance with the spirit of the Code may have implications for institutional investors' resources. These should be sufficient to allow them to fulfill their responsibilities effectively, commensurate with the benefits derived. The duty of institutional investors is to their end-beneficiaries and/or clients and not to the wider public.

The Code may also be applied by overseas investors, including Sovereign Wealth Funds. The ISC would welcome their commitment to the Code and may also list those that choose to sign up on the ISC's website. The Code will be reviewed biennially by the ISC in line with the FRC's review process for the Combined Code.

Principle 1: Institutional investors should publicly disclose their policy on how they will discharge their stewardship responsibilities

Guidance

The policy should include:

- How investee companies will be monitored. In order for monitoring to be effective, where necessary, an active dialogue may need to be entered into with the investee company's board.

- The strategy on intervention.

- Internal arrangements, including how stewardship is integrated with the wider investment process.

- The policy on voting and the use made of, if any, proxy voting or other voting advisory service, including information on how they are used (see Principle 6).

- The policy on considering explanations made in relation to the Combined Code.

Principle 2: Institutional investors should have a robust policy on managing conflicts of interest in relation to stewardship and this policy should be publicly disclosed.

<u>Guidance</u>

An institutional investor's duty is to act in the interests of all clients and/or beneficiaries when considering matters such as engagement and voting.

Conflicts of interest will inevitably arise from time to time, which may include when voting on matters affecting a parent company or client.

Institutional investors should put in place and maintain a policy for managing conflicts of interest.

Principle 3: Institutional investors should monitor their investee companies

<u>Guidance</u>

Investee companies should be monitored to determine when it is necessary to enter into an active dialogue with their boards. This monitoring should be regular, and the process clearly communicable and checked periodically for its effectiveness.

As part of this monitoring, institutional investors should:

- seek to satisfy themselves, to the extent possible, that the investee company's board and sub-committee structures are effective, and that independent directors provide adequate oversight; and

- maintain a clear audit trail, for example, records of private meetings held with companies, of votes cast, and of reasons for voting against the investee company's management, for abstaining, or for voting with management in a contentious situation.

Institutional investors should endeavour to identify problems at an early stage to minimise any loss of shareholder value. If they have concerns they should seek to ensure that the appropriate members of the investee company's board are made aware of them.

Institutional investors may not wish to be made insiders. They will expect investee companies and their advisers to ensure that information that could affect their ability to deal in the shares of the company concerned is not conveyed to them without their agreement.

Principle 4: Institutional investors should establish clear guidelines on when and how they will escalate their activities as a method of protecting and enhancing shareholder value

<u>Guidance</u>

Institutional investors should set out the circumstances when they will actively intervene and regularly assess the outcomes of doing so. Intervention should be considered regardless of whether an active or passive investment policy is followed. In addition, being underweight is not, of itself, a reason for not intervening. Instances when institutional investors may want to intervene include when they have concerns about the company's strategy and performance, its governance or its approach to the risks arising from social and environmental matters.

Initial discussions should take place on a confidential basis. However, if boards do not respond constructively when institutional investors intervene, then institutional investors will consider whether to escalate their action, for example, by:

- holding additional meetings with management specifically to discuss concerns;

- expressing concerns through the company's advisers;

- meeting with the Chairman, senior independent director, or with all independent directors;

- intervening jointly with other institutions on particular issues;

- making a public statement in advance of the AGM or an EGM;

- submitting resolutions at shareholders' meetings; and

- requisitioning an EGM, possibly to change the board.

Principle 5: Institutional investors should be willing to act collectively with other investors where appropriate

<u>Guidance</u>

At times collaboration with other investors may be the most effective manner in which to engage.

Collaborative engagement may be most appropriate at times of significant corporate or wider economic stress, or when the risks posed threaten the ability of the company to continue.

Institutional investors should disclose their policy on collective engagement.

Institutional investors when participating in collective engagement should have due regard to their policies on conflicts of interest and insider information.

Principle 6: Institutional investors should have a clear policy on voting and disclosure of voting activity

Guidance

Institutional investors should seek to vote all shares held. They should not automatically support the board.

If they have been unable to reach a satisfactory outcome through active dialogue then they should register an abstention or vote against the resolution. In both instances, it is good practice to inform the company in advance of their intention and the reasons why.

Institutional investors should disclose publicly voting records and if they do not explain why.

Principle 7: Institutional investors should report periodically on their stewardship and voting activities

Guidance

Those that act as agents should regularly report to their clients details on how they have discharged their responsibilities. Such reports will be likely to comprise both qualitative as well as quantitative information. The particular information reported, including the format in which details of how votes have been cast are be presented, should be a matter for agreement between agents and their principals.

Transparency is an important feature of effective stewardship. Institutional investors should not, however, be expected to make disclosures that might be counterproductive. Confidentiality in specific situations may well be crucial to achieving a positive outcome.

Those that act as principals, or represent the interests of the end-investor, should report at least annually to those to whom they are accountable on their policy and its execution.

Those that sign up to this Code should consider obtaining an independent audit opinion on their engagement and voting processes having regard to the standards in AAF 01/06[3] and SAS 70.[4] The existence of such assurance certification should be publicly disclosed.

[3] Assurance reports on internal controls of service organisations made available to third parties
[4] Statement on Auditing Standards No.70: Reports on the processing of transactions by service organizations

FINANCIAL REPORTING COUNCIL

THE UK STEWARDSHIP CODE

JULY 2010

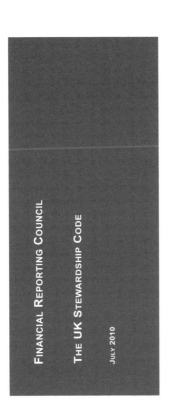

PREFACE

The Stewardship Code aims to enhance the quality of engagement between institutional investors and companies to help improve long-term returns to shareholders and the efficient exercise of governance responsibilities. Engagement includes pursuing purposeful dialogue on strategy, performance and the management of risk, as well as on issues that are the immediate subject of votes at general meetings.

The Code sets out good practice on engagement with investee companies to which the FRC believes institutional investors should aspire. It provides an opportunity to build a critical mass of UK and overseas investors committed to the high quality dialogue with companies needed to underpin good governance. By creating a sound basis of engagement it should create a much needed stronger link between governance and the investment process, and lend greater substance to the concept of "comply or explain" as applied by listed companies. The FRC therefore sees it as complementary to the UK Corporate Governance Code for listed companies, as revised in June 2010.

Institutional shareholders are free to choose whether or not to engage but their choice should be a considered one based on their investment approach. Their managers or agents are then responsible for ensuring that they comply with the terms of the mandate as agreed.

Disclosures made by institutions under the Code should assist companies to understand the approach and expectations of their major shareholders. They should also assist those issuing mandates to institutional fund managers to make a better informed choice, thereby improving the functioning of the market and facilitating the exercise of responsibility to end-investors.

As with the UK Corporate Governance Code, the Code should be applied on a "comply or explain" basis. In reporting terms this entails providing a statement on the institution's website that contains:

- a description of how the principles of the Code have been applied, and

- disclosure of the specific information listed under Principles 1, 5, 6 and 7; or

- an explanation if these elements of the Code have not been complied with.

It should be noted that compliance with the Code does not constitute an invitation to manage the affairs of investee companies or preclude a decision to sell a holding, where this is considered in the best interest of end-investors.

1

The Code is addressed in the first instance to firms who manage assets on behalf of institutional shareholders such as pension funds, insurance companies, investment trusts and other collective investment vehicles. The FRC expects those firms to disclose on their websites how they have applied the Code. Institutions that manage several types of fund need to make only one statement.

However the responsibility for monitoring company performance does not rest with fund managers alone. Pension fund trustees and other owners can do so either directly or indirectly through the mandates given to fund managers. Their actions can have a significant impact on the quality and quantity of engagement with UK companies. The FRC therefore strongly encourages all institutional investors to report if and how they have complied with the Code.

Principle 1 of the Code states that institutional investors that make use of proxy voting and other advisory services should disclose how they are used. The FRC encourages those service providers in turn to disclose how they carry out the wishes of their clients by applying the principles of the Code that are relevant to their activities.

The FRC recognises that not all parts of the Code will be relevant to all institutional investors, while smaller institutions may judge that some of its principles and guidance are disproportionate in their case. In these circumstances, they should take advantage of the "comply or explain" approach and set out why this is the case.

Specifically, the "explain" option means that overseas investors who follow other national or international standards that have similar objectives should not feel application of the Code duplicates or confuses their responsibilities. Disclosures made in respect of those standards can also be used to demonstrate the extent to which they have complied with the Code. In a similar spirit, UK institutions that apply the Code should use their best efforts to apply its principles to overseas holdings.

The FRC will retain on its website a list of those investors that have published a statement on their compliance or otherwise with the Code, and requests that they notify the FRC when they have done so. The FRC also considers that it would be good practice for each institution to name in its statement an individual who can be contacted for further information and by those interested in collective engagement.

The FRC will carry out regular monitoring of the take-up and application of the Code.

The FRC expects the content of the Code to evolve over time to reflect developments in good engagement practice, in the structure and operation of the market, and the broader regulatory framework, and it will need to give further consideration to issues raised in response to the consultation on this Code in the same light. A decision on the timing of the first review of the content of the Code will be taken in the second half of 2011.

Financial Reporting Council
July 2010

THE PRINCIPLES OF THE CODE

Institutional investors should:

- publicly disclose their policy on how they will discharge their stewardship responsibilities.

- have a robust policy on managing conflicts of interest in relation to stewardship and this policy should be publicly disclosed.

- monitor their investee companies.

- establish clear guidelines on when and how they will escalate their activities as a method of protecting and enhancing shareholder value.

- be willing to act collectively with other investors where appropriate.

- have a clear policy on voting and disclosure of voting activity.

- report periodically on their stewardship and voting activities.

THE UK STEWARDSHIP CODE

Principle 1

Institutional investors should publicly disclose their policy on how they will discharge their stewardship responsibilities.

Guidance

The disclosure should include:

- how investee companies will be monitored. In order for monitoring to be effective an active dialogue may, where necessary, need to be entered into with the investee company's board;

- the strategy on intervention;

- internal arrangements, including how stewardship is integrated with the wider investment process;

- the policy on voting and the use made of, if any, proxy voting or other voting advisory service, including information on how they are used; and

- the policy on considering explanations made in relation to the UK Corporate Governance Code.

Principle 2

Institutional investors should have a robust policy on managing conflicts of interest in relation to stewardship and this policy should be publicly disclosed.

Guidance

An institutional investor's duty is to act in the interests of all clients and/or beneficiaries when considering matters such as engagement and voting.

Conflicts of interest will inevitably arise from time to time, which may include when voting on matters affecting a parent company or client.

Institutional investors should put in place and maintain a policy for managing conflicts of interest.

Principle 3

Institutional investors should monitor their investee companies.

Guidance

Investee companies should be monitored to determine when it is necessary to enter into an active dialogue with their boards. This monitoring should be regular, and the process clearly communicable and checked periodically for its effectiveness.

As part of this monitoring, institutional investors should:

* seek to satisfy themselves, to the extent possible, that the investee company's board and committee structures are effective, and that independent directors provide adequate oversight, including by meeting the chairman and, where appropriate, other board members;

* maintain a clear audit trail, for example, records of private meetings held with companies, of votes cast, and of reasons for voting against the investee company's management, for abstaining, or for voting with management in a contentious situation; and

* attend the General Meetings of companies in which they have a major holding, where appropriate and practicable.

Institutional investors should consider carefully explanations given for departure from the UK Corporate Governance Code and make reasoned judgements in each case. They should give a timely explanation to the company, in writing where appropriate, and be prepared to enter a dialogue if they do not accept the company's position.

Institutional investors should endeavour to identify problems at an early stage to minimise any loss of shareholder value. If they have concerns they should seek to ensure that the appropriate members of the investee company's board are made aware of them.

Institutional investors may not wish to be made insiders. They will expect investee companies and their advisers to ensure that information that could affect their ability to deal in the shares of the company concerned is not conveyed to them without their agreement.

106

Principle 4

Institutional investors should establish clear guidelines on when and how they will escalate their activities as a method of protecting and enhancing shareholder value.

Guidance

Institutional investors should set out the circumstances when they will actively intervene and regularly assess the outcomes of doing so. Intervention should be considered regardless of whether an active or passive investment policy is followed. In addition, being underweight is not, of itself, a reason for not intervening. Instances when institutional investors may want to intervene include when they have concerns about the company's strategy and performance, its governance or its approach to the risks arising from social and environmental matters.

Initial discussions should take place on a confidential basis. However, if boards do not respond constructively when institutional investors intervene, then institutional investors will consider whether to escalate their action, for example, by:

* holding additional meetings with management specifically to discuss concerns;

* expressing concerns through the company's advisers;

* meeting with the chairman, senior independent director, or with all independent directors;

* intervening jointly with other institutions on particular issues;

* making a public statement in advance of the AGM or an EGM;

* submitting resolutions at shareholders' meetings; and

* requisitioning an EGM, in some cases proposing to change board membership.

Principle 5

Institutional investors should be willing to act collectively with other investors where appropriate.

Guidance

At times collaboration with other investors may be the most effective manner in which to engage.

Collaborative engagement may be most appropriate at times of significant corporate or wider economic stress, or when the risks posed threaten the ability of the company to continue.

Institutional investors should disclose their policy on collective engagement.

When participating in collective engagement, institutional investors should have due regard to their policies on conflicts of interest and insider information.

Principle 6

Institutional investors should have a clear policy on voting and disclosure of voting activity.

Guidance

Institutional investors should seek to vote all shares held. They should not automatically support the board.

If they have been unable to reach a satisfactory outcome through active dialogue then they should register an abstention or vote against the resolution. In both instances, it is good practice to inform the company in advance of their intention and the reasons why.

Institutional investors should disclose publicly voting records and if they do not explain why.

Principle 7

Institutional investors should report periodically on their stewardship and voting activities.

Guidance

Those that act as agents should regularly report to their clients details of how they have discharged their responsibilities. Such reports will be likely to comprise qualitative as well as quantitative information. The particular information reported, including the format in which details of how votes have been cast are presented, should be a matter for agreement between agents and their principals.

Transparency is an important feature of effective stewardship. Institutional investors should not, however, be expected to make disclosures that might be counterproductive. Confidentiality in specific situations may well be crucial to achieving a positive outcome.

Those that act as principals, or represent the interests of the end-investor, should report at least annually to those to whom they are accountable on their policy and its execution.

Those that sign up to this Code should consider obtaining an independent audit opinion on their engagement and voting processes having regard to the standards in AAF 01/06[1] and SAS 70[2]. The existence of such assurance certification should be publicly disclosed.

---

[1] Assurance reports on internal controls of service organisations made available to third parties.
[2] Statement on Auditing Standards No.70: Reports on the processing of transactions by service organizations.

FINANCIAL REPORTING COUNCIL
5TH FLOOR
ALDWYCH HOUSE
71-91 ALDWYCH
LONDON WC2B 4HN
TEL: +44 (0)20 7492 2300
FAX: +44 (0)20 7492 2301
WEBSITE: www.frc.org.uk

ISBN 978-1-84798-335-0

9 781847 983350

UP/FRC-BI10008

10

Code

Corporate Governance

FRC Financial Reporting Council

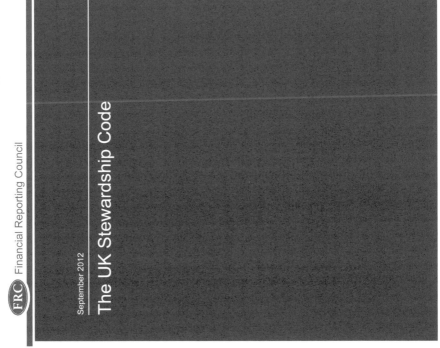

September 2012

The UK Stewardship Code

Contents

Stewardship and the Code

1. Stewardship aims to promote the long term success of companies in such a way that the ultimate providers of capital also prosper. Effective stewardship benefits companies, investors and the economy as a whole.

2. In publicly listed companies responsibility for stewardship is shared. The primary responsibility rests with the board of the company, which oversees the actions of its management. Investors in the company also play an important role in holding the board to account for the fulfilment of its responsibilities.

3. The UK Corporate Governance Code identifies the principles that underlie an effective board. The UK Stewardship Code sets out the principles of effective stewardship by investors. In so doing, the Code assists institutional investors better to exercise their stewardship responsibilities, which in turn gives force to the "comply or explain" system.

4. For investors, stewardship is more than just voting. Activities may include monitoring and engaging with companies on matters such as strategy, performance, risk, capital structure, and corporate governance, including culture and remuneration. Engagement is purposeful dialogue with companies on these matters as well as on issues that are the immediate subject of votes at general meetings.

5. Institutional investors' activities include decision-making on matters such as allocating assets, awarding investment mandates, designing investment strategies, and buying or selling specific securities. The division of duties within and between institutions may span a spectrum, such that some may be considered asset owners and others asset managers.

6. Broadly speaking, asset owners include pension funds, insurance companies, investment trusts and other collective investment vehicles. As the providers of capital, they set the tone for stewardship and may influence behavioural changes that lead to better stewardship by asset managers and companies. Asset managers, with day-to-day responsibility for managing investments, are well positioned to influence companies' long-term performance through stewardship.

7. Compliance with the Code does not constitute an invitation to manage the affairs of a company or preclude a decision to sell a holding, where this is considered in the best interest of clients or beneficiaries.

110

Application of the Code

1. The UK Stewardship Code traces its origins to "The Responsibilities of Institutional Shareholders and Agents: Statement of Principles," first published in 2002 by the Institutional Shareholders Committee (ISC), and which the ISC converted to a code in 2009. Following the 2009 Walker Review of governance in financial institutions, the FRC was invited to take responsibility for the UK Code. In 2010, the FRC published the first version of the UK Stewardship Code, which closely mirrored the ISC code. This edition of the Code does not change the spirit of the 2010 Code.

2. The Code is directed in the first instance to institutional investors, by which is meant asset owners and asset managers with equity holdings in UK listed companies. Institutional investors may choose to outsource to external service providers some of the activities associated with stewardship. However, they cannot delegate their responsibility for stewardship. They remain responsible for ensuring those activities are carried out in a manner consistent with their own approach to stewardship. Accordingly, the Code also applies, by extension, to service providers, such as proxy advisors and investment consultants.

3. The FRC expects signatories of the Code to publish on their website, or if they do not have a website in another accessible form, a statement that:

    - describes how the signatory has applied each of the seven principles of the Code and discloses the specific information requested in the guidance to the principles; or

    - if one or more of the principles have not been applied or the specific information requested in the guidance has not been disclosed, explains why the signatory has not complied with those elements of the Code.

4. Disclosures under the Code should improve the functioning of the market for investment mandates. Asset owners should be better equipped to evaluate asset managers, and asset managers should be better informed, enabling them to tailor their services to meet asset owners' requirements.

5. In particular the disclosures should, with respect to conflicts of interest, address the priority given to client interests in decision-making; with respect to collective engagement, describe the circumstances under which the signatory would join forces with other institutional investors to ensure that boards acknowledge and respond to their concerns on critical issues and at critical times; and, with respect to proxy voting agencies, how the signatory uses their advice.

6. The statement of how the Code has been applied should be aligned with the signatory's role in the investment chain.

7. Asset owners' commitment to the Code may include engaging directly with companies or indirectly through the mandates given to asset managers. They should clearly communicate their policies on stewardship to their managers. Since asset owners are the primary audience of asset managers' public statements as well as client reports on stewardship, asset owners should seek

8. An asset manager should disclose how it delivers stewardship responsibilities on behalf of its clients. Following the publication in 2011 of the Stewardship Supplement to Technical Release AAF 01/06, asset managers are encouraged to have the policies described in their stewardship statements independently verified. Where appropriate, asset owners should also consider having their policy statements independently verified.

9. Overseas investors who follow other national or international codes that have similar objectives should not feel the application of the Code duplicates or confuses their responsibilities. Disclosures made in respect of those standards can also be used to demonstrate the extent to which they have complied with the Code. In a similar spirit, UK institutions that apply the Code should use their best efforts to apply its principles to overseas equity holdings.

10. Institutional investors with several types of funds or products need to make only one statement, but are encouraged to explain which of their funds or products are covered by the approach described in their statements. Where institutions apply a stewardship approach to other asset classes, they are encouraged to disclose this.

11. The FRC encourages service providers to disclose how they carry out the wishes of their clients with respect to each principle of the Code that is relevant to their activities.

12. Signatories are encouraged to review their policy statements annually, and update them where necessary to reflect changes in actual practice.

13. This statement should be easy to find on the signatory's website, or if they do not have a website in another accessible form, and should indicate when the statement was last reviewed. It should include contact details of an individual who can be contacted for further information and by those interested in collective engagement. The FRC hosts on its website the statements of signatories without their own website.

14. The FRC retains on its website a list of asset owners, asset managers and service providers that have published a statement on their compliance or otherwise with the Code, and requests that signatories notify the FRC when they have done so, and when the statement is updated.

15. The FRC regularly monitors the take-up and application of the Code. It expects the content of the Code to evolve over time to reflect developments in good stewardship practice, the structure and operation of the market, and the broader regulatory framework. Unless circumstances change, the FRC does not envisage proposing further changes to the Code until 2014 at the earliest.

to hold their managers to account for their stewardship activities. In so doing, they better fulfil their duty to their beneficiaries to exercise stewardship over their assets.

Financial Reporting Council
September 2012

The Principles of the Code

So as to protect and enhance the value that accrues to the ultimate beneficiary, institutional investors should:

1. publicly disclose their policy on how they will discharge their stewardship responsibilities.

2. have a robust policy on managing conflicts of interest in relation to stewardship which should be publicly disclosed.

3. monitor their investee companies.

4. establish clear guidelines on when and how they will escalate their stewardship activities.

5. be willing to act collectively with other investors where appropriate.

6. have a clear policy on voting and disclosure of voting activity.

7. report periodically on their stewardship and voting activities.

Comply or Explain

1. As with the UK Corporate Governance Code, the UK Stewardship Code should be applied on a "comply or explain" basis.

2. The Code is not a rigid set of rules. It consists of principles and guidance. The principles are the core of the Code and the way in which they are applied should be the central question for the institutional investor as it determines how to operate according to the Code. The guidance recommends how the principle might be applied.

3. Those signatories that choose not to comply with one of the principles, or not to follow the guidance, should deliver meaningful explanations that enable the reader to understand their approach to stewardship. In providing an explanation, the signatory should aim to illustrate how its actual practices contribute to good stewardship and promote the delivery of the institution's or its clients' investment objectives. They should provide a clear rationale for their approach.

4. The Financial Services Authority requires any firm authorised to manage funds, which is not a venture capital firm, and which manages investments for professional clients that are not natural persons, to disclose "the nature of its commitment" to the Code or "where it does not commit to the Code, its alternative investment strategy" (under Conduct of Business Rule 2.2.3[1]).

5. The FRC recognises that not all parts of the Code are relevant to all signatories. For example, smaller institutions may judge that some of its principles and guidance are disproportionate in their case. In these circumstances, they should take advantage of the "comply or explain" approach and set out why this is the case.

6. In their responses to explanations, clients and beneficiaries should pay due regard to the signatory's individual circumstances and bear in mind in particular the size and complexity of the signatory, the nature of the risks and challenges it faces, and the investment objectives of the signatory or its clients.

7. Whilst clients and beneficiaries have every right to challenge a signatory's explanations if they are unconvincing, they should not evaluate explanations in a mechanistic way. Departures from the Code should not be automatically treated as breaches. A signatory's clients and beneficiaries should be careful to respond to the statements from the signatory in a manner that supports the "comply or explain" process and bears in mind the purpose of good stewardship. They should put their views to the signatory and both parties should be prepared to discuss the position.

[1] http://fsahandbook.info/FSA/html/handbook/COBS/2/2

4 The UK Stewardship Code (September 2012)

The UK Stewardship Code

Principle 1

Institutional investors should publicly disclose their policy on how they will discharge their stewardship responsibilities.

Guidance

Stewardship activities include monitoring and engaging with companies on matters such as strategy, performance, risk, capital structure, and corporate governance, including culture and remuneration. Engagement is purposeful dialogue with companies on those matters as well as on issues that are the immediate subject of votes at general meetings.

The policy should disclose how the institutional investor applies stewardship with the aim of enhancing and protecting the value for the ultimate beneficiary or client.

The statement should reflect the institutional investor's activities within the investment chain, as well as the responsibilities that arise from those activities. In particular, the stewardship responsibilities of those whose primary activities are related to asset ownership may be different from those whose primary activities are related to asset management or other investment-related services.

Where activities are outsourced, the statement should explain how this is compatible with the proper exercise of the institutional investor's stewardship responsibilities and what steps the investor has taken to ensure that they are carried out in a manner consistent with the approach to stewardship set out in the statement.

The disclosure should describe arrangements for integrating stewardship within the wider investment process.

Principle 2

Institutional investors should have a robust policy on managing conflicts of interest in relation to stewardship which should be publicly disclosed.

Guidance

An institutional investor's duty is to act in the interests of its clients and/or beneficiaries.

Conflicts of interest will inevitably arise from time to time, which may include when voting on matters affecting a parent company or client.

Institutional investors should put in place, maintain and publicly disclose a policy for identifying and managing conflicts of interest with the aim of taking all reasonable steps to put the interests of their client or beneficiary first. The policy should also address how matters are handled when the interests of clients or beneficiaries diverge from each other.

Principle 3

Institutional investors should monitor their investee companies.

Guidance

Effective monitoring is an essential component of stewardship. It should take place regularly and be checked periodically for effectiveness.

When monitoring companies, institutional investors should seek to:

- keep abreast of the company's performance;
- keep abreast of developments, both internal and external to the company, that drive the company's value and risks;
- satisfy themselves that the company's leadership is effective;
- satisfy themselves that the company's board and committees adhere to the spirit of the UK Corporate Governance Code, including through meetings with the chairman and other board members;
- consider the quality of the company's reporting; and
- attend the General Meetings of companies in which they have a major holding, where appropriate and practicable.

Institutional investors should consider carefully explanations given for departure from the UK Corporate Governance Code and make reasoned judgements in each case. They should give a timely explanation to the company, in writing where appropriate, and be prepared to enter a dialogue if they do not accept the company's position.

Institutional investors should endeavour to identify at an early stage issues that may result in a significant loss in investment value. If they have concerns, they should seek to ensure that the appropriate members of the investee company's board or management are made aware.

Institutional investors may or may not wish to be made insiders. An institutional investor who may be willing to become an insider should indicate in its stewardship statement the willingness to do so, and the mechanism by which this could be done.

Institutional investors will expect investee companies and their advisers to ensure that information that could affect their ability to deal in the shares of the company concerned is not conveyed to them without their prior agreement.

Principle 4

Institutional investors should establish clear guidelines on when and how they will escalate their stewardship activities.

Guidance

Institutional investors should set out the circumstances in which they will actively intervene and regularly assess the outcomes of doing so. Intervention should be considered regardless of whether an active or passive investment policy is followed. In addition, being underweight is not, of itself, a reason for not intervening. Instances when institutional investors may want to intervene include, but are not limited to, when they have concerns about the company's strategy, performance, governance, remuneration or approach to risks, including those that may arise from social and environmental matters.

Initial discussions should take place on a confidential basis. However, if companies do not respond constructively when institutional investors intervene, then institutional investors should consider whether to escalate their action, for example, by:

- holding additional meetings with management specifically to discuss concerns;
- expressing concerns through the company's advisers;
- meeting with the chairman or other board members;
- intervening jointly with other institutions on particular issues;
- making a public statement in advance of General Meetings;
- submitting resolutions and speaking at General Meetings; and
- requisitioning a General Meeting, in some cases proposing to change board membership.

Principle 5

Institutional investors should be willing to act collectively with other investors where appropriate.

Guidance

At times collaboration with other investors may be the most effective manner in which to engage.

Collective engagement may be most appropriate at times of significant corporate or wider economic stress, or when the risks posed threaten to destroy significant value.

Institutional investors should disclose their policy on collective engagement, which should indicate their readiness to work with other investors through formal and informal groups when this is necessary to achieve their objectives and ensure companies are aware of concerns. The disclosure should also indicate the kinds of circumstances in which the institutional investor would consider participating in collective engagement.

Principle 6

Institutional investors should have a clear policy on voting and disclosure of voting activity.

Guidance

Institutional investors should seek to vote all shares held. They should not automatically support the board.

If they have been unable to reach a satisfactory outcome through active dialogue then they should register an abstention or vote against the resolution. In both instances, it is good practice to inform the company in advance of their intention and the reasons why.

Institutional investors should disclose publicly voting records.

Institutional investors should disclose the use made, if any, of proxy voting or other voting advisory services. They should describe the scope of such services, identify the providers and disclose the extent to which they follow, rely upon or use recommendations made by such services.

Institutional investors should disclose their approach to stock lending and recalling lent stock.

Principle 7

Institutional investors should report periodically on their stewardship and voting activities.

Guidance

Institutional investors should maintain a clear record of their stewardship activities.

Asset managers should regularly account to their clients or beneficiaries as to how they have discharged their responsibilities. Such reports will be likely to comprise qualitative as well as quantitative information. The particular information reported and the format used, should be a matter for agreement between agents and their principals.

Asset owners should report at least annually to those to whom they are accountable on their stewardship policy and its execution.

114

Transparency is an important feature of effective stewardship. Institutional investors should not, however, be expected to make disclosures that might be counterproductive. Confidentiality in specific situations may well be crucial to achieving a positive outcome.

Asset managers that sign up to this Code should obtain an independent opinion on their engagement and voting processes having regard to an international standard or a UK framework such as AAF 01/06[2]. The existence of such assurance reporting should be publicly disclosed. If requested, clients should be provided access to such assurance reports.

The FRC is responsible for promoting high quality corporate governance and reporting to foster investment. We set the UK Corporate Governance and Stewardship Codes as well as UK standards for accounting, auditing and actuarial work. We represent UK interests in international standard-setting. We also monitor and take action to promote the quality of corporate reporting and auditing. We operate independent disciplinary arrangements for accountants and actuaries; and oversee the regulatory activities of the accountancy and actuarial professional bodies.

Financial Reporting Council
5th Floor, Aldwych House
71-91 Aldwych
London WC2B 4HN
+44 **(0)20 7492 2300**

www.frc.org.uk

UP/FRC-BI12002

---

[2] Assurance reports on internal controls of service organisations made available to third parties: http://www.icaew.com/en/technical/audit-and-assurance/assurance/technical-release-aaf-01-06

10 The UK Stewardship Code (September 2012)

資料3－4

The FRC's mission is to promote transparency and integrity in business. The FRC sets the UK Corporate Governance and Stewardship Codes and UK standards for accounting and actuarial work; monitors and takes action to promote the quality of corporate reporting; and operates independent enforcement arrangements for accountants and actuaries. As the Competent Authority for audit in the UK the FRC sets auditing and ethical standards and monitors and enforces audit quality.

Consultation

FRC Financial Reporting Council

January 2019

Proposed Revision to the UK Stewardship Code

Annex A - Revised UK Stewardship Code

INTRODUCTION

The UK Stewardship Code ('the Code') has been reshaped to set new and substantially higher expectations for stewardship. The Code focuses on developing stewardship to deliver sustainable value for beneficiaries, the economy and society. It aims to stimulate greater demand for an engaged approach to stewardship and investment decision-making which is aligned to the investment time-horizons of beneficiaries, which are often long-term.

The Code reflects the changing nature of UK investments and builds on significant developments in sustainable finance, responsible investment and stewardship since 2012.[1] It makes explicit reference to environmental, social and governance (ESG) factors, and now requires signatories to integrate stewardship into their investment approach. The Code also now states that signatories should report on their own purpose, values and culture, and use the resources, rights and influence available to them to exercise stewardship beyond UK listed equity.

The structure of the Code is now similar to the UK Corporate Governance Code, with numbered Sections, Principles and Provisions accompanied by Guidance. The Code is applicable to a range of different entities in the investment community – asset managers, owners and service providers. Finally, all signatories will be required to provide more detailed reporting on their stewardship activities and how effectively they have achieved their stated objectives.

The Code remains underpinned by the Financial Conduct Authority (FCA) Conduct of Business Sourcebook and incorporates the requirements of the EU Shareholder Rights Directive II (SRD II).[2] The requirements of the Code are more demanding than SRD II, and it is the intention of the FRC that in reporting against the Code, signatories to the Code will have regard to any relevant reporting requirements of the laws, rules, regulations and administrative provisions that transpose SRD II.[3]

1. Defining stewardship

Stewardship is the responsible allocation and management of capital across the institutional investment community to create sustainable value for beneficiaries, the economy and society. Stewardship activities include monitoring assets and service providers, engaging issuers and holding them to account on material issues, and publicly reporting on the outcomes of these activities.

This definition identifies the primary purpose of stewardship as looking after the assets of beneficiaries that have been entrusted to the care of others. It also broadens the scope of the Code to be applicable beyond UK listed equity assets.

---

1 The Code was last updated in 2012. In addition, see commentary on stewardship in *The Kay Review of UK Equity Markets and Long-term Decision Making – Final Report*, July 2012.
2 FCA COBS 2.2.3 requires any firm authorised to manage funds, which is not a venture capital firm and which manages investments for professional clients that are not natural persons, to disclose clearly on its website the nature of its commitment to the Code or, where it does not commit, its alternative investment strategy.
3 Directive 2017/828 of the European Parliament and of the Council of 17 May 2017, amending Directive 2007/36/EC. Laws, regulations and administrative provisions to implement the EU Shareholder Rights' Directive II (SRD II) must be put in place by member states by 10 June 2019. [At the time of publication, under proposals the UK to withdraw from the EU, the UK intends to transpose SRD II into UK law and regulation. The FRC will amend references to SRD II that are currently in the Guidance accordingly.] Signatories should have regard to these when reporting against the Code.

2. Who the Code is for

The Code is written for asset owners, asset managers and entities providing services to the institutional investment community, including: investment consultants, proxy advisers and other service providers that want to demonstrate their commitment to stewardship.

The Code does not prescribe a single approach, but allows signatories to demonstrate high-quality stewardship that is aligned with each signatory's business model, objectives and activities to fulfil obligations to beneficiaries and clients.

Institutional investors cannot delegate their responsibility for stewardship. They remain responsible for ensuring those activities are carried out in a manner consistent with their own approach to stewardship. Accordingly, the Code requires signatories to explain how they have ensured service providers have supported their stewardship objectives.[4]

3. Key changes in the 2019 UK Stewardship Code

a. Purpose, objectives and governance

Signatories are asked to develop their organisational purpose and disclose their stewardship objectives and governance. A well-defined purpose will enable signatories to articulate their role in the institutional investment community and demonstrate how the alignment of purpose, values, strategy and culture enables them to fulfil their stewardship objectives directed towards the needs of their clients and beneficiaries. This focus on purpose aligns the Code with the 2018 UK Corporate Governance Code, builds on the FRC's observations in its report, *Corporate Culture and the Role of Boards*, and seeks to encourage embedding behaviour conducive to effective stewardship across signatories' businesses.[5][6]

b. Stewardship beyond UK listed equity

The Code has long been, and remains, closely tied to the UK Corporate Governance Code. Investors, particularly those with UK listed equity holdings, should engage constructively and discuss with investee companies any departures from recommended practice in the UK Corporate Governance Code. Holding companies to account through the exercise of shareholder rights remains core to the Code. Yet capital is allocated to a range of asset types over which investors have different terms, rights and levels of influence. The Code aims to encourage the application of the Principles across asset classes, including but not limited to listed and private equity holdings, bonds, infrastructure and alternatives. Signatories should use the resources, rights and influence available to them to exercise stewardship, no matter how capital is invested.

c. Inclusion of environmental, social and governance (ESG) factors

The Code now makes explicit reference to ESG factors. Signatories are expected to take into account material ESG factors, including climate change, when fulfilling their stewardship responsibilities. This change follows multiple developments to this end, including: clarification by the Law Commission that it is within trustees' duties to take account of material ESG factors;[7] amendments by the Department for Work and Pensions to the Occupational Pension Schemes (Investment and Disclosure) (Amendment) Regulations 2018 require consideration of ESG issues;[8] the growth of over 400 policy instruments in the largest 50 economies to support investors to consider long-term value drivers, including ESG

---

4 For key terms see the Glossary.
5 FRC, *UK Corporate Governance Code*, July 2018.
6 FRC, *Corporate Culture and the Role of Boards Report of Observations*, July 2016.
7 The Law Commission, *Fiduciary Duties of Investment Intermediaries*, June 2014. See also The Law Commission, *Pension Funds and Social Investment*, June 2017.
8 DWP, *Clarifying and strengthening trustees' investment duties*, June 2018.

factors,[9] and explicit reference to ESG issues in international stewardship codes issued since the last revision of the UK Stewardship Code.

d. Differentiation between roles

The Code is written for asset owners, asset managers and entities providing services to the institutional investment community, including: investment consultants, proxy advisers and other service providers that want to demonstrate their commitment to stewardship. The Provisions are tailored to different roles within the investment community.

e. Reporting on policies, activities and outcomes

Reporting will now be in two parts:

1) a Policy and Practice Statement upon signing the Code;
2) an annual Activities and Outcomes Report.

This will enable signatories to demonstrate the nature, extent and effectiveness of their stewardship more clearly to clients and beneficiaries for greater transparency and accountability.

4. Structure of the Code

The Code follows a similar structure to the UK Corporate Governance Code of Sections, Principles and Provisions. The Code is supported by Guidance.

Sections: numbered Sections of the Code group Principles and Provisions together under common themes.

Principles: to be followed on an 'apply and explain' basis. This means that all signatories are required to apply the Principles and make a clear statement to explain how they have done so, in a manner that will enable their stakeholders to evaluate how the Principles have been applied.

Provisions: to be followed on a 'comply or explain' basis. This means that signatories are expected to comply with the Provisions and explain how they have done so. Signatories that choose not to comply with a Provision should explain why and disclose what alternative approach they have taken. Non-compliance with a Provision is an opportunity to present a credible alternative approach to help the reader to understand the rationale and evaluate their response. This may include if, and when, the signatory expects to comply in the future.

Guidance: provides suggested ways in which the Principles and Provisions can be followed and how signatories can report against them. It includes links to the requirements of SRD II to be set out in UK legislation.

5. How to apply the Code

While most of the Code is applicable across different entities in the investment community, they have been tailored to three broad categories of Code signatories:

Asset owners: institutional investors responsible for protecting and enhancing assets on behalf of beneficiaries.

Examples of activities asset owners undertake related to their stewardship responsibilities include: setting investment beliefs, asset allocation, awarding investment mandates, designing investment strategies, and monitoring the performance and behaviours of service

---

9 PRI, *Responsible Investment Regulation Map*, 2018

providers who act on their behalf. Some asset owners may also carry out the stewardship activities described below under asset managers.

Asset managers: individuals or organisations who have the responsibility for the day-to-day management of assets.

Examples of activities asset managers undertake related to their stewardship responsibilities include: establishing investment processes, monitoring assets, engagement, voting (for shareholders), as well as monitoring the performance of service providers who act on their behalf and reporting on how they have fulfilled their stewardship responsibilities.

Service providers: individuals or organisations that do not manage investments directly or do not have fiduciary responsibility, but play a key role in the investment community as they provide services that enable clients to deliver quality stewardship.

Service provider activity that is considered to fall within this scope includes, but is not limited to: engagement, voting recommendations and execution, research and data provision, advice, and provision of reporting frameworks and standards.

Signatories in more than one category

Some signatories will have responsibilities that require them to follow Principles and Provisions across multiple categories. To determine the most appropriate way to follow the Code, signatories should report against the Principles and Provisions that apply to their main activities.

6. Becoming a signatory to the Code

The FRC requires a named contact for stewardship to be publicly disclosed and all reporting against the Code to be approved by the signatories' board.

Signatories will not be accepted to the Code without providing a named contact and confirming signatories' board approval.

Policy and Practice Statement (the Statement)

Entities will be required to submit a Statement to the FRC which:

- confirms the primary category of Principles and Provisions that can best be applied against the signatories' activities (asset manager, asset owner, service provider);
- identifies any other Principles or Provisions that are relevant to them;
- discloses relevant policies and explains how their practices enable them to apply all the Principles and comply with the relevant Provisions.

Annual Activities and Outcomes Report (the Report)

After one year of being a signatory to the Code, and annually thereafter, signatories must submit a Report which:

- details compliance with their Statement and any departures from this;
- describes activities they have undertaken to implement the Provisions in the preceding 12 months;
- provides an evaluation of how well stewardship objectives have been met, and/or have enabled clients to meet theirs, and the outcomes achieved.

7. Reporting and assessment

The Code does not include a separate Principle or Provision on disclosure and reporting. Instead it is a requirement of the Code that, through their Statement and Report, signatories must provide public disclosures about their stewardship policies and practices, and their assessment of how effectively their activities have enabled them to achieve their stated objectives. Signatories' Statements and Reports will be made publicly available.

The FRC recognises that some signatories may follow other reporting frameworks or requirements which meet the reporting expectations of the Code. To avoid duplication and unnecessary burden, signatories may signpost to these reports to fulfil, in part, the reporting requirements for the Code. The FRC will to continue to monitor and assess stewardship disclosures against the Code.

1 PURPOSE, OBJECTIVES AND GOVERNANCE

Principles

A. Signatories must develop their organisational purpose and disclose how their purpose, strategy, values and culture enable them to fulfil their stewardship objectives.

B. Signatories must develop and disclose their stewardship approach and objectives, and how they serve the interests of clients and beneficiaries.

C. Signatories' governance, processes, resources and remuneration must support the delivery of their stewardship objectives.

D. Signatories must establish policies to manage conflicts of interest, which put the interests of beneficiaries and/or clients first.

Provisions

	Asset owner	Asset manager
1.	Signatories should clearly disclose if, and how, stewardship policies and practices differ across asset allocation.	Signatories should clearly disclose if, and how, stewardship policies and practices differ at a fund level or between asset classes.
2.	Signatories should explain what activities they undertake to interact with other stakeholders and exercise their role as stewards of the market.	
3.	Signatories should have appropriate governance policies and/or structures to enable the delivery of their stewardship obligations.	
4.	Signatories should ensure their workforce has appropriate experience, qualifications and/or oversight to deliver their stewardship obligations.	
5.	Signatories should explain how they ensure the organisation has appropriate incentives in place for the delivery of the investment strategy and stewardship objectives.	
6.	Signatories should explicitly state their stewardship objectives and their expectations of stewardship activities when inviting tenders, selecting service providers and designing mandates.	
7.	Signatories should disclose their conflicts of interest policy and how it has been applied.	
8.	Signatories should disclose how they review and assure their stewardship objectives, and policies, processes, activities and reported outcomes.	

2 INVESTMENT APPROACH

Principles

E. Signatories must integrate stewardship with their investment approach and demonstrate how they take into account material ESG factors, including climate change.

F. Signatories must actively demonstrate how prospective and current investments are aligned with their stewardship approach.

Provisions

	Asset owner	Asset manager
9.	Signatories should disclose the structures and processes they have in place to ensure that information gathered through stewardship activities is factored directly into investment decision-making.	
10.	Signatories should state their investment time horizon.	
11.	Signatories should ensure that the investment and stewardship mandates that they issue appropriately reflect the investment time horizon of their beneficiaries and demonstrate how they take ESG issues into account.	Signatories should align their investment and stewardship activities appropriately with the client's investment time horizon and demonstrate how the organisation takes ESG issues into account.
12.	Signatories should disclose their investment beliefs.	
13.	Signatories should provide clear and actionable criteria for managers to assess assets against, including prior to investment, to ensure they are appropriate investments to make in accordance with their investment and stewardship strategy.	Signatories should evaluate assets, including prior to investment, to assess whether they are appropriate investments to make in accordance with their investment and stewardship strategy.

3 ACTIVE MONITORING

Principles

G. Signatories must actively monitor the performance of the assets for which they are responsible and/or the managers and service providers that they use.

Provisions

	Asset owner	Asset manager
14.	Signatories should actively monitor issues that may impact the value of assets held over the investment time horizon of beneficiaries and/or clients, identify key priorities, and use this information to inform their stewardship activities and communication with managers and/or service providers.	
15.	Signatories should actively monitor asset managers to ensure that assets managed on their behalf are aligned with their investment and stewardship policies.	Signatories should actively monitor how assets are managed and aligned with clients' investment and stewardship policies.
16.	Signatories should actively monitor service providers to ensure that their services enable effective stewardship.	

120

4 CONSTRUCTIVE ENGAGEMENT AND CLEAR COMMUNICATION

Principles

H. Signatories must undertake constructive engagement to maintain or enhance the value of assets.

I. Signatories must communicate clearly with clients and beneficiaries.

Provisions

	Asset owner	Asset manager
17.		Signatories should establish and publicly disclose an engagement policy.
18.	Signatories should describe how they integrate engagement into their investment strategy.	
19.	Signatories should describe what methods they use for engagement, and escalation if required, to enhance the value of assets.	
20.	Signatories should state the extent to which they participate in collaborative engagement.	
21.	Signatories should disclose engagement activity undertaken on their behalf and communicate to beneficiaries about how they have fulfilled their stewardship responsibilities.	Signatories should proactively communicate with clients about how assets managed on their behalf are aligned with asset owners' and the asset managers' investment and stewardship policies.
22.	Signatories should describe how they take account of beneficiaries' needs and the extent to which they seek to engage with beneficiaries to understand their views.	Signatories should engage asset owners to understand their needs, including their investment strategy, policy, beliefs and approach to stewardship.

5 EXERCISE RIGHTS AND RESPONSIBILITIES

Principles

J. Signatories must actively exercise their rights and responsibilities.

Provisions

	Asset owner	Asset manager
23.	Signatories should explain how they exercise ownership rights across different markets and asset classes.	
24.		Signatories should indicate which, if any, proxy voting adviser(s) they use, the scope of services procured and how advice/information received is used as part of the signatories' stewardship activities.
25.	Signatories should explain their policy on voting shares in listed assets, including: • the extent to which the fund sets its own voting policies; • the extent to which voting decisions are executed by another entity; • how they monitor service providers' voting on their behalf; • how the asset owner monitors the voting rights it has; • the funds' approach to stock lending and recalling lent stock for voting; • votes withheld if applicable.	Signatories should explain their policy on voting shares in listed assets, including: • any house voting policy set by the manager; • the extent to which voting decisions are executed by another entity; • how they monitor voting on their behalf; • how the asset manager monitors the voting rights it has; • how the manager seeks to mitigate 'empty voting'; • the funds' approach to stock lending and recalling lent stock for voting; • votes withheld if applicable; • the policy on allowing clients to direct voting in segregated and pooled accounts; • the use of default recommendations and the extent to which clients may override the house voting policy.
26.	Signatories should disclose their voting records.	
27.	Signatories should explain their policy on bond engagement, including the extent to which they engage pre- and post-issuance of bonds.	

SERVICE PROVIDERS

Service providers do not manage investments directly or have fiduciary responsibility; however, they play a key role in the investment community and, therefore, they must provide services that allow clients to deliver quality stewardship.

Signatories will also be required to make a statement upon signing and provide an annual report of their activities. The Provisions are broad and must be tailored to the services which the entity offers.

Service provider activity considered to fall within this scope includes, but is not limited to: engagement, voting recommendations and execution, research and data provision, advice, and provision of reporting frameworks and standards.

Principles

A. Signatories must develop their purpose and state how their purpose, strategy, values and culture enable them to promote effective stewardship.
B. Signatories must ensure they execute their role in the investment community in a manner that promotes and enables effective stewardship.
C. Signatories' governance, processes, resources and remuneration (including fee structures) must support them to promote and enable effective stewardship.
D. Signatories must establish policies to manage conflicts of interest, which put the interests of clients first.

Provisions

1.	Signatories must indicate the range of services they offer, and how they serve the interests of clients and enable them to deliver effective stewardship.
2.	Signatories must inform clients about the accuracy of their services and demonstrate service quality by providing information about how products and services are prepared to best support clients' stewardship.
3.	Signatories should explain what activities they undertake to work with other stakeholders and exercise their role as stewards of the market.
4.	Signatories should ensure their workforce has appropriate experience, qualifications and/or oversight to deliver their services.
5.	Signatories should disclose their conflicts of interest policy and how it has been applied.
6.	Signatories should establish a code of conduct.

11

GUIDANCE

Provides more detailed direction and examples of disclosure being sought under each Provision.

1 PURPOSE, OBJECTIVES AND GOVERNANCE

	Asset owner	Asset manager
1.	This Provision seeks to encourage clearer and more transparent disclosure on the scope of signatories' stewardship activities. Signatories may have different investment approaches and stewardship practices across assets and funds. For example, some firms may only mandate and/or seek to undertake stewardship activities for a proportion of their investments. The scope of signatories' stewardship should be clearly disclosed.	
2.	In addition to their effective stewardship of assets, we expect Code signatories to fulfil their role as stewards of the market, meaning that they support well-functioning financial markets in whatever function they serve. The effective implementation of stewardship requires constructive coordination of many market participants working towards positive outcomes for stewardship and sustainable financial markets. Signatories should explain what activities they undertake to support effective stewardship and positive outcomes that contribute to building a sustainable financial system, which both manages systemic risks and drives capital towards more sustainable investments. Activities may include, but are not limited to: engagement with other participants in the financial market, policymakers, regulators and other relevant industry initiatives.	
3.	Signatories should disclose: • how stewardship policies and practices are developed and approved within the organisation; • the level of authority and accountability of those with stewardship responsibilities; • an overview of team size and structure, as well as how they are integrated with other functions and teams in the organisation. Note: Provision 9 asks for further detail on specific processes and activities signatories undertake to integrate stewardship with investment approach and decision-making.	
4.	In disclosing against this Provision, signatories are expected to demonstrate that they have established the human resourcing, training and oversight required for individuals within their chosen structure to deliver their stewardship objectives. Examples of information signatories may choose to disclose to demonstrate this can include an overview of relevant skills and experience held across the team, as well as responsibilities and their oversight.	
5.	*Reporting against this Provision should seek to satisfy requirements in SRD II: chapter 1b, article 3h, 2 (b).*	Signatories should disclose that they are incentivised to align investment strategy and decision-making with the profile and duration of the liabilities of the asset owner, particularly with respect to long-term liabilities.
6.	Signatories should explain how they integrate stewardship expectations in the tender and selection process, and how they design mandates for managers and service providers (as applicable) to deliver in the best interests of beneficiaries. This should include asking the recipient of Requests for Proposals for: • the organisation's view/approach to stewardship; • the processes and resources used to deliver stewardship activities at team level(s).	

12

Asset owner	Asset manager
7.	Conflicts of interest may arise from, but are not limited to:
	• affiliations between the ownership structure of a pension fund and/or fiduciary manager and assets held and assets held (for asset owners);
	• affiliations between the ownership structure of an asset management firm and assets held (for asset managers);
	• business relationships between the asset owner and/or asset manager and assets, e.g. investee companies;
	• cross-directorships, e.g. the director of an asset manager is also the director of an investee company.
	Reporting against this Provision should seek to satisfy requirements in SRD II, chapter 1b, article 3g, 1 (a) and 3.
8.	Signatories should obtain assurance of their stewardship processes and reported outcomes. Assurance may be undertaken by an external party, or as part of the signatories' internal audit processes based upon relevant international standards. Signatories should make a statement that assurance has been undertaken and, if not, an explanation as to why. If requested, clients should be provided with access to assurance reports on the signatories' stewardship activities and reported outcomes.

2 INVESTMENT APPROACH

	Asset owner	Asset manager
9.		This Provision expects the signatory to demonstrate how their stewardship is integrated with their investment approach / decision-making. Examples of actions signatories could take and disclose include:
		• regular cross-team meetings and presentations;
		• sharing information gathered through stewardship activities across platforms that are accessible to stewardship/ESG and investment teams;
		• encouraging stewardship/ESG and investment teams to join engagement meetings and roadshows;
		• delegating some engagement dialogue to portfolio managers (if not already within portfolio managers' remit);
		• joint engagement meetings between stewardship/ESG team and portfolio managers (where these functions are not already integrated);
		• involving portfolio managers when defining an engagement programme and developing voting decisions.
		Where funds have different approaches, signatories may wish to indicate the proportion of assets under management to which they integrate stewardship with investment decision-making.
10.	Signatories should recognise their responsibility to preserve and enhance value that is aligned in the interest of beneficiaries over an appropriate time horizon; in most cases a long-term perspective is required.	
11.	Signatories should explain how their approach to investment and stewardship is aligned with the investment time horizon of beneficiaries, including how they take material ESG factors into account. *Reporting against this Provision should seek to satisfy requirements in SRD II, chapter 1b, article 3h, 1.*	Signatories should explain how their approach to investment and stewardship is aligned with the investment time horizon of beneficiaries, including how they take material ESG factors into account. *Reporting against this Provision should seek to satisfy requirements in SRD II, chapter 1b, article 3i, 1.*
12.	Signatories may have beliefs about how investment markets function and which factors lead to good investment outcomes. Investment beliefs, supported by research and experience, can help focus investment approach / decision-making. Signatories should develop and disclose the investment beliefs which set the direction for their investment principles, strategy, policy and practice.	
13.	Signatories should explain how and what they communicate as criteria for managers for pre-investment monitoring. Examples of criteria may include, but are not limited to: • if investment in listed equity shares with no or dual class voting rights is suitable for their stewardship policies; • the extent of engagement on ESG issues pre-issuance and issuer creditworthiness for bonds.	Signatories should explain how they assess assets prior to investment. Integrating criteria could result in adjustments to areas such as selection, weighting or asset allocation. Examples of criteria may include, but are not limited to: • if investment in listed equity shares with no or dual class voting rights is suitable for their stewardship policies; • the extent of engagement on ESG issues pre-issuance and issuer creditworthiness for bonds.

3 ACTIVE MONITORING

	Asset owner	Asset manager
14.	Signatories should explain: • what tools or processes they use to monitor issues* that may impact asset value over the investment time horizon of beneficiaries they serve; • the rationale or method they use to prioritise issues and actions taken as a result. This may include how key issues feed into engagement or investment decision-making. * Issues to monitor across different asset classes include, but are not limited to: company strategy and performance; capital structure, reporting and audit quality; directors' application of section 172 of the Companies Act 2006, adherence to the UK Corporate Governance Code and/or other governance codes; leadership effectiveness, risk and value drivers, material environmental, social and corporate governance factors (including culture, remuneration and diversity) debt to equity ratio, cash flows, compliance with covenants and contracts. *Reporting against this Provision should seek to satisfy requirements in SRD II: chapter 1b, article 3g, 1(a).*	
15.	Signatories' explanation should include, but is not limited to: • Asset managers' assessment of investment risk and value drivers • Portfolio composition • Policy on securities lending • Engagement • Portfolio turnover costs • Use of proxy advisers • General description of voting behaviour • Explanation of significant votes • Vote disclosure *Reporting against this Provision should seek to satisfy requirements in SRD II: chapter 1b, article 3h (d) and chapter 1b, article 3g (b).*	Signatories' explanation should include, but is not limited to: • Assessment of investment risk and value drivers • Portfolio composition • Policy on securities lending • Engagement • Portfolio turnover costs • Use of proxy advisers • General description of voting behaviour • Explanation of significant votes • Vote disclosure *Reporting against this Provision should seek to satisfy requirements in SRD II: chapter 1b, article 3g (b).*
16.	Signatories should: • disclose which services they procure to support their stewardship; • explain what actions they take to monitor service providers; • describe what actions, if any, they have taken because of monitoring.	

4 CONSTRUCTIVE ENGAGEMENT AND CLEAR COMMUNICATION

	Asset owner	Asset manager
17.	A signatory's engagement policy may be part of another policy, such as a stewardship and/or responsible investment policy. A signatory's engagement policy should describe their approach to engagement as it applies to their assets and investment strategy.	
18.		This Provision is applicable to asset owners in instances where they have directly employed investment staff to undertake stewardship activities, such as voting, screening and engagement activities. Engagement should be undertaken with a clearly defined purpose, primarily based on an investment case to maintain or enhance the value of assets. Issues to engage across different asset classes include, but are not limited to: company strategy and performance; capital structure, reporting and audit quality; directors' application of section 172 of the Companies Act 2006, adherence to the UK Corporate Governance Code and/or other governance codes; leadership effectiveness, risk and value drivers, material environmental, social and corporate governance factors (including culture, remuneration and diversity) debt to equity ratio, cash flows, compliance with covenants and contracts. *Reporting against this Provision should seek to satisfy requirements in SRD II, Chapter 1b, article 3g, 1 and chapter 1b, article 3g, 2.*
19.		Signatories should make use of methods of engagement which they consider effective to meet their stewardship objectives and disclose how they have done so. Signatories should engage with relevant entities to maintain and enhance value across asset classes, with clear, precise objectives and a constructive approach. Signatories should seek to engage with companies in advance of casting any votes against. Successful engagement is not a requirement of disclosure against this Provision, but signatories should be able to indicate their perceived success and how this has been measured against stated objectives. Progress of engagements to date should be reflected in annual activity reporting, recognising that engagements will often take place over years. Care should be taken when handling privileged material which could be considered as insider information. *For listed equity assets:* Where a major shareholder divests, the investor should disclose their reason(s) to the company's board. Engagement with companies may include, but is not limited to: one-to-one meetings, attending Annual and Extraordinary General Meetings, and collaborative engagements with other investors. *For bondholders:* Bondholders should initiate dialogue with the bond issuer to engage on covenant design, as well as work with equity holders as part of their engagement strategy. Examples of escalation may include: • holding additional meetings with management; • raising key issues through the company's advisers; • meeting with the chairman or other board members; • jointly intervening with other institutions; • making a public statement in advance of General Meetings; • submitting resolutions and speaking at General Meetings; • requisitioning a General Meeting; • proposing to change board membership in some cases. *Reporting against this Provision should seek to satisfy requirements in SRD II, chapter 1b, article 3g, 1 and chapter 1b, article 3g, 2.*

	Asset owner	Asset manager
20.	Signatories should state whether or not they participate in collaborative engagement with other investors and/or other market participants. Where signatories do undertake collaborative engagements, they should: • disclose their policy on collaborative engagement; • indicate to which markets and funds and/or asset classes the policy applies; • indicate issues they plan to prioritise for collaborative engagement in the forthcoming year; • state their objective(s) for collaborative engagements in which they plan to participate or have already done so; • disclose the number of collaborative engagements they have participated in during the previous year; • give an assessment of the effectiveness of the collaborative engagements they have participated in against their stated objectives.	
21.	Signatories should indicate how, and with what regularity, they appraise their appointed managers and service providers and their satisfaction with the investment and stewardship activities undertaken on their behalf. Signatories should communicate with signatories about how this activity enables them to meet the needs of beneficiaries.	Signatories should indicate how, the stewardship activities undertaken on behalf of their clients are aligned with their clients' investment and stewardship policies, as well as their own, and how this enables the signatory to meet clients' needs.
22.	Signatories should determine the extent and method of the engagement with beneficiaries as appropriate for the fund size, structure and approach. Where signatories do not seek to engage beneficiaries, they should disclose their rationale for not doing so. Where signatories seek to engage beneficiaries, they should disclose the methods they have used to gather member views and the extent to which member preferences are incorporated into the investment strategy.	Signatories should engage clients to understand their needs, including their investment strategy, policy and beliefs, and approach to stewardship.

5 EXERCISE RIGHTS AND RESPONSIBILITIES

23.	Signatories should explain how they use their ownership rights as stewards across asset classes in which they are invested, e.g. bonds, private equity and others as appropriate.
24.	Signatories should describe the services they procure, if any, from voting advisory services: including identifying the providers, the scope of services and extent to which they follow voting recommendations made by such services. Signatories should indicate which, if any, proxy voting adviser(s) they use, the scope of services procured and how advice/information received is used as part of the signatories' stewardship activities.
25.	This Provision expects disclosure to demonstrate that the asset owner and/or manager has processes in place to ensure that it knows what stock and voting rights it has and exercises them accordingly, which is made more difficult when there is separation of the economic and voting rights of shares. 'Empty voting' may occur when shares are bought and sold between the record date and the general meeting date, and when stock lending. Asset owners and asset managers may take different approaches to stock lending and recalling lent stock for voting. Signatories should also disclose their policies (if any) on empty voting, stock lending and recalling lent stock for voting. *Reporting against this Provision should seek to satisfy requirements in SRD II, chapter 1b, article 3g, 1-2.*
26.	Signatories should publicly disclose voting records, including votes for, against, withheld and abstentions. Records should include rationale for voting decisions, particularly where: • there is a vote against the board; • a vote is withheld; or • the vote is not in line with voting policy. Records should be published regularly, on the signatories' website, and in a format that can be easily accessed and interpreted. *Reporting against this Provision should seek to satisfy requirements in SRD II, chapter 1b, article 3g, 1(b).*
27.	This Provision expects disclosure to demonstrate the extent to which signatories invested in bonds seek to exercise stewardship. Signatories should describe what actions, if any, they take to engage with issuers as bondholders. Examples may include working equity with portfolio managers. Where the signatory does not seek to undertake bondholder engagement they should disclose their approach.

SERVICE PROVIDERS

1.	Signatories may provide a range of services, including: vote execution, voting advice, research and data analysis, and consultancy. Signatories should indicate which services they offer to asset owners and asset managers to support their stewardship objectives. We recognise also that some service providers are part of larger organisations, e.g. an investment consultant that is part of a larger consultancy firm. Where service providers offer engagement services they should set out an engagement policy and how this supports clients' stewardship.
2.	*Reporting against this Provision should seek to satisfy requirements in SRD II, chapter 1b, article 3j, 2.*
3.	In addition to their effective stewardship of assets, we expect Code signatories to fulfil their role as stewards of the market, meaning that they support well-functioning financial markets in whatever function they serve. The effective implementation of stewardship requires constructive coordination of many market participants working towards positive outcomes for stewardship and sustainable financial markets. Signatories should explain what activities they undertake to support effective stewardship and positive outcomes that contribute to building a sustainable financial system, which both manages systemic risks and drives capital towards more sustainable investments. Activities may include, but are not limited to: engagement with other participants in the financial market, policymakers, regulators, representative bodies and relevant industry initiatives.
4.	Signatories should explain how they ensure they have the necessary resources in place, including teams with the appropriate levels of seniority, integration, qualifications and experience to deliver their stewardship objectives.
5.	*Reporting against this Provision should seek to satisfy requirements in SRD II, chapter 1b, article 3j, 2(g).*
6.	*Reporting against this Provision should seek to satisfy requirements in SRD II, chapter 1b, article 3j, 1.*

126

20

GLOSSARY OF CODE TERMS

Asset manager	An individual or organisation to whom the responsibility for the day-to-day management of assets is delegated by an individual or institutional asset owner. The asset manager will act based on instructions given to them in an investment mandate, with discretion to buy and sell assets on behalf of another entity or person.
Asset owner	An institutional investor responsible for protecting assets on behalf of beneficiaries.
Beneficiary	An individual, natural person who derives an economic benefit from investments held with an investment intermediary or under a contract with a financial services provider.
Bond	A debt security issued by a company or national government and sold to investors.
Client	A person or organisation that receives a service from another person or organisation in return for payment.
COBS	Conduct of Business Sourcebook. The section of the FCA's Handbook that deals with business standards.
Engagement	Communication between different stakeholders, e.g. between asset owners and beneficiaries or investors and investee companies.
Equity	A share or stock in the share capital of an incorporated company.
ESG	An abbreviation for environmental, social and governance.
Fiduciary duty	The obligation to manage other people's money in their best interests, e.g. an asset manager executing their role in clients' and beneficiaries' best interests.
Institutional investor	Legal entities invested in funds or mandates, including pension schemes, charities, insurance companies and endowment funds.
Investment consultant	An individual or organisation undertaking consultancy and/or fiduciary management services. Investment consultancy is the provision of advice to institutional investors on investment strategy, asset allocation and asset manager product selection.
Investment strategy	Decisions and actions to implement investment beliefs, e.g. investors' decisions and subsequent actions to be taken on asset allocation, approach to risk, and use of risk hedging instruments.

Proxy adviser	A person or organisation that analyses, on a professional and commercial basis, company disclosure and, where relevant, other information of listed companies with a view to informing investors' voting decisions by providing research, advice or voting recommendations that relate to the exercise of voting rights.
Service provider	Service providers do not manage investments directly or have fiduciary responsibility. However, they play a key role in the investment community. Service provider activity considered to fall within the scope of the 2019 UK Stewardship Code includes, but is not limited to engagement, voting recommendations and execution, research and data provision, advice, and provision of reporting frameworks and standards.
Stewardship	Stewardship is the responsible allocation and management of capital across the institutional investment community to create sustainable value for beneficiaries, the economy and society. Stewardship activities include monitoring assets and service providers, engaging issuers and holding them to account on material issues, and publicly reporting on the outcomes of these activities.
Stakeholder	In the context of this Code, a stakeholder is an entity or person with an interest or concern in effective stewardship.
Responsible investment	An approach to investing that aims to incorporate ESG factors into investment decision-making to better manage investment risk and opportunities, as well as to contribute to a more sustainable economy.

Financial Reporting Council
8th Floor
125 London Wall
London
EC2Y 5AS

+44 (0)20 7492 2300

www.frc.org.uk

21

Singapore Stewardship Principles

For Responsible Investors

November 2016

STEWARDSHIP ASIA

Preamble

The Importance of Investor Stewardship

Stewardship is about building and growing sustainable businesses to produce long-term benefits for all stakeholders, and in the process contributing to the community and economy as a whole. It goes beyond short-term considerations and includes the sustainability of a company's long-term performance.

Stewardship is important for the wider business and investment ecosystem, including investors and investee companies. In today's context, the investment value-chain linking ultimate asset owners to investee companies is increasingly complex. Many countries are seeing a trend towards fragmented ownership, especially in listed companies, with many shareholders each holding a small proportion of shares. Coupled with increasingly shorter shareholding tenure, the ownership mentality is arguably being eroded and replaced by a prevalent short-term view of investment and portfolio management. Hence, the emphasis on stewardship is relevant and timely.

The Stewardship Principles

These Stewardship Principles aim, by articulating the core behaviour and actions associated with investor stewardship, to enable investors to be active and responsible shareholders. They provide a view on the activities and functions that stewards should carry out, and how these should relate to the boards and management of investee companies.

They are not intended to be rigid rules to be enforced or prescriptive measures to be adhered to, nor are they intended to constitute a code. They are stated as broad principles, with suggested ways that these principles could be applied. Articulating and sharing stewardship activities, and the level of commitment to these Stewardship Principles, are matters that are left to each individual investor to adopt, on a wholly voluntary basis.

Adopting these Stewardship Principles ought not to be interpreted as an invitation for investors to manage the affairs of an investee company or to interfere in its operations. It underscores the role of the investors as responsible shareholders who appropriately engage the board and management of investee companies, and other shareholders, so as to ensure the long-term success of the companies.

The Responsible Investors

For the purpose of these Principles, the term "investors" is used in a broad sense to include institutional investors who are asset owners and asset managers.

For investors, stewardship extends beyond attendance and voting at shareholders' meetings. It may involve responsibilities and activities that include actively monitoring and engaging with investee companies on a range of matters and issues. These may include the mandate for the board, performance and performance measurement, risk management, capital structure and corporate

governance. Engagement with investee companies should be proactive and conducted on both a routine basis and during times of concern or crisis.

Asset owners are the providers of capital to investee companies. Asset owners, at various parts of the investment value chain, are in effect stewards of assets entrusted to them by their own clients who are the ultimate owners and beneficiaries. By subscribing to these Stewardship Principles, and encouraging their corresponding asset managers and/or investee companies to exercise sound stewardship, asset owners can enhance the long term economic welfare generated within the investment ecosystem.

Asset managers act as agents on behalf of their clients. Though they are not the owners of the assets, asset managers are in effect stewards who are entrusted with the assets under management. Asset managers, given their mandate to manage investments, are more directly connected to investee companies. They are well-positioned to influence the long-term performance of companies through stewardship. By subscribing to these Stewardship Principles, asset managers can play an instrumental role in fostering effective stewardship between investors and investee companies.

Investors may choose to outsource to external service providers some of the activities associated with stewardship but they remain responsible for activities to be carried out in a manner consistent with their own approach to stewardship. Accordingly, service providers such as proxy advisors and investment consultants are encouraged to subscribe to these Stewardship Principles.

It is understandable that not all the Stewardship Principles are relevant to all market participants in the same way. The value chain is differentiated, and there are different applications for ultimate owners, asset owners, and asset managers, among others. Not all principles or guidance might be carried out to the fullest extent or be applied to the same degree. These Stewardship Principles are most applicable to Singapore-based institutional investors with equity holdings in Singapore-listed companies. These Principles, however, would also apply to other investor groups and to service providers that provide advice on investment and corporate governance to investors, including proxy advisors and investment consultants as indicated above.

A Matter of Principle

Ultimately, the effectiveness of these Stewardship Principles hinges upon their application in the right spirit rather than compliance merely in form. They are not intended to be a "box-ticking" exercise. They are also not intended, even unwittingly, to constitute an administrative burden to those who subscribe to these Principles. These Stewardship Principles are intended to help shape positive corporate behaviour and to benefit all stakeholders in the long term, by encouraging investors to be responsible and active stewards who contribute positively to the welfare of the economy, community and society at large.

129

STEWARDSHIP PRINCIPLES

The following seven Principles provide useful guidance to responsible investors towards fostering good stewardship in discharging their responsibilities and creating sustainable long-term value for all stakeholders.

1. **Take a stand on stewardship.**

    Responsible investors establish and articulate their policies on their stewardship responsibilities.

2. **Know your investment.**

    Responsible investors communicate regularly and effectively with their investee companies.

3. **Stay active and informed.**

    Responsible investors actively monitor their investee companies.

4. **Uphold transparency in managing conflicts of interest.**

    Responsible investors make known their approach to managing conflicts of interest.

5. **Vote responsibly.**

    Responsible investors establish clear policies on voting and exercise their voting rights in a responsible fashion.

6. **Set a good example.**

    Responsible investors document and provide relevant updates on their stewardship activities.

7. **Work together.**

    Responsible investors are willing to engage responsibly with one another where appropriate.

130

Principle 1: Take a stand on stewardship

Responsible investors establish and articulate their policies on their stewardship responsibilities.

GUIDANCE

1.1 Investors should clearly articulate their policies concerning their responsibilities as shareholders. Where applicable, these policies could be stated plainly on the investor's corporate website.

1.2 The stewardship policies should explain the methods by which investors will ensure that investment activities (including outsourced activities) are performed in line with their chosen approach to stewardship.

1.3 The policies should explain the rationale for their approach to stewardship; how it enhances and protects value for their clients and ultimate beneficiaries; and how it may be applied to various aspects of the investment process.

1.4 Investors should take steps to satisfy themselves that they adhere to their own stewardship approach in carrying out investment activities.

Principle 2: Know your investment

Responsible investors communicate regularly and effectively with their investee companies.

GUIDANCE

2.1 Investors should have meaningful and effective communications with investee companies. These communications should ensure mutual understanding and achievement of objectives, so as to meet the aims of long-term value creation, capital efficiency, and sustainable growth.

2.2 As part of these communications, investors could satisfy themselves that the investee company's board and board committee structures are effective, and that independent directors provide adequate oversight.

2.3 Investors may engage with their investee companies on a full spectrum of topics, including strategy, long-term performance, risk, financials, culture and remuneration, social and environmental considerations, and corporate governance.

2.4 Investors should have a policy for managing disclosures of material information that could lead to a breach of listing rules or other relevant legislation. The policy should indicate whether in exceptional circumstances they are willing to be made insiders, and the mechanism by which this could be done.

Principle 3: Stay active and informed

Responsible investors actively monitor their investee companies.

GUIDANCE

3.1 Investors should have monitoring activities in place so that issues may be identified and addressed early to avoid any consequential loss in investment value.

3.2 The monitoring process should cover both financial and non-financial factors as appropriate to the investee company. Should investors have concerns about the investee companies on these factors, particularly with regard to non-financial disclosures, they should raise these concerns directly with the investee companies and seek to address them.

3.3 Where investors observe any deviation from applicable corporate governance practices, including Singapore's Code of Corporate Governance, they should carefully consider the explanations given for the deviation, assess the reasons, and if necessary, take action as they see fit.

3.4 Where there is need for follow-up engagement, it should preferably begin with a confidential discussion. However, if the investee company does not respond constructively, investors may consider escalating their actions. Investors should have policies in place on escalation of engagement.

Principle 4: Uphold transparency in managing conflicts of interest

Responsible investors make known their approach to managing conflicts of interest.

GUIDANCE

4.1 Asset owners and asset managers should have clear written policies on identifying and managing conflicts of interest. These policies should be stated plainly on the investor's corporate website, and they should emphasise the asset owner's and asset manager's duty to act in the interests of its clients and/or beneficiaries and to be consistent with client mandates in fulfilling its fiduciary responsibilities.

4.2 When conflicts of interest arise, asset owners and asset managers should take all reasonable steps to prioritise their clients' and/or beneficiaries' interests over their own interest.

4.3 Investors should communicate to their service providers the need to disclose all potential conflicts of interest and to explain how they are managed.

Principle 5: Vote responsibly

Responsible investors establish clear policies on voting and exercise their voting rights in a responsible fashion.

GUIDANCE

5.1 Investors should actively seek to participate in the general meetings of investee companies, and exercise their voting rights responsibly and on an informed basis.

5.2 Investors should have a clear view on how to vote proxies relating to the investments they manage or own. These policies should include both general policies and specific policies on voting issues, and they should ensure that proxies are voted in the best interest of their clients, beneficiaries and/or investee companies.

5.3 Investors should maintain records of the votes exercised, and any deviation from their voting policies should be documented.

5.4 Investors should have clear policies on communicating information pertinent to voting, such as voting policies, votes exercised, and records of votes cast.

5.5 Investors should maintain records of voting outcomes.

Principle 6: Set a good example

Responsible investors document and provide relevant updates on their stewardship activities.

GUIDANCE

6.1 Asset owners and asset managers should proactively inform their clients, beneficiaries and/or investee companies about their approaches to stewardship, how they carry out their stewardship responsibilities and the extent to which they adhere to their own stewardship policies or to these Principles. This information could be communicated in the form of annual or more frequent updates.

6.2 Investors should maintain a record of ways in which they have carried out their stewardship responsibilities. This record could be shared on the investors' website.

Principle 7: Work together

Responsible investors are willing to engage responsibly with one another where appropriate.

GUIDANCE

7.1 Investors may, on occasion, find that collaboration with other investors, subject to regulations on disclosure, may be the most effective manner in which to engage their investee companies.

7.2 Collective engagement through formal or informal groups may be the most appropriate means of ensuring that investee companies are aware of concerns at times of significant corporate or wider economic stress, or when there are risks that threaten to destroy significant value.

7.3 Should collective engagement become appropriate, investors should disclose their rationale for doing so, including the circumstances which have prompted their action.

Singapore Stewardship Principles (SSP) for Responsible Investors

Working Group

Members	Association of Chartered Certified Accountants
	Asia Pacific Real Estate Association
	CFA Singapore
	CPA Australia
	Hermes Equity Ownership Services Ltd
	Investment Management Association of Singapore
	Institute of Singapore Chartered Accountants
	Securities Investors Association (Singapore)
	Singapore Institute of Directors
	Singapore Venture Capital and Private Equity Association
	Stewardship Asia Centre
Supported By	Monetary Authority of Singapore
	Singapore Exchange

STEWARDSHIP ASIA PUBLICATIONS

Stewardship Principles for Family Businesses

Fostering Success, Significance and Sustainability

Contents

About Stewardship Asia Centre

Stewardship Asia Centre is a non-profit organisation supported by Temasek, committed to working with partners to uplift stewardship and foster effective governance across Asia.

Preamble

Stewardship matters for successful and enduring family businesses

Stewardship is a defining hallmark of businesses that achieve success, significance and sustainability.

In crux, stewardship encapsulates the essence of responsible and meaningful value creation in a sustainable way to benefit stakeholders, as well as the larger community that they are a part of. It underscores the importance of an ownership mindset, a long-term perspective and an inclusive approach. These stewardship elements undergird and reflect the business leaders' motivation and commitment to nurture and grow what they are entrusted with, such that it can be handed over in a better shape to successors.

Stewardship is particularly pertinent to family businesses (FBs), which form a key component of economic activity around the world. This is especially relevant in Asia, where FBs remain the mainstay of business ownership, and families continue to be influential players in the business landscape, as owners as well as managers. Successful and sustainable FBs create wealth and growth for the family across generations. In their stewardship journey, such great and lasting FBs leave a rich legacy, contributing significantly to the multiplier effects such as knowledge creation, economic development and capacity building of human and social capital to benefit society in the long run.

FBs are very diverse in nature - ranging from small, medium local enterprises to huge conglomerates that operate across industries and countries. For our purpose here, we broadly define FBs to include companies with the presence of family members as shareholders as well as board members and managers who are able to influence strategic decisions. We use the term FBs to include family companies, family firms and organisations.

Notwithstanding their diversity in scale and nature, FBs in general face some common challenges:

- Responding and adapting to the vortex of disruptive changes stemming from the global and local fronts, while still maintaining the sense of purpose that propelled them to success

- Maintaining coherence and harmony as ownership becomes more fragmented over time

- Attracting, retaining and "professionalising" talents that constitute the human capital essential for FBs to maintain their competitive edge

- Transitioning successfully during periods of leadership renewal, especially for firms where the influence of the founder-leaders dominate

- Guarding against the pitfalls of hubris and complacency on one hand, and a reluctance to adapt due to inertia to changes on the other

- Upholding high standards of resource management and corporate governance

Faced with such challenges and an increasingly demanding business environment, stewardship has become all the more relevant and important. Well-stewarded FBs emerge over time as engaged, forward-looking and adaptable enterprises. They are able to leverage their inherent strengths and competitive advantages. Guided by their values, such FBs remain resilient in the face of changing times and disruptions, overcoming adversity and outperforming their competitors.

Stewardship is, however, always a journey. Every generation of FBs faces unique circumstances, challenges and opportunities. A FB with a successful stewardship experience in one generation does not guarantee its continual success into the next. Hence, for FBs striving towards success, significance and sustainability, a resolve to continually imbibe, propagate and reinforce stewardship concepts and actions is vital, and remains relevant and timely.

The approach of Stewardship Principles for Family Businesses

Undertaking this exercise is a challenging process as the concept of FBs contains some inherent paradoxes. Firstly, at the level of aspirations, the notions of "family business" and "business family" have different implications – the former prioritising family while the latter prioritising business interests. Secondly, at the level of strategy, conflating short-term and long-term perspectives is often difficult as motivations differ within and across owners, family members and non-family employees. While being cognisant of these paradoxes, it is nevertheless relevant, useful and possible to establish a set of general principles, which could help FBs on their stewardship journey.

After collating and translating the collective wisdom and knowledge gleaned from an extensive review of literature, as well as consultation with subject matter experts and business families regionally and internationally, we have distilled and organised the insights into seven broad principles. Termed the Stewardship Principles for Family Businesses, they aim to articulate the mindset and attitudes, as well as behaviours and practices that would foster success, significance and sustainability for FBs. These Principles intend and hope to inspire reflections and actions for those who are committed to stewarding their organisations towards sustainable success. As broad principles, they highlight the dimensions that FBs can focus on to develop a stewardship orientation and culture in their organisations with a long-term perspective.

The Principles are not meant to serve as a formula for success or a blueprint for all contexts. As situations differ across organisations, their adoption will require translation and adaptation to make them applicable, useful and effective. Further, these Principles are not doctrinal or prescriptive. They are intended to serve as useful and relevant guides, like "sign-posts" along the stewardship journey for the FBs. In this sense, the Principles will evolve and improve over time, so as to stay useful and relevant for FBs striving for success, significance and sustainability.

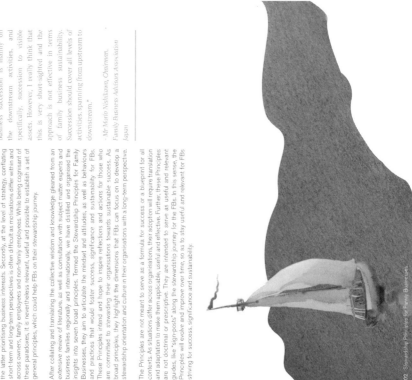

"Traditionally, the focus of business succession is mainly on the downstream activities, and specifically, succession to visible assets. However, I really think that this is very short-sighted and the approach is not effective in terms of family business sustainability. Succession should cover all levels of activities spanning from upstream to downstream."

- Mr Mario Nishikawa, Chairman,
Family Business Advisors Association
Japan

02 Stewardship Principles for Family Businesses

134

Stewardship Principles for Family Businesses

PRINCIPLE 1
Driven by purpose, anchored on values

PRINCIPLE 2
Cultivate an ownership mentality

PRINCIPLE 3
Integrate short-term and long-term perspectives

PRINCIPLE 4
Expect changes, nurture agility and strengthen resilience

PRINCIPLE 5
Embrace inclusiveness and build strong stakeholder relationships

PRINCIPLE 6
Do well, do good, do right; contributing to community

PRINCIPLE 7
Be mindful of succession

PRINCIPLE 1
Driven by a sense of purpose, anchored on values

Successful and enduring FBs establish clarity on the purpose of their existence. Their business decisions and operations are driven by a strong commitment in purpose, anchored on their values. These values, which are built, strengthened and passed down over time, are the fundamentals that act like compass bearings uniting the components of FBs in action. They will help reconcile seemingly conflicting family and business identities and interests.

In practice

a. Articulate and communicate clearly the purpose of the FB and responsible wealth creation. This could be transmitted through the family constitution, business philosophy, organisational vision, mission statement and shared stories.

b. Live out the organisational purpose and values consistently such that they are embedded in the daily language, actions and thinking processes of all stakeholders.

c. Facilitate the value-alignment process on an ongoing basis for both existing and new stakeholders. This ensures that the transcendental purpose, values and founder's mentality will continue to be inscribed as the company grows.

d. Provide opportunities for employees to formulate and review the company's mission and values together. This can enhance shared interpretations and encourage collective enactment.

e. Affirm those who exemplify the values of FBs. Educate those who deviate from them. This allows everyone to visualise how the shared purpose and values will look like when they are put into action.

PRINCIPLE 2
Cultivate an ownership mentality

Successful and enduring FBs build a culture that instils the ownership mentality. Owners and employees take responsibility and action as well as develop a sense of collective pride to forge proactive and integrative solutions to complex, problems and dynamic situations. They see the organisation as an extension of themselves, are willing to be change agents, and act within their locus of control with the interest of the company in mind. They engage and galvanise the diverse parts of the organisation towards a common destination with a collective sense of success and failure.

In practice

a. Instil a culture that emphasises personal as well as collective accountability. Employees are clear of their individual roles as well as shared responsibilities. This enhances ownership, mitigates conflicts and promotes collaboration.

b. Value the diversity of perspectives. Translate promising ideas into concrete actions whenever applicable. This instils a sense of belonging and pride in employees.

c. Associate ownership mentality with the drive to take good care of the family business. Family owners should not misconstrue ownership as having the entitlement to use company resources to benefit themselves.

d. Adopt an ownership structure that fulfils the objective of capital injection as well as family control. This allows FBs to continue to exercise some degree of autonomy over business direction and investment decisions.

e. Embrace the responsibility for creating long-term social and economic value to a wider group of stakeholders, and not just myopically focusing on family wealth to foster ownership mentality amongst all those who play a role in the success of the business.

135

PRINCIPLE 3
Integrate short-term and long-term perspectives

Successful and enduring FBs do not neglect long-term considerations in the face of pressure from increasing short-termism. They are known to adopt a long-term orientation towards spending and investment, favouring sustainable growth over quick gains.

In practice

a. Ensure that short-term decisions are in line with the long-term goals – act today with tomorrow in mind. Be mindful of intergenerational equity and understand the costs and opportunities involved. This maintains coherence across all initiatives over time.

b. Contemplate the long-term consequences of actions. Spend prudently, invest patiently, re-invest strategically and take calculated risks to reap social and financial rewards in the future.

c. Exercise sound governance while growing wealth. Consider having a range of mechanisms that allow regular check-ins and management of the business portfolio. Investment and divestment criteria should be transparent and rigorous to build long-term confidence amongst stakeholders.

d. Understand the history of the family business and the lessons that global development can offer. Leverage the longstanding competitive advantages so that they can continue to contribute towards the long-term development of the business.

e. Look beyond short-term profitability and temporary gains. Focus on the preservation of intangible values such as kinship and loyalty for the long-term success and legacy building.

PRINCIPLE 4
Expect changes, nurture agility and strengthen resilience

Successful and enduring FBs anticipate changes in the business environment and demands, and continually seek to nurture adaptive skills. This is not only to prepare themselves to address challenges, but also to build capacity to leverage opportunities brought forth by disruptive changes, new market imperatives and emerging technologies.

In practice

a. Conduct horizon scanning and scenario planning. Understand emerging threats, opportunities and evolving customer needs. Re-calibrate what matters and enact change.

b. Exercise agility. Arrest and reverse inefficacious decisions. Remove emotional attachments to outmoded beliefs, structures, processes or relationships.

c. Cultivate a growth mindset instead of passively guarding current wealth and traditional practices. Exercise strategic flexibility and draw upon accumulated reserves to develop new market niches at the opportune moment.

d. Nurture resilience in response to the onslaught of disruptive innovations. Improvise existing resources to devise innovative solutions. Invest in research and development so as to create a leading edge in identified niche areas.

e. Foster the mindset of lifelong learning to avoid stagnation. Learning includes not only raising the bar of competency and professionalism, but more importantly in inculcating business acumen, perspectives and values. It can be facilitated through organised training, family gatherings, team-building activities, peer coaching, apprenticeship or mentorship.

PRINCIPLE 5
Embrace inclusiveness and build strong stakeholder relationships

Successful and enduring FBs believe that stable and strong relationships with and amongst various stakeholders need to be established and carefully maintained. When resolving internal conflicts, FBs leverage family harmony to promote business unity and vice-versa – creating virtuous loops that are difficult to be emulated by non-family businesses. They also reinforce the stability of the social network when interfacing with external stakeholders.

In practice

a. Cultivate an organisational culture that promotes open communication and tolerance, where family and non-family employees can share ideas and resolve differences in a consensual manner via conflict resolution mechanisms. Examples of arbitration mechanisms include people-centred policies, family council and soft persuasion.

b. Exercise good nurturing. Impart values such as financial discipline and family harmony to the next generation. This paves the way for the development of good relationships amongst family members, which has bearings on how potential family conflicts can be mitigated in future.

c. Develop longstanding relationships with internal and external stakeholders. Care for the family and non-family members alike to promote reciprocal trust, kindness and compassion. Foster win-win collaboration with external partners in a responsible manner to cement rapport.

d. Ensure professionalism in the quality of governance. Demonstrate commitment towards business interests to mitigate conflicts associated with complicated or excessive family ownership. Examples of sound governance include embracing board diversity as well as rewarding employees, or exercising hiring decisions based on merit and not entitlement.

e. Conduct stakeholder analysis. Engage identified stakeholders on a sustained basis to ensure value alignment, problem identification and conflict resolution. Engagement platforms can include annual general meetings, voluntary disclosure reports, collective dialogues, informal meetings and family governance mechanisms.

PRINCIPLE 6
Do well, do good, do right; contributing to community

Successful and enduring FBs adopt a broader definition of success to include doing well, doing good, and doing right as they grow. They see businesses as an integral part of society. They strive to create a positive economic, social and environmental sustainability in mind to reinforce and core values will be preserved and transmitted.

In practice

a. Safeguard and enhance the reputation of the family brand. Focus on a "quality first" approach by delivering quality products that are manufactured with integrity and environmental sustainability in mind to reinforce customer loyalty and project a positive corporate image.

b. Integrate social responsibility into the corporate philosophy of FBs. Identify the social causes that FBs can resonate with. To create real impact, these commitments should be embedded as mainstream and not piecemeal business activities. Social responsibility is not to be seen as a separate part of the business operation, but part of the overall stewardship mindset of the business.

c. Encourage both management and employees to be involved in volunteering efforts to sustain a connection with the community. Create a visible social imprint by promoting such volunteerism on various media to perpetuate the family legacy and attract like-minded partners.

d. Evaluate the impact of the philanthropic pursuits, relating it to the intent of the efforts. This can ensure coherence between business goals and societal contributions, thus gaining more long-term support and alignment for doing good.

e. Uplift the communities from which FBs draw their resources from. Collaborate with multiple parties to understand gaps so as to give more meaningfully. This can promote mutual benefits and build sustainable relationships.

136

Conclusion

Stewardship has never been more relevant to FBs than it is today. In a volatile, uncertain, complex and ambiguous environment, it is becoming increasingly challenging for FBs to foster success, sustainability and significance. A central question that we want to address in this document is:

"How does Family Business thrive and sustain growth while enhancing the wealth of its stakeholders and the well-being of the societies in which it operates over the long term?"

The distillation of the Seven Stewardship Principles is an attempt to demystify how successful and enduring FBs have managed to do well over the years, despite the onslaught of challenges. As what the Principles posit, fundamentals such as purpose and values remain important, and so are long-term and forward-looking strategies.

As what we have alluded to earlier, stewardship is a journey and the business context is dynamic. Along this vein, these Principles can be viewed as 'living principles' which can be prospectively enriched by continued dialogue. We welcome subject matter experts and FBs to embark on this journey with us to sharpen our understanding collectively, and be partners in the endeavour to promote and foster stewardship.

"Whether it is family executives in businesses or whether it is business families, they are simply for me, responsible businesses that they have to learn to be professional so that they can be sustainable. In the end, it is all about governance, about transparency, about wanting to safeguard the legacy and learning all the good values in doing well, doing good and doing right."

Ms Claire Chiang, Co-founder, Banyan Tree Hotels & Resorts

PRINCIPLE 7
Be mindful of succession

Successful and enduring FBs truly see leadership transition in a timely and effective manner as a critical aspect of good stewardship. They deliberate, plan and execute their leadership renewal in ways that minimise destabilising shocks and increase the stakeholders' acceptance of the new leadership. Having a robust succession plan is crucial in the context of FBs as succession frequently affects the family dynamics and survivability of the business.

"We have to have humanity, tolerance, compassion, kindness in the way we conduct business, because we always talk about wanting to do something good for society. And you can only do something good to society if you also have an open relationship to each other and a warm heart."

Dr Harald Link, Chairman, B. Grimm

In practice

a. View succession as a protracted and continual process. Communicate current concerns and future expectations of FBs. This allows a more coherent transgenerational business strategy to be formulated during leadership transitions.

b. Facilitate successful transition to the next generation of leaders by beginning the mentoring process of potential successors early. This provides sufficient time for the new generation to gain a nuanced understanding of the business and a broader perspective of the environment.

c. Assess the capabilities and character of potential family successors. Appoint a successor who reflects the right values and motivation, on top of honouring meritocracy so that the founder's mentality will be preserved and that the business will continue to grow.

d. Adopt a more holistic view of succession, which encompasses household and family succession, management succession and asset succession. Asset succession can include both the tangible (physical and financial capital) and intangible (philosophy, culture, expertise and network) aspects.

e. Create a healthy environment where the older and younger generations can exchange views with veracity. Gradually, the younger generation should be given more opportunities to make strategic decisions as they acquire more competencies.

f. Keep an open mind towards including external expertise in both the aspects of successors and succession. External successors can bring new perspectives, competencies and networks. External professional help such as consultants can help FBs put together a more robust succession plan.

137

Acknowledgements

The development of the Stewardship Principles for Family Businesses has been the result of intensive research and extensive consultation. More than one hundred journal articles and research reports on family businesses covering a wide range of industries across and beyond Asia were reviewed.

Following from the literature review, the first draft of the Stewardship Principles was distilled and shared during the focus group meeting held at the 2018 Stewardship Asia Roundtable. Comprising eminent local and overseas family businesses, professional associations, academic institutions and think tanks, these participants from various countries provided invaluable insights and thoughtful comments on the draft. The draft was then refined after taking into consideration their qualitative inputs.

We would like to thank all our illustrious meeting participants for sharing generously and contributing significantly to the crafting of the Stewardship Principles. Many brought their wealth of knowledge and experience to the discussion and provided us with nuanced expositions of stewarding FBs. Some carefully reviewed the draft and provided intellectual inputs that helped us to incorporate multiple perspectives. Some provided editorial inputs that helped us articulate the principles in ways that could resonate better with family businesses. All participants had in one way or another helped us along this journey and we could not thank them enough for their time and expertise.

Stewardship Asia Centre
5/02 Orchard Road, #06-16, Tower 2, The Atrium @Orchard, Singapore 238891

Korea Stewardship Code

Principles on the Stewardship Responsibilities of Institutional Investors

December 16, 2016

Korea Stewardship Code Council

Korea Stewardship Code Council Chair & Members

As of November 18, 2016
(Alphabetical Order)

Role	Name	Current Position
Chair	Cho, Myeong Hyeon	Professor, Korea University Business School President, Korea Corporate Governance Service
Members	Ahn, Soo Hyun	Professor, Hankuk University of Foreign Studies Law School
	Chung, Yoon Mo	Research Fellow, Korea Capital Market Institute
	Hong, Sung Gi	Compliance Officer, Mirae Asset Global Investments
	Kim, Hyungseok	Associate Research Fellow, Korea Corporate Governance Service
	Kim, Jin Eok	Head of Legislative Affairs Department, Korea Financial Investment Association
	Lee, Wonil	CEO, Zebra Investment Management
	Park, Yoo Kyung	Director, APG Asset Management
	Shin, Jhinyoung	Professor, Yonsei University School of Business
	Shin, Seong Mook	Chief Compliance Officer, Samsung Asset Management
	Song, Min Kyung	Research Fellow, Korea Corporate Governance Service
Staff	Lim, Ja Young	Researcher, Korea Corporate Governance Service

139

Principles on the Stewardship Responsibilities of Institutional Investors

Korean Stewardship Code Council, November 18, 2016

Objectives of the "Principles" and their Implications

1. The responsibility institutional investors bear in taking care of or managing assets entrusted by others (stewardship responsibilities, hereafter) refers to a sense of responsibility to promote the mid- to long-term interests of their clients and ultimate beneficiaries by pursuing the mid- to long-term value enhancement and sustainable growth of investee companies.

2. Successful implementation of stewardship responsibilities not only induces the mid- to long-term development of investee companies, contributes to enhancing investor returns, but also supports the sound and substantial growth and development of capital markets and the overall economy.

3. Institutional investors are responsible for monitoring whether or not the board of directors faithfully exercises the responsibilities bestowed upon it and, where necessary, carrying out constructive engagement such as an active dialogue with the board. The board of directors exercises its responsibilities by supervising management on behalf of the company and shareholders.

4. The aim of the "Principles on the Stewardship Responsibilities of Institutional Investors" (the Principles, hereafter) is to propose key principles that are crucial for institutional investors to effectively exercise their stewardship responsibilities, and concrete details for these principles.

5. Activities in implementing stewardship responsibilities (stewardship activities, hereafter) have broad scope, including but not limited to the exercise of voting rights. The activities range from monitoring key management issues such as an investee company's business strategy and outcome, risk management, and corporate governance, to consultation with the board of directors, etc., as well as more proactive activities concerning shareholder proposals, litigations, etc. Engagement activities of institutional investors include a wide spectrum of shareholder activities geared towards "clear and constructive goals" in conducting a dialogue with investee companies.

6. Institutional investors are broadly categorized into "asset owners" and "asset managers". Asset managers routinely implement stewardship responsibilities through investment management and dialogue with investee companies. Asset managers namely include asset management companies. Asset owners can carry out stewardship activities by proposing key principles and mobilizing methods such as instructions, evaluations, etc. to ensure that asset managers effectively implement their monitoring and engagement activities. Pension funds and insurance companies are major types of asset owners.

7. Assuming the burden of the responsibility, duty, and an appropriate level of remuneration in fulfilling stewardship responsibilities is essential to the sound growth of investee companies, the protection and enhancement of mid- to long-term investment returns, and the continuous development and advancement of the capital markets. Investors, asset owners, asset managers, and relevant authorities, etc. need to share a common understanding on this point.

8. Stewardship activities do not signify any undue intervention in day-to-day operations of investee companies. Moreover, institutional investors can consider selling their shares should it be deemed in the best interests of their clients and beneficiaries.

9. In order to minimize any legal uncertainties that institutional investors may face during the course of their stewardship activities, institutional investors, relevant authorities, etc. need to make collaborative efforts to categorize shareholder activities in order to make it clear which category of activities is subject to relevant laws and regulations, etc.

Application of the "Principles"

1. The Principles basically apply to domestic and overseas institutional investors holding shares of publicly listed companies in Korea; in other words, asset owners and asset managers.

2. Institutional investors take on ultimate stewardship responsibilities even when they entrust all or part of their stewardship activities to external investors or other (advisory) service providers. Institutional investors should monitor and supervise to ensure that outsourced activities are executed in accordance with their own stewardship policy. Hence, the Principles apply to proxy advisors, investment advisors, etc. that provide (advisory) services related to the detailed contents of the Principles.

3. The Principles are not legally binding. Hence, the Principles apply only to institutional investors, among the aforementioned parties, that agree with the intention

and contents of and that voluntarily affirm participation in the Principles by accepting and implementing them (participating institutional investors, hereafter).

⁴ Participating institutional investors, etc. should comply with the Principles, but when they cannot comply exceptionally, they should explain the reasons ("comply or explain"). When participating institutional investors, etc. cannot adhere to any details set forth in the Principles due to their business model, investment policy, etc., they should provide the reason, sufficiently explain alternatives to stewardship activities to their clients and beneficiaries, and publicly disclose the contents.

⁵ Participating institutional investors, etc. should publicly disclose matters listed below on their website, and periodically review and update the contents where necessary. Should they decide to participate in the Principles or should there be any updates or changes on the website, they should immediately notify these to the Korea Corporate Governance Service with the last updated date, and website address.

· Intention to accept and implement the Principles;
· Details on how to implement each Principle and guideline;

· Details that are required to be publicly disclosed by the Principles and guidelines;
· When there are any unimplemented Principle and guideline, or when there is any undisclosed item that is required to be disclosed under each Principle and guideline, the reasons for the failure to apply it and alternatives to stewardship activities; and
· Whether or not the institutional investor applies the Principles across-the-board to all funds it manages, and related details when there are differences in their application, implementation, and standards.

⁶ Participating institutional investors, etc. may concurrently utilize their disclosed policies and implementation report made in adherence to similar overseas stewardship codes (or Principles of Responsible Investment, PRI) to fulfil the disclosure and reporting requirement of the Principles. But if there are differences in the detailed contents of the Principles and overseas codes, these must be reflected.

⁷ The Korea Corporate Governance Service should periodically examine trends in participation in and implementation of the Principles in order to gauge the overall level of stewardship activities in the capital markets. Furthermore, it should publicly disclose on its own website the list of participating institutional investors, etc. and the website of each investor. This will enable capital market participants, etc. to easily check information on institutional investors, based on which they will be able to select institutional investors that fit their investment preferences, and monitor how well the

investor implements stewardship responsibilities. In addition, the Korea Corporate Governance Service should periodically monitor and improve the detailed contents of the Principles by taking into account best practices and cultures from Korea and overseas related to stewardship activities, capital market development stage, overseas stewardship codes, and domestic and international regulatory trends, etc.

8. Participating institutional investors, etc. should designate staff in charge of policies, procedures, and disclosures related to stewardship responsibilities, and publicly disclose the staff's name and contact information.

Principles

In order to enhance the mid- to long-term value and sustainable growth of investee companies and further the mid- to long-term interests of their clients and ultimate beneficiaries, institutional investors should comply with the Principles stated below.

1. **Institutional investors, as a steward of assets entrusted by their clients, beneficiaries, etc, to take care of and manage, should formulate and publicly disclose a clear policy to faithfully implement their responsibilities.**

2. **Institutional investors should formulate and publicly disclose an effective and clear policy as to how to resolve actual or potential problems arising from conflicts of interest in the course of their stewardship activities.**

3. **Institutional investors should regularly monitor investee companies in order to enhance investee companies' mid- to long-term value and thereby protect and raise their investment value.**

4. **While institutional investors should aim to form a consensus with investee companies, where necessary, they should formulate internal guidelines on the timeline, procedures, and methods for stewardship activities.**

5. **Institutional investors should formulate and publicly disclose a voting policy that includes guidelines, procedures, and detailed standards for exercising votes in a faithful manner, and publicly disclose voting records and the reasons for each vote so as to allow the verification of the appropriateness of their voting activities.**

6. **Institutional investors should regularly report their voting and stewardship activities to their clients or beneficiaries.**

7. **Institutional investors should have the capabilities and expertise required to implement stewardship responsibilities in an active and effective manner.**

Principle 1
Institutional investors, as a steward of assets entrusted by their clients, beneficiaries, etc, to take care of and manage, should formulate and publicly disclose a clear policy to faithfully implement their responsibilities.

Guidelines

Institutional investors are responsible for acting in the mid- to long-term interests of their clients and beneficiaries by using their deep understanding of investee companies and the economic, social, and business environment, etc. for active communication and shareholder activities in order to pursue the value enhancement and growth of investee companies.

The activities which institutional investors carry out to implement their responsibilities as a manager and steward of the assets entrusted to them should include proactive engagement activities such as monitoring potential problems, constructive dialogue and, where necessary, productive proposals geared towards problem-solving.

Institutional investors should formulate and publicly disclose a documented policy on how they understand stewardship responsibilities, and what are the effective and concrete methods for exercising their responsibilities, etc. This policy should include the principles and guidelines, investment management philosophy, rights and duties, and organization and procedures related to their stewardship activities.

The stewardship responsibility policy should consider what position institutional investors take in the overall investment chain running from capital suppliers such as clients and beneficiaries to investee companies. In particular, stewardship activities of asset managers such as asset management companies, etc. differ from those of asset owners such as pension funds, insurance companies, etc. that in most cases manage external asset managers. Asset owners can not only directly engage in shareholder activities, but can also utilize indirect means such as selection of competent asset managers, and provision of instructions, evaluations, and feedback. Asset managers' shareholder activities should comply with the standards and requirements set out by their clients who are asset owners. In this regard, close communication between asset owners and asset managers is important, and the relevant matters should be included in the "policy".

Principle 2

Institutional investors should formulate and publicly disclose an effective and clear policy as to how to resolve actual or potential problems arising from conflicts of interest in the course of their stewardship activities.

Guidelines

Institutional investors have the duty to act in the best interests of their clients and beneficiaries.

During the course of their stewardship activities, institutional investors may face a conflict-of-interest situation where their own interests with investee companies prevent them from faithfully promoting the best interests of clients or beneficiaries. Such examples namely include when their ownership or governance structure, or their trade and contractual relationships make casting against votes difficult at the investee company's shareholder meetings.

To effectively address actual conflict-of-interest problems that have arisen or may possibly arise in the course of stewardship activities, institutional investors should review them in minute detail and then formulate and publicly disclose a documented policy. This policy should stipulate matters related to the principles and guidelines, concrete methods, rights and duties, and procedures, etc. for conflict-of-interest monitoring and management.

To manage conflict-of-interest problems, institutional investors in general can adopt various means, including publicly disclosing the relevant policies and detailed guidelines, working with a third-party organization, adopting other methods set forth in Korea's Financial Investment Services and Capital Markets Act and related regulations. Institutional Investors should properly utilize these methods in order to secure enhanced confidence of their clients and beneficiaries.

When an institutional investor entrusts its activities to external service providers, their "policy" should reflect matters related to selection, monitoring, evaluation, and administration of the entrusted investment manager or advisor, and the scope of shareholder activities entrusted, etc.

When an institutional investor manages collective investment vehicles in various asset classes and types that are different in terms of the time horizon, investment management philosophy, etc., the "policy" can reflect the consequent differences in the principles, guidelines, procedures, etc.

Principle 3
Institutional investors should regularly monitor investee companies in order to enhance investee companies' mid- to long-term value and thereby protect and raise their investment value.

Guidelines

Institutional investors should monitor investee companies on a regular basis and review the effectiveness of their monitoring activities to promote the value enhancement and continuous growth of investee companies.

Institutional investors need to include for monitoring all factors that could affect the value and sustainable growth of investee companies; for example, not only financial factors such as capital structures, business performances, etc., but also non-financial factors such as corporate governance, business strategy, etc.

Institutional investors should take into consideration their investment policy and internal capacity to determine the appropriate scope for the monitoring of the aforementioned financial and non-financial factors so as to ensure effective stewardship activities.

Institutional investors should make due effort to detect in advance any risk factors that may cause material damage to the investee company's value. If they confirm any risk factors or other matters of concern, they should seek appropriate solutions through constructive communication such as prior consultation in advance of shareholders meetings, etc.

For the reasons stated above, regular monitoring of investee companies is one of the core elements of stewardship responsibilities in seeking to improve investee companies' value and to enhance the interests of their clients and beneficiaries.

Principle 4
While institutional investors should aim to form a consensus with investee companies, where necessary, they should formulate internal guidelines on the timeline, procedures, and methods for stewardship activities.

Guidelines

Institutional investors must endeavor to form a consensus with investee companies with regard to key financial and non-financial management matters based on their pursuit of the mid- to long-term value enhancement of the investee company and their investment and stewardship policies, etc.

In case concerns remain unresolved after sufficient consultation with investee companies, institutional investors should review whether to step up their engagement within the scope of their internal policies.

Institutional investors should take into account investee companies' circumstances, investment policy, and internal capacity, etc. and devise an internal guideline that sets out the scope, procedures, and standards of their communication and engagement activities.

In their active engagement process, institutional investors should beware of the possibility of breaching the regulation banning the use of undisclosed material information set forth in the Financial Investment Services and Capital Markets Act. In particular, they should not use inside information that could substantially affect the investee company's value by attempting to use privileged information to achieve trading gains.

Principle 5.
Institutional investors should formulate and publicly disclose a voting policy that includes guidelines, procedures, and detailed standards for exercising votes in a faithful manner, and publicly disclose voting records and the reasons for each vote so as to allow the verification of the appropriateness of their voting activities.

Guidelines

Institutional investors should reflect in their voting policy information concerning their stock lending and the recall of lent stock if it is deemed to affect matters related to their exercise of voting rights.

Institutional investors should make an effort to exercise their voting rights on all shares held, and it is not appropriate to automatically vote in favor of management-proposed resolutions.

Institutional investors should make their for/against voting decision based on the result of sufficient data collection and analysis, in-depth review, dialogue and engagement, etc., with regard to investee companies, and it is advisable to have a discussion with investee companies concerning their voting decision where necessary.

Institutional investors should build up internal resources, organizational structures, and professional capacity to ensure that their voting rights are exercised in order to enhance the mid- to long-term value of investee companies and to advance the interests of clients and beneficiaries, while relevant principles and information should be included in the voting policy to be explained hereunder.

Institutional investors should formulate and publicly disclose a documented voting policy that includes guidelines, procedures, and detailed standards with regard to the disclosure of their voting activities and records. The detailed standards for voting activities should not solely be comprised of a mechanical checklist, but be designed to contribute to the mid- to long-term value enhancement of investee companies.

The voting policy should include policies on preventing conflicts of interest set out in Principle 2 with regard to any potential conflicts of interest institutional investors may face when exercising their votes.

Institutional investors can devise a voting policy that provides a different set of detailed standards and guidelines for each type of collective investment vehicles with varying management targets and philosophies.

Institutional investors should publicly disclose their voting results and concrete reasons for votes for, against, neutral, and abstentions via an appropriate method so that their clients and beneficiaries, etc. can easily check the appropriateness of the voting activity.

Institutional investors should publicly disclose whether or not they use proxy advisory services and, if they use them, the service scope, application method, identity of the provider, and the extent of their reliance on the provider's recommendations.

Even in the case where institutional investors use proxy advisory services, they are ultimately responsible for exercising their votes according to their own responsibility and judgment as a steward.

145

Principle 6.
Institutional investors should regularly report their voting and stewardship activities to their clients or beneficiaries.

Guidelines

Institutional investors should keep a record of their stewardship activities, including their exercise of voting rights, and maintain the record for a certain period.

Asset managers in principle should regularly report their stewardship policy and the implementation of such policy to clients and beneficiaries such as asset owners, etc.

Asset owners should report to their clients and beneficiaries their stewardship policy and matters concerning the actual implementation of this policy at least annually.

Institutional investors should make an effort to ensure that their stewardship policy and its actual implementation can be effectively reported, and if there are certain reporting scope and form agreed between them and their clients and beneficiaries, these should be followed. Where appropriate and agreed by their clients and beneficiaries, institutional investors can disclose their shareholder activities on the website or in the annual report as a way to enhance the transparency and accountability of such reporting.

Institutional investors should set out the concrete scope and standards of disclosure on how they implement stewardship responsibilities, etc. in a manner that can be easily monitored and trusted by their clients and beneficiaries. In such cases, the overall impact any detailed disclosure could have on asset value can be considered.

Principle 7.
Institutional investors should have the capabilities and expertise required to implement stewardship responsibilities in an active and effective manner.

Guidelines

Institutional investors need to build up their capacity and expertise that will enable them to deepen their understanding of investee companies and to carry out constructive shareholder activities in order to promote the mid- to long-term development and sustainability of investee companies based on active dialogue and shareholder activities.

To that end, institutional investors should design an appropriate organizational structure, inject internal resources, and make a continuous effort to develop and improve the capacity and expertise of these resources.

An asset owner who entrusts stewardship activities to an asset manager should seek ways to oversee the asset manager and pay an appropriate level of remuneration to allow the asset manager to accumulate the capacity for effective engagement with investee companies through dialogue and shareholder activities.

In light of available internal resources and financial conditions, institutional investors can use external services for professional advice in seeking to implement their stewardship responsibilities.

Institutional investors can establish forums, etc. with the aim of stimulating debates and discussions and to pursue mutual interests, as well as to share and learn relevant experiences and opinions about successful shareholder engagement cases, to improve their expertise and the quality of their shareholder activities.

Recommendations

1. As the organization that examines and monitors the trend of the implementation of the Korea Stewardship Code, it is recommended that the Korea Corporate Governance Service examine the appropriateness of the Code's detailed contents every two years.

2. When the participants of the Korea Stewardship Code or the market at large request, or when the need arises, it is recommended that the Korea Corporate Governance Service prepare and publicly release explanatory documents and undertake measures to introduce overseas examples in order to assist in the understanding and actual implementation of the Code's detailed contents.

3. The Korea Stewardship Code stipulates that the Korea Corporate Governance Service examine and monitor market trends as part of its work. Apart from this work, it is recommended for future discussion the need to examine the implementation of the Code by participating institutional investors separately, as well as the organization in charge, and the scope of its work.

147

THE PRINCIPLES

Stewardship

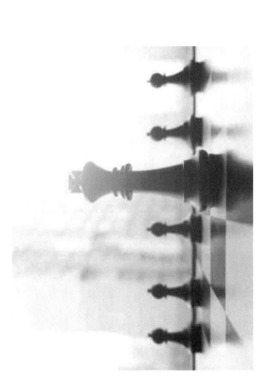

STEWARDSHIP FRAMEWORK FOR INSTITUTIONAL INVESTORS :

Principle A: Institutional investors are accountable to those whose money they invest.

Principle B: Institutional investors should demonstrate how they evaluate corporate governance factors with respect to the companies in which they invest.

Principle C: Institutional investors should disclose, in general terms, how they manage potential conflicts of interest that may arise in their proxy voting and engagement activities.

Principle D: Institutional investors are responsible for proxy voting decisions and should monitor the relevant activities and policies of third parties that advise them on those decisions.

Principle E: Institutional investors should address and attempt to resolve differences with companies in a constructive and pragmatic manner.

Principle F: Institutional investors should work together, where appropriate, to encourage the adoption and implementation of the Corporate Governance andStewardship principles.

STEWARDSHIP FRAMEWORK FOR INSTITUTIONAL INVESTORS

Principle A. Institutional investors are accountable to those whose money they invest.

A.1 Asset managers are responsible to their clients, whose money they manage. Asset owners are responsible to their beneficiaries.

A.2 Institutional investors should ensure that they or their managers, as the case may be, oversee client and/or beneficiary assets in a responsible manner.

Principle B. Institutional investors should demonstrate how they evaluate corporate governance factors with respect to the companies in which they invest.

B.1 Good corporate governance is essential to long-term value creation and risk mitigation by companies. Therefore, institutional investors should adopt and disclose guidelines and practices that help them oversee the corporate governance practices of their investment portfolio companies. These should include a description of their philosophy on including corporate governance factors in the investment process, as well as their proxy voting and engagement guidelines.

B.2 Institutional investors should hold portfolio companies accountable to the Corporate Governance Principles set out in this document, as well as any principles established by their own organization. They should consider dedicating resources to help evaluate and engage portfolio companies on corporate governance and other matters consistent with the long-term interests of their clients and/or beneficiaries.

B.3 On a periodic basis and as appropriate, institutional investors should disclose, publicly or to clients, the proxy voting and general engagement activities undertaken to monitor corporate governance practices of their portfolio companies.

B.4 Asset owners who delegate their corporate governance-related tasks to their asset managers should, on a periodic basis, evaluate how their managers are executing these responsibilities and whether they are doing so in line with the owners' investment objectives.

Principle C: Institutional investors should disclose, in general terms, how they manage potential conflicts of interest that may arise in their proxy voting and engagement activities.

C.1 The proxy voting and engagement guidelines of investors should generally be designed to protect the interests of their clients and/or beneficiaries in accordance with their objectives.

C.2 Institutional investors should have clear procedures that help identify and mitigate potential conflicts of interest that could compromise their ability to put their clients' and/or beneficiaries' interests first.

C.3 Institutional investors who delegate their proxy voting responsibilities to asset managers should ensure that the asset managers have appropriate mechanisms to identify and mitigate potential conflicts of interest that may be inherent in their business.

Principle D. Institutional investors are responsible for proxy voting decisions and should monitor the relevant activities and policies of third parties that advise them on those decisions.

D.1 Institutional investors that delegate their proxy voting responsibilities to a third party have an affirmative obligation to evaluate the third party's processes, policies and capabilities. The evaluation should help ensure that the third party's processes, policies and capabilities continue to protect the institutional investors' (and their beneficiaries' and/or clients') long-term interests, in accordance with their objectives.

D.2 Institutional investors that rely on third-party recommendations for proxy voting decisions should ensure that the agent has processes in place to avoid/mitigate conflicts of interest.

Principle E: Institutional investors should address and attempt to resolve differences with companies in a constructive and pragmatic manner.

E.1 Institutional investors should disclose to companies how to contact them regarding voting and engagement.

E.2 Institutional investors should engage with companies in a manner that is intended to build a foundation of trust and common understanding.

E.3 As part of their engagement process, institutional investors should clearly communicate their views and any concerns with a company's practices on governance-related matters. Companies and investors should identify mutually held objectives and areas of disagreement, and ensure their respective views are understood.

E.4 Institutional investors should disclose, in general, what further actions they may take in the event they are dissatisfied with the outcome of their engagement efforts.

Principle F: Institutional investors should work together, where appropriate, to encourage the adoption and implementation of the Corporate Governance and Stewardship Principles.

F.1 As corporate governance norms evolve over time, institutional investors should collaborate, where appropriate, to ensure that the framework continues to represent their common views on corporate governance best practices.

F.2 Institutional investors should consider addressing common concerns related to corporate governance practices, public policy and/or shareholder rights by participating, for example, in discussions as members of industry organizations or associations.

150

Stewardship Principles for Institutional Investors

Chapter 1   Institutional Investors and Their Duties

Institutional investors can be classified into two types based on their business models:

1. "Asset owners" (e.g. insurance companies, pension funds) which invest with their proprietary capital or funds collected from clients or beneficiaries; and

2. "Asset managers" (e.g. investment trust, investment consulting companies, etc.) which provide assistance to clients on management and investment/utilization of funds.

With financial services gradually becoming diversified, capital providers not only engage directly in trading of relevant assets (including securities such as stocks and bonds or other assets) but also achieve various investment objectives through the assistance of institutional investors.

Nowadays, the investment chain is frequently complicated and institutional investors can greatly influence the market and investee companies through fund management. An institutional investor, when making an investment or carrying out its fiduciary duty, shall base on fund provider's (may contain clients, beneficiaries or shareholders of the institutional investors) long-term interests, monitor the operation of an investee company and participate in corporate governance through attendance at shareholders' meetings, exercise of voting rights, engagement in appropriate dialogue and interact with management, including board of directors or executives, of the investee company. Such is "stewardship" of an institutional investor referred to in these Principles.

Institutional investors may outsource part of their stewardship activities (e.g. to provide voting advice or to cast proxy votes) to other professional service providers (e.g. proxy advisory firms or custodian banks). However, institutional investors shall not be released from their existing stewardship responsibilities to their clients and beneficiaries. The institutional investor must, through effective communications, agreements or monitoring, ensure that service providers act in accordance with their requests, so that the rights and benefits of their clients and beneficiaries are protected.

Chapter 2   Objectives of the Principles

The Principles, through provision of a principle-based framework and guidance, are intended to encourage institutional investors to apply their expertise and influence, and fulfill their duties as asset owners or managers, so as to enhance long-term value for themselves and capital providers. The institutional investors, through monitoring, engaging in dialogue and interacting with investee companies, as well as efforts to enhance investment value, are also able to improve the quality of corporate governance of the investee companies, thus creating an overall positive effect on the development of industry, economy and society.

The Principles encourage institutional investors valuing stewardship to endorse and comply with relevant principles (Please refer to Chapter 3). All institutional investors, that are, asset owners or managers, investing in securities issued by Taiwanese companies (including but not limited to TWSE listed, TPEx listed, emerging or public companies), regardless of whether they are domestic or foreign, government- or private-owned, are encouraged to be signatories.

Chapter 3 Endorsement and "Comply or Explain"

Institutional investors are encouraged to publicly endorse the Principles to demonstrate their intention to support the Principles. Public endorsement means an institutional investor discloses a statement of how the Principles has been applied (hereinafter the "statement") on its website and a website designated by the Corporate Governance Center, and it becomes a signatory after notifying the Corporate Governance Center of the above. Foreign institutional investors who are signatories of other national or international codes/principles with similar objectives may refer back to their home country reporting or statements and notify the Corporate Governance Center to become a signatory of the Principles.

A statement shall at least include the following:

1. A brief introduction of the business of an institutional investor;
2. A brief description of the status of compliance with each principle set forth under Chapter 4 herein;
3. Letterhead or signature of an institutional investor (the institutional investor may publicly endorse the Principles in the name of its business group or as an individual company);
4. Date of announcement (endorsement date) or update.

The institutional investor shall complete a brief description of status of its compliance with each principle mentioned in the preceding paragraph 2 within six months starting from the endorsement date and notify the Corporate Governance Center. Please refer to the Attachment for a sample statement.

A signatory may also disclose information to stakeholders by means of press releases,

press conferences or others. The Corporate Governance Center will consolidate a list of signatories, statements, and links to signatories' websites where they disclose information according to the guidelines for compliance with the Principles (refer to Chapter 5) and publish on a website designated by the Corporate Governance Center.

A signatory is advised to update its statement and other information disclosed according to the guidelines for compliance with the Principles depending on its business content and actual status in compliance with the Principles. If an update occurs, the Corporate Governance Center must be notified. The information disclosed by each signatory will form a reference point for future updates or ongoing facilitation of the Principles by the Corporate Governance Center.

Signatories are not required to fully comply with all six principles under Chapter 4 but rather apply a "comply or explain" basis which aims to retain flexibility, so that the Principles may be abided by more institutional investors. If a signatory is unable to comply with certain principles stipulated under Chapter 4, it must provide a reasonable explanation in its statement or incorporate such explanation on its website or reports such as business report or annual report, provided that relevant disclosures must be made in an ethical and transparent manner.

Chapter 4　Stewardship Principles

Principle 1　Establish and disclose stewardship policies

Principle 2　Establish and disclose policies on managing conflicts of interest

Principle 3　Regularly monitor investee companies

Principle 4　Maintain an appropriate dialogue and interaction with investee companies

Principle 5　Establish clear voting policies and disclose voting results

Principle 6　Periodically disclose to clients or beneficiaries about status of fulfilment of stewardship responsibilities

Chapter 5　Guidelines for Compliance with Principles

The following guidelines are references for signatories to comply with the six principles set forth under Chapter 4.

Principle 1 Establish and disclose stewardship policies

Guideline 1-1　When establishing stewardship policies, an institutional investor is advised to contemplate its role in an investment chain, its nature of business and how to protect rights and benefits of its clients and beneficiaries.

Guideline 1-2　Disclosure of stewardship policies is advised to at least include the following:

1. A brief introduction of business;
2. Duties to clients or beneficiaries;
3. Stewardship activities, e.g. frequency and methods of monitoring investee companies, interaction with management, participation in shareholders' meetings and voting;
4. Status and management measures of outsourcing stewardship activities;
5. Manner and frequency of status disclosure of stewardship fulfilment.

Principle 2 Establish and disclose policies on managing conflicts of interest

Guideline 2-1　A policy on managing conflicts of interest aims to ensure that an institutional investor operates in the interests of its clients or beneficiaries.

Guideline 2-2 A policy on managing conflicts of interest is advised to at least include the following:

1. Possible situations of conflicts of interest;
2. How conflicts of interest in each situation are managed.

Guideline 2-3 Situations of conflicts of interest may include the following:

1. Where an institutional investor, for its own benefits, makes a decision or carries out an activity to the disadvantage of clients or beneficiaries.
2. Where an institutional investor, for benefits of certain clients or beneficiaries, makes a decision or carries out an activity to the disadvantage of other clients, beneficiaries or stakeholders.

Guideline 2-4 Measures of managing conflicts of interest may include training, delegation of duties, information security, firewalls, control mechanisms regarding detection and monitoring, reasonable remuneration policies, and remedial measures.

Guideline 2-5 An institutional investor is advised to consolidate and explain to clients or beneficiaries, either regularly or when considered necessary, about causes and handling measures for major incidents of conflicts of interest which have taken place.

Principle 3 Regularly monitor investee companies

Guideline 3-1 The purpose of monitoring investee companies is such that impacts of relevant information on long-term values of investee companies, clients or beneficiaries may be assessed, so that an institutional investor's manner and time of further dialogue and interaction with the investee companies

can be determined. It may also form a reference for future investment decisions.

Guideline 3-2 In determining the content, extent and frequency of monitoring investee companies, an institutional investor is advised to consider its purposes of investment, cost and benefits. Information such as industry profile, opportunities and risks, shareholding structure, operational strategies, business profile, financial position, results of operation, cash flow, stock price, environmental impacts, social issues and corporate governance may be monitored.

Principle 4 Maintain an appropriate dialogue and interaction with investee companies

Guideline 4-1 The purpose of an institutional investor's dialogue and interaction with investee companies is such that it may better understand the views of management of the investee companies regarding material issues and obtain mutual feedback, so as to strengthen corporate governance.

Guideline 4-2 An institutional investor is advised to determine the manner and time of dialogue and interaction with investee companies by taking its purpose, cost and benefits of the investment and significance of particular issues of concern to it into account. The manners of dialogue and interaction between an institutional investor and its investee company may include the following:

1. Written or verbal communications with management;
2. Public statements on specific issues;
3. Expression of opinions at shareholders' meetings;
4. Submitting motions at shareholders' meetings;

5. Casting votes at shareholders' meetings.

Guideline 4-3 Under circumstances where an institutional investor judges it necessary to take action, it may act collectively with other institutional investors, so as to protect the rights and interests of clients or beneficiaries.

Principle 5 Establish clear voting policies and disclose voting results

Guideline 5-1 The purpose that an institutional investor exercises its voting right is to express opinion on each motion at a shareholder's meeting of investee companies. Specifically, the institutional investor is advised to carefully exercise voting rights of stocks it holds or manages in relation to motions which have significant impacts on rights and benefits of its clients and beneficiaries.

Guideline 5-2 Voting rights shall be exercised based on information obtained from investee companies by taking long-term joint interests of clients, beneficiaries and investee companies into account. An institutional investor shall not always vote in favor of, against or abstain from motions, but shall judge each motion individually. Voting rights shall be exercised objectively even in the case where a voting recommendation report has been obtained from a proxy advisory firm.

Guideline 5-3 A voting policy may include the following:

1. Threshold for exercising voting rights as determined in contemplation of cost and benefit. For instance, voting rights will only be exercised if shareholding reaches a certain percentage or amount;

2. To the best of an institutional investors' ability, prudently evaluate

each motion of a shareholders' meeting before casting votes and communicate in advance with the management of an investee company when necessary;

3. Define types of motions which an institutional investor may support, oppose to or may only deliver its abstention from in principle;

4. A statement that an institutional investor does not necessarily support motions proposed by management;

5. Extent to which an institutional investor obtains and adopts voting recommendation reports made by proxy advisory firms;

Guideline 5-4 An institutional investor is advised to carefully record and analyze voting rights exercised in accordance with relevant policies, so as to facilitate disclosure of the voting activities, which may be disclosed in aggregate. For instance, votes cast in favor, against or abstaining from various types of motions made by investee companies.

Principle 6 Periodically disclose to clients or beneficiaries about status of fulfilment of stewardship responsibilities

Guideline 6-1 An institutional investor is advised to carefully record its stewardship activities to form a basis of assessment and improvement for its stewardship policy, action and disclosure.

Guideline 6-2 When regularly disclosing to its clients or beneficiaries a status of its fulfilment of stewardship duty according to agreement with or request of its clients or beneficiaries, an institutional investor may disclose relevant

information may be made in written, electronic or any other form which can be easily accessible and readable.

Guideline 6-3 Under a situation where clients and beneficiaries are vast in number or the provision of status of fulfilment of stewardship duty is not specified in an agreement, an institutional investor is advised to disclose its stewardship activities annually on its website or in its reports such as business report and annual report. The content is advised to include:

1. A statement on "Stewardship Principles for Institutional Investors" and explanations for non-compliance with certain principles;
2. Attendance in person or by proxy at shareholders' meetings of an investee company;
3. Voting activities (as specified under Guideline 5-4);
4. Contact channel for stakeholders such as clients, beneficiaries, investee companies or other institutional investors to reach a signatory;
5. Other material events (e.g. dialogue and interaction with an investee company or relevant opinions and actions on special events).

Guideline 6-4 If investment or stewardship activities are not directly performed by a signatory, for instance where management of a fund is fully entrusted to an asset manager by an asset owner, measures taken to ensure the trustee's compliance with a stewardship policy is advised to be explained when disclosing the stewardship activities to the clients or beneficiaries.

Attachment

Sample Statement on

"Stewardship Principles for Institutional Investors"

※ Note:

This sample is for reference only. A signatory is advised to disclose and update its statement according to actual circumstances and its business model. Institutional investors shall complete a brief description of status of their compliance with each stewardship principle within six months starting from the endorsement date and notify the Corporate Governance Center. Foreign institutional investors who are signatories of other national or international codes/principles with similar objectives can refer back to their home country reporting or statements to demonstrate the status of compliance with each Stewardship Principle.

The ○○'s (name of institution) main business is _____ and is an asset owner / asset manager / or other (e.g. service provider or industrial association). ○○ hereby represents to comply with "Stewardship Principles for Institutional Investors". Compliance with the six principles is detailed below (or will be provided within six months starting from the endorsement date):

Principle 1 Establish and disclose stewardship policies

The operational objective of ○○ is to achieve maximum benefits for the clients / beneficiaries / shareholders through conducting the businesses of (business). To achieve such an objective, the stewardship policies set forth by ○○ include but not limited to its responsibilities to clients / beneficiaries / shareholders and disclosure of fulfillment of stewardship duties. Please visit (website) for details of stewardship policies.

Principle 2 Establish and disclose policies on managing conflicts of interest

To ensure that ○○ executes its businesses in the interest of its clients or beneficiaries, ○○ establishes policies on managing conflicts of interest, including types of conflicts of interest and management approach. Please visit (website) for details of policy content on managing conflicts of interest and handling of material conflicts of interest.

Principle 3 Regularly monitor investee companies

To ensure that sufficient and valid information can be obtained by ○○ for assessing the nature, timeline and degree of dialogue and interaction with investee companies and to form a sound basis for investment decisions of ○○, ○○ focuses on issues regarding the investee companies, such as related news, financial performance, industry profile, operational strategy, activities for environmental protection, social responsibilities and corporate governance.

Principle 4 Maintain an appropriate dialogue and interaction with investee companies

Through appropriate dialogue and interaction with investee companies, ○○ will further understand and communicate with management, including board of directors or executives, about risks faced by industry and strategies adopted, and strive to reach consensus with the investee companies on creating long-term values. ○○ communicates annually with management of investee companies through conference calls, face-to-face meetings, participation in institutional investors' roadshows or attendance at shareholders' meetings or significant extraordinary general meetings. If it is likely that an investee company may violate principles of corporate governance on specific issues or damage long-term values of clients / beneficiaries / shareholders of ○○, ○○ will, when considered necessary, inquire with management of the investee company about compliance handling and does not give up its rights to act collectively with other investors to protect their interests.

Principle 5 Establish clear voting policies and disclose voting results

In order to achieve maximum benefits for clients / beneficiaries / shareholders, ○○ has established a clear voting policy and is a proactive voter at shareholders' meetings. The Company does not necessarily support proposals made by management. Please

13

refer to _____ (website) for (aggregated) details of voting activities.

Principle 6 Periodically disclose to clients or beneficiaries about status of fulfilment of stewardship responsibilities

The stewardship activities are disclosed by ○○ on its website （or concurrently in its annual report / business report） on a regular basis, including this statement, explanation on non-compliance with stewardship principles, attendance at shareholders' meetings of investee companies, voting activities, and other material matters.

Signatory ○○ **(name of institution)**

Month/Date/Year

14

157

158

第13号「敵対的買収に関する法規制」　　　　　　　　2006 年 5 月
　　　　報告者　中東正文名古屋大学教授

第14号「証券アナリスト規制と強制情報開示・不公正取引規制」 2006 年 7 月
　　　　報告者　戸田暁京都大学助教授

第15号「新会社法のもとでの株式買取請求権制度」　　2006 年 9 月
　　　　報告者　藤田友敬東京大学教授

第16号「証券取引法改正に係る政令等について」　　　2006年12月
　　　（ＴＯＢ、大量保有報告関係、内部統制報告関係）
　　　　報告者　池田唯一　金融庁総務企画局企業開示課長

第17号「間接保有証券に関するユニドロア条約策定作業の状況」 2007 年 5 月
　　　　報告者　神田秀樹　東京大学大学院法学政治学研究科教授

第18号「金融商品取引法の政令・内閣府令について」　2007 年 6 月
　　　　報告者　三井秀範　金融庁総務企画局市場課長

第19号「特定投資家・一般投資家について—自主規制業務を中心に—」 2007 年 9 月
　　　　報告者　青木浩子　千葉大学大学院専門法務研究科教授

第20号「金融商品取引所について」　　　　　　　　　2007年10月
　　　　報告者　前田雅弘　京都大学大学院法学研究科教授

第21号「不公正取引について−村上ファンド事件を中心に−」 2008 年 1 月
　　　　報告者　太田 洋 西村あさひ法律事務所パートナー・弁護士

第22号「大量保有報告制度」　　　　　　　　　　　　2008 年 3 月
　　　　報告者　神作裕之　東京大学大学院法学政治学研究科教授

第23号「開示制度（Ⅰ）—企業再編成に係る開示制度および　2008 年 4 月
　　　集団投資スキーム持分等の開示制度—」
　　　　報告者　川口恭弘 同志社大学大学院法学研究科教授

第24号「開示制度（Ⅱ）—確認書、内部統制報告書、四半期報告書—」 2008 年 7 月
　　　　報告者　戸田　暁　京都大学大学院法学研究科准教授

第25号「有価証券の範囲」　　　　　　　　　　　　　2008 年 7 月
　　　　報告者　藤田友敬　東京大学大学院法学政治学研究科教授

第26号「民事責任規定・エンフォースメント」　　　　2008 年10月
　　　　報告者　近藤光男　神戸大学大学院法学研究科教授

第27号「金融機関による説明義務・適合性の原則と金融商品販売法」2009 年 1 月
　　　　報告者　山田剛志　新潟大学大学院実務法学研究科准教授

第28号「集団投資スキーム（ファンド）規制」　　　　2009 年 3 月
　　　　報告者　中村聡 森・濱田松本法律事務所パートナー・弁護士

第 29 号「金融商品取引業の業規制」　　　　　　　　　　　2009 年 4 月
　　　　　報告者　黒沼悦郎　早稲田大学大学院法務研究科教授

第 30 号「公開買付け制度」　　　　　　　　　　　　　　　2009 年 7 月
　　　　　報告者　中東正文　名古屋大学大学院法学研究科教授

第 31 号「最近の金融商品取引法の改正について」　　　　2011 年 3 月
　　　　　報告者　藤本拓資　金融庁総務企画局市場課長

第 32 号「金融商品取引業における利益相反　　　　　　　2011 年 6 月
　　　　―利益相反管理体制の整備業務を中心として―」
　　　　　報告者　神作裕之　東京大学大学院法学政治学研究科教授

第 33 号「顧客との個別の取引条件における特別の利益提供に関する問題」2011 年 9 月
　　　　　報告者　青木浩子　千葉大学大学院専門法務研究科教授
　　　　　　　　　松本譲治　ＳＭＢＣ日興証券　法務部長

第 34 号「ライツ・オファリングの円滑な利用に向けた制度整備と課題」2011 年 11 月
　　　　　報告者　前田雅弘　京都大学大学院法学研究科教授

第 35 号「公開買付規制を巡る近時の諸問題」　　　　　　2012 年 2 月
　　　　　報告者　太田 洋 西村あさひ法律事務所弁護士・NY州弁護士

第 36 号「格付会社への規制」　　　　　　　　　　　　　2012 年 6 月
　　　　　報告者　山田剛志　成城大学法学部教授

第 37 号「金商法第 6 章の不公正取引規制の体系」　　　　2012 年 7 月
　　　　　報告者　松尾直彦　東京大学大学院法学政治学研究科客員
　　　　　　　　　教授・西村あさひ法律事務所弁護士

第 38 号「キャッシュ・アウト法制」　　　　　　　　　　2012 年 10 月
　　　　　報告者　中東正文　名古屋大学大学院法学研究科教授

第 39 号「デリバティブに関する規制」　　　　　　　　　2012 年 11 月
　　　　　報告者　神田秀樹　東京大学大学院法学政治学研究科教授

第 40 号「米国 JOBS 法による証券規制の変革」　　　　　2013 年 1 月
　　　　　報告者　中村聡 森・濱田松本法律事務所パートナー・弁護士

第 41 号「金融商品取引法の役員の責任と会社法の役員の責任　2013 年 3 月
　　　　―虚偽記載をめぐる役員の責任を中心に―」
　　　　　報告者　近藤光男　神戸大学大学院法学研究科教授

第 42 号「ドッド=フランク法における信用リスクの保持ルールについて」2013 年 4 月
　　　　　報告者　黒沼悦郎　早稲田大学大学院法務研究科教授

第 43 号「相場操縦の規制」　　　　　　　　　　　　　　2013 年 8 月
　　　　　報告者　藤田友敬　東京大学大学院法学政治学研究科教授

第 44 号「法人関係情報」　　　　　　　　　　　　　　　2013 年 10 月
　　　　　　報告者　川口恭弘　同志社大学大学院法学研究科教授
　　　　　　　　　　平田公一　日本証券業協会常務執行役

第 45 号「最近の金融商品取引法の改正について」　　　　2014 年 6 月
　　　　　　報告者　藤本拓資　金融庁総務企画局企画課長

第 46 号「リテール顧客向けデリバティブ関連商品販売における民事責任　2014 年 9 月
　　　　　　―「新規な説明義務」を中心として―」
　　　　　　　　　報告者　青木浩子　千葉大学大学院専門法務研究科教授

第 47 号「投資者保護基金制度」　　　　　　　　　　　　2014 年 10 月
　　　　　　報告者　神田秀樹　東京大学大学院法学政治学研究科教授

第 48 号「市場に対する詐欺に関する米国判例の動向について」　2015 年 1 月
　　　　　　報告者　黒沼悦郎　早稲田大学大学院法務研究科教授

第 49 号「継続開示義務者の範囲―アメリカ法を中心に―」　2015 年 3 月
　　　　　　報告者　飯田秀総　神戸大学大学院法学研究科准教授

第 50 号「証券会社の破綻と投資者保護基金　　　　　　　2015 年 5 月
　　　　　　―金融商品取引法と預金保険法の交錯―」
　　　　　　　　　報告者　山田剛志　成城大学大学院法学研究科教授

第 51 号「インサイダー取引規制と自己株式」　　　　　　2015 年 7 月
　　　　　　報告者　前田雅弘　京都大学大学院法学研究科教授

第 52 号「金商法において利用されない制度と利用される制度の制限」2015 年 8 月
　　　　　　報告者　松尾直彦　東京大学大学院法学政治学研究科
　　　　　　　　　　　　　　　客員教授・弁護士

第 53 号「証券訴訟を巡る近時の諸問題　　　　　　　　　2015 年 10 月
　　　　　　―流通市場において不実開示を行った提出会社の責任を中心に―」
　　　　　　報告者　太田 洋 西村あさひ法律事務所パートナー・弁護士

第 54 号「適合性の原則」　　　　　　　　　　　　　　　2016 年 3 月
　　　　　　報告者　川口恭弘　同志社大学大学院法学研究科教授

第 55 号「金商法の観点から見たコーポレートガバナンス・コード」2016 年 5 月
　　　　　　報告者　神作裕之　東京大学大学院法学政治学研究科教授

第 56 号「ＥＵにおける投資型クラウドファンディング規制」2016 年 7 月
　　　　　　報告者　松尾健一　大阪大学大学院法学研究科准教授

第 57 号「上場会社による種類株式の利用」　　　　　　　2016 年 9 月
　　　　　　報告者　加藤貴仁　東京大学大学院法学政治学研究科准教授

第58号「公開買付前置型キャッシュアウトにおける　　　　2016年11月
　　　　価格決定請求と公正な対価」
　　　　　　報告者　藤田友敬　東京大学大学院法学政治学研究科教授

第59号「平成26年会社法改正後のキャッシュ・アウト法制」2017年1月
　　　　　　報告者　中東正文　名古屋大学大学院法学研究科教授

第60号「流通市場の投資家による発行会社に対する証券訴訟の実態」2017年3月
　　　　　　報告者　後藤　元　東京大学大学院法学政治学研究科准教授

第61号「米国における投資助言業者（investment adviser）　2017年5月
　　　　　の負う信認義務」
　　　　　　報告者　萬澤陽子　専修大学法学部准教授・当研究所客員研究員

第62号「最近の金融商品取引法の改正について」　　　　　2018年2月
　　　　　　報告者　小森卓郎　金融庁総務企画局市場課長

第63号「監査報告書の見直し」　　　　　　　　　　　　　2018年3月
　　　　　　報告者　弥永真生　筑波大学ビジネスサイエンス系
　　　　　　　　　　　　　　　ビジネス科学研究科教授

第64号「フェア・ディスクロージャー・ルールについて」　2018年6月
　　　　　　報告者　大崎貞和　野村総合研究所未来創発センターフェロー

第65号「外国為替証拠金取引のレバレッジ規制」　　　　　2018年8月
　　　　　　報告者　飯田秀総　東京大学大学院法学政治学研究科准教授

第66号「一般的不公正取引規制に関する一考察」　　　　　2018年12月
　　　　　　報告者　松井秀征　立教大学法学部教授

第67号「仮想通貨・ＩＣＯに関する法規制・自主規制」　　2019年3月
　　　　　　報告者　河村賢治　立教大学大学院法務研究科教授

第68号「投資信託・投資法人関連法制に関する問題意識について」2019年5月
　　　　　　報告者　松尾直彦　東京大学大学院法学政治学研究科
　　　　　　　　　　　　　　　客員教授・弁護士

第69号「「政策保有株式」に関する開示規制の再構築について」2019年7月
　　　　　　報告者　加藤貴仁　東京大学大学院法学政治学研究科教授

第70号「複数議決権株式を用いた株主構造のコントロール」2019年11月
　　　　　　報告者　松井智予　上智大学大学院法学研究科教授

第71号「会社法・証券法における分散台帳の利用　　　　　2020年2月
　　　　　　―デラウェア州会社法改正などを参考として」
　　　　　　報告者　小出　篤　学習院大学法学部教授

購入を希望される方は、一般書店または当研究所までお申し込み下さい。
当研究所の出版物案内は研究所のホームページ http://www.jsri.or.jp/ にてご覧いた
だけます。

金融商品取引法研究会研究記録　第 72 号

スチュワードシップコードの目的とその多様性

令和 2 年 5 月 22 日

定価（本体 500 円＋税）

編　者　　金 融 商 品 取 引 法 研 究 会
発行者　　公益財団法人　日本証券経済研究所
　　　　　東京都中央区日本橋 2-11-2
　　　　　　　　　　　　〒 103-0027
　　　　　電話　03（6225）2326 代表
　　　　　URL: http://www.jsri.or.jp

ISBN978-4-89032-688-4　C3032　¥500E